Holiday & Travel Security Handbook

Other titles by Des Conway

The Home Security Handbook
How to keep your home and family safe from crime

Will show you how you can reduce the risk of becoming a crime statistic. You can successfully audit and review your home and lifestyle, identify a range of threats and risks and provide effective countermeasures to avoid the threat and reduce the risk.

The Personal Security Handbook
How to keep yourself and your family safe from crime

Will show you how to ensure that you don't become the victim of a crime. You can protect yourself against credit card theft and fraud, from physical harm, keep you car secure and deal with a host of other issues by performing a security review on various aspects of your life, identifying any vulnerabilities and resolving them using simple, affordable and achievable measures.

howtobooks

Please send for a free copy of the latest catalogue to:
How To Books
3 Newtec Place, Magdalen Road
Oxford OX4 1RE, United Kingdom
Email: info@howtobooks.co.uk
www.howtobooks.co.uk

Holiday & Travel Security Handbook

D. G. Conway

howtobooks

IT'S YOUR DECISION

This book contains general advice. Laws and circumstances change, people differ and experts learn new techniques, so advice will evolve and change over time. You may have a totally different lifestyle to everyone else in the country, or you may have strange allergies and a love for dangerous sports. Because there is only one 'you', this book has to offer **advice** only, and you must treat it as such. You must decide if you want to act on any of this advice. You must make sure that any actions are appropriate to you, and check current rules and regulations with the relevant experts to make sure that you do the right thing for you.

Published by How To Books Ltd
3 Newtec Place, Magdalen Road,
Oxford OX4 1RE, United Kingdom
Tel: (01865) 793806. Fax: (01865) 248780
email: info@howtobooks.co.uk
www.howtobooks.co.uk

British Library Cataloguing in Publication Data
A catalogue record for this book is available from the British Library.

Produced for How To Books by Deer Park Productions, Tavistock
Cover design by Baseline Arts Ltd, Oxford
Typeset by Kestrel Data, Exeter
Printed and bound in Great Britain by Bell & Bain Ltd, Glasgow

NOTE: The material contained in this book is set out in good faith for general guidance and no liability can be accepted for loss or expense incurred as a result of relying in particular circumstances on statements made in this book. Laws and regulations are complex and liable to change, and readers should check the current position with the relevant authorities before making personal arrangements.

Contents

1 Introduction

We all know that society is less than perfect and that crime could touch us all. Almost anyone can tell you tales of crime and disorder. People fear crime and other threats, they feel helpless because they think that there is nothing they can do to protect themselves, but that is wrong! There is a lot that the average person can do to protect themselves, their family and their property at home and abroad. This *Holiday & Travel Security Handbook* will teach you how to make your journey as safe as it can be.

Origins of This Book

Discussing what friends would buy if they won the lottery, there were dreams of fast cars and big houses, but almost all of them dreamed of using their fortune to buy a 'secure and safe lifestyle.'

They were ordinary people, leading ordinary lives who should have had no real security worries. I asked what special threats they thought they faced and how they thought sudden wealth would give them security? Most of their concerns could be listed under two main classifications:

1. Aspects of their lifestyle that I thought were already within their control.
2. Headline-grabbing crimes, which they were very unlikely to encounter.

In other words, they were worrying about nothing, because with the right information, preparation and guidance they could easily make significant improvements to their security at minimal cost.

Lack of understanding and knowledge

Statistics can be worrying, but they can help us too. Look at these statistics:

- Complaints about holiday crime have more than doubled in the last couple of years.

- Poor holiday resort hygiene leaves about one in five holidaymakers and travellers with food poisoning or gastric infections.

- Among younger male travellers, violent attacks have increased by 30% over the last year, usually when both victim and attacker were intoxicated.

These might worry you, but I want to train you to view this sort of information differently – I want you to use it to identify opportunities! When looking at the information above, this is how I read them:

- **Complaints about holidays have doubled**. If the quality of holiday arrangements or destinations is falling, acquaint yourself with the formal complaint procedure before you go. Forewarned is forearmed.

- **One in five become sick through poor hygiene.** If poor resort hygiene is leaving holidaymakers and travellers sick, learn how to identify questionable hygiene or suspect food and drink to protect yourself and your family.

- **Attacks on young men up 30%.** If drunken young men on holiday become involved in fights, they should adopt a more mature outlook and view alcohol as a pleasurable drink, not a cheap and quick way to get drunk. More importantly, you should avoid clubs and bars full of drunken young men.

By learning how to look, and picking up the messages behind those statistics and news stories and acting on them, you and your family will be significantly safer. As you work through this book, you will identify a number of risks, threats and vulnerabilities then decide how to remove, reduce or avoid them.

You may for example adopt the following countermeasures to the problems above.

- ✔ Read the complaints procedure for your holiday company, knowing it will help you to get problems resolved quickly. Be ready to take pictures or video footage of problems as evidence in case you need to take things further when you get home. Take the name and address of other travellers affected by the problem; a group of people will have more impact on your holiday company and have a better chance of interesting the media than one individual voice.

✔ Do some research on food hygiene. Find out what is good practice and make sure that your resort is following best practice. Don't be afraid to ask to see the kitchens; if they have nothing to hide they should not mind showing you. Keep an eye out for rats and mice, droppings, insects, poorly stored food, rubbish and a lack of cleanliness and personal hygiene among staff. If you see it, complain about it. Know what foods and drinks are safest, and know what to avoid (covered later in this book).

✔ If you are a young man, learn the lesson about drunken fights and assaults (see *The Personal Security Handbook*). A holiday is supposed to be a relaxing break, not a series of vague memories hidden in an alcoholic haze, all of which seem to be associated with a range of mysterious battle injuries! If you want a holiday and not a one-way ticket to a foreign hospital or the local jail, drink sociably but don't drink yourself into a fight.

If you introduce these countermeasures, you will probably make yourself at least 50% less likely to become the victim of holiday problems, which isn't a bad result considering you have only read a few pages!

Do you have to have a high IQ? Do you have to be wealthy? Do you have to speak multiple languages or be a trained travel agent to improve your holiday security? No – and that's as hard as it gets.

As you review different aspects of your security, you will need to record any problems you identify. You may develop your own style and method of recording the vulnerabilities, threats and risks, but until then you may want to use the suggested 'form' below.

Use a new form to record each vulnerability, threat or risk that you identify. (From this point on, for clarity I will call any vulnerability, threat or risk a 'problem'.) Making a record of any problems will help you to control and manage them as you gradually resolve them and improve your security.

Fill in the title, and the identified 'problem', with any necessary explanation in the next box. Lastly, add any possible countermeasures you have identified. You may take them from the examples I list in the book if they are relevant to you, or

3

Holiday Planning Review Mr A. Biggins – 2nd to 29th Feb 20XX

PROBLEM
Passport nearly expired or will expire while I am abroad.

OTHER INFORMATION
Newspaper reports indicate that there is a minimum five-week backlog
of postal passport applications which means I cannot get a new passport
by post.

POSSIBLE COUNTERMEASURES
a) Cancel the holiday.
b) The passport office says anyone attending the London office in
   person gets a new passport that day, if all documents are in order. The
   applicant may be waiting for up to 8 hours in a queue for their new
   passport.

---

you may add countermeasures that are appropriate to you and your unique
circumstances and lifestyle.

Recording each problem on a new form allows you to:

• Keep a record of all vulnerabilities, threats and risks identified.

• Gradually review and refine your understanding of the problems as you
  research them.

• As you better understand the problems, you will be able to add to and refine
  the proposed countermeasures. For example, you may find that due to staff
  sickness, anyone who arrives at the passport office after 2pm will not be seen.

• Review and sort the forms, which will enable you to place the countermeasures in priority order.

• With additional analysis you can select the countermeasures you wish to
  implement to resolve any problem. By crossing out the discarded countermeasures you will arrive at a record that shows the problem and the selected
  countermeasure(s).

■ ■

Countermeasures

a) ~~Cancel the holiday.~~

b) The passport office says anyone attending the London office in person gets a new passport that day, if all documents are in order. The applicant may be waiting for up to 8 hours in a queue for their new passport.

Work through this book, reading each section until you understand the problems and the process you will be asked to follow. When you are sure you fully understand it, work through and compile a list of problems and counter-measures specific to you and your lifestyle and circumstances. Make a note of any additional problems you spot that may be unique and appropriate to your lifestyle, holiday or travel plans. When you identify an *additional* threat or risk, record it then use the same common sense process to define a counter-measure.

Definitions

■ ■

If we have a common understanding and definition of some basic terms, we will be able to make better progress.

Security

In the *Security Handbook* series of books, security is the application of methods and procedures that are used to make our lifestyle secure against any vulner-ability, threat or risk. By applying security appropriately, we will achieve safety.

Vulnerability

A 'vulnerability' is the avenue that a threat uses to reach you and cause you harm. If you are careless with your passport and traveller's cheques they may be stolen, but if you take care of them they will be safe.

Threat

A threat is any occurrence that could cause you harm, loss or distress. Threats may be imposed on us by crimes such as theft, robbery, accident or illness. Though most people tend to think of threats from criminal activity or accident, we will also address other threats, for example earthquake, fire, flood and disease.

Risk

Risk is the extent of our exposure to the threats to which we are vulnerable. Risk can be measured in two ways: the impact of the threat or the likelihood of falling victim to that threat.

The impact of a threat is a measure of the damage, injury or loss it could inflict if we fell victim to that threat. For example, the impact of somebody stealing my passport at home is that I will have to get a new one. If they steal it the day I am due to go on holiday, the impact increases because I cannot go on holiday without a passport. If it is stolen while I am abroad, the impact could be greater still. I may be put in prison for illegally entering that country because I cannot prove who I am, and I may not be able to get back into the UK because I have no passport to prove my nationality.

The likelihood of a threat is a measure of the frequency with which we are exposed to it and may become a victim of it. For example, being targeted by an international gang of terrorists, who plan to kidnap somebody and demand ten million pounds in ransom, would be a major threat. However, the likelihood of that happening to me is so low that I won't be losing any sleep over it. I don't have ten million pounds and any international terrorist would know that. I am of no significance to them, so though kidnapping and murder are decidedly serious and unwelcome, because I am not a senior politician, president of a huge corporation or national leader, I am pretty sure they won't be looking for me.

Countermeasures

A countermeasure is something that you can do to improve your safety and security. My aim is to teach you how to identify problems, then how to propose solutions that are appropriate to you and your problems. To do that I will discuss potential problems, then suggest a range of possible countermeasures. None of the lists I produce is exhaustive – they simply illustrate some possible solutions. The lists will be a guide for you when considering your unique circumstances and lifestyle, but you will need to spend some time identifying your vulnerabilities, threats and risks, then finding a countermeasure that is appropriate to your lifestyle and circumstances.

Generally when you identify a threat, there are four things that you can do about it:

- Ignore it and hope it goes away.

- Take action to reduce the risk.

- Take action to avoid the risk.

- Take action to remove it – without taking new and unnecessary risks.

For any given vulnerability, threat and risk some options might not be acceptable because of the intrusive impact they will have on your lifestyle. By under-standing the threat, recognising the options and making use of your skill, experience and knowledge, you can amend a proposed countermeasure or introduce a new one to suit your circumstances. Throughout this book, that will be your primary objective.

- To recognise the sort of problems that are out there and how they can affect you and your lifestyle.

- To look beyond the examples listed, to recognise additional or modified problems to which you are vulnerable due to your unusual or unique circumstances.

- To study those problems and to identify how you can avoid, remove or reduce them.

- To compile an action plan that sets out the actions you have to take or preparations and plans you have to complete to avoid, reduce or remove the risks.

- To continually monitor your life, so that you can recognise change which will be a trigger to performing another security review, to ensure that your lifestyle remains as safe and secure as it can.

Safety

Safety is the status we all want to achieve. Safety can be defined as a circumstance in which vulnerabilities have been removed or reduced to insignificant levels, and threats and risks have been removed by the application of sensible, achievable and affordable countermeasures.

Non-security problems

While performing a security review people often identify problems that are not security related. For example, while checking your hotel in the holiday brochure you may see that fire alarms and fire escapes are not mentioned.

Obviously you should not ignore these problems. They are not strictly security related, but they are a potential threat to us so we have to take action. In this case, call the tour operator or travel agent and ask them to confirm the presence of fire alarms, sprinklers and fire escapes in the resort hotel.

Review Method

The method I propose is easy to follow. The book is broken down into chapters and sections, where each one concentrates on a different aspect of your holiday and travel security. A security review is completed in simple stages.

Stage 1: Review security

You will review an aspect of your security during which you will identify and record any problems that you find.

Stage 2: Prioritise problems

When you have finished the review, you will need to prioritise the problems that you have identified and recorded. When completed, you will have listed them in order of severity, putting those that present the greatest threat to you and your lifestyle at the top of the list, and those that present the least threat at the bottom of the list. This prioritisation process allows you to concentrate on resolving the problems that will give you the greatest possible reward for your efforts, making best use of your limited resources.

Stage 3: Define countermeasures

In stage 2 you prioritised the problems to allow you to concentrate on those that offer the greatest threat to your security. In this stage, you take each problem and attempt to identify and define sensible, achievable and affordable counter-measures that will resolve the problem to your satisfaction. You may come up with only one possible countermeasure, or a list of three alternative counter-measures. Record them all.

Stage 4: Adopt and prioritise countermeasures

For each problem you should consider the possible countermeasures that you identified and recorded. Look at the options and decide which counter-measure(s) you want to introduce. That decision will be based on a range of considerations, including:

- **Benefit** – try to decide by how much any proposed countermeasure will improve your security and safety. A countermeasure that delivers marginal benefits should possibly be shelved while you concentrate on a counter-measure that will deliver greater benefits. However, if you have ten minutes free and can easily introduce that simple countermeasure delivering that marginal benefit, you may as well do it, as long as it is not diverting effort away from a higher priority countermeasure that will significantly improve your security when delivered.

- **Cost** – try to identify the financial cost of introducing each countermeasure. The cost may be easy to identify. For example, 'paying for a good-quality hire car from an international company while at home' will cost £35 per day. Sometimes there are hidden costs, which have to be identified and included. For example, insuring the car for all adults in the party who have agreed to take it in turns to drive may cost £50 per week per person. So there is a hidden cost of an extra £250 to include all drivers.

- **Resources** – you may not have the skills to introduce the selected counter-measure. If you are paying somebody to do it you will get three independent quotes, and pick the quote that offers best value – which may not be the cheapest. As with any purchase, you should also consider reputation and recommendation, quality, availability and your feelings. When dealing with people, I always consider my 'gut feelings' about them. No matter how well he may be recommended, no matter how low he may bid, if I just don't trust him or I feel there is something not quite right, I won't use him.

- **Degree of risk** – you should also consider the level of risk you will be taking by not introducing a countermeasure. For example, if you don't bother checking for a fire alarm and sprinkler system at the hotel, you could lose your whole family.

Stage 5: Implement

When all of the decisions have been made, you have to implement the selected countermeasures in the order you decided upon. That countermeasure may be simple, such as renewing your passport. It may be more involved, such as investigating the symptoms of malaria and putting together a holiday first-aid kit.

This is the most vital stage of the process, the time when you act to protect yourself against the vulnerabilities, threats and risks that you have identified during the lifestyle security review process.

Review Pace

The sooner you review your security and implement countermeasures, the safer you will be, but don't rush the process. Take your time to read each section of this book carefully. Think about each problem that is discussed and consider how that problem or others like it could affect you. When you fully understand them, you will have a valuable insight into the way apparently inconsequential, innocent acts, omissions and decisions could put your security and safety at risk.

When you have finished reading this book, using the examples and descriptions given and your intimate knowledge of your unique lifestyle, you will be able to identify and prioritise the specific problems that could turn you into a victim. More importantly, you will have learned to look at everyday situations in a new way. You will be able to identify where new risks and threats lie, which will allow you to take steps to avoid them. Knowing that not only allows you to make changes to reduce or remove your exposure, it also allows you to continually review your life, identifying and avoiding new threats as they occur.

What You Will Need

To understand and be able to undertake an effective security review, you will need:

- This book and the methodology and explanations contained in it.

- Constant access to, and a close and detailed understanding of, the person and lifestyle of the subject of the review. Which means you can easily review your own lifestyle, you could review a close family member but almost certainly couldn't effectively review the lifestyle of a total stranger.

- Time to read the book, to consider the range and type of problems discussed and to take more time to think through and identify how any of the issues raised could affect your particular lifestyle.

- The ability to decide on the relevance and threat level to your lifestyle of the risks discussed, while taking a broader view to decide if you are subject to other more specific and unique threats and risks.

- A notepad and pencil or other means of recording problems as you discover them as well as assigning appropriate and possible countermeasures.

- The time, knowledge, skill, finances and resources to implement any counter-measure that you select.

Other than that there are no specialist skills or knowledge required to be able to perform a security review. But you must:

- Recognise and understand that there are threats and risks all around us.

- Accept that some of your activities will make you more vulnerable and hence at a greater risk of becoming a victim.

- Learn how to identify potential threats and risks in 'your world'.

- Learn how to identify acceptable and possible countermeasures that you can use to reduce or remove your exposure to those threats and risks.

- Remain alert to your surroundings, particularly in relation to some of your activities and actions.

• Become equally aware of the activities and behaviour of the people around you, and be prepared to take action to avoid developing or potential risks.

When To Do It

If you have never reviewed your holiday and travel security, do it now. After that, you should perform a formal security review before any foreign holiday or business trip, and before any lengthy UK absence. You should also review your plans if there is a significant change to them, for example if there are reports of a typhoid epidemic or hurricane at your proposed destination.

2 Planning

Almost everyone takes a holiday, many of them abroad. Some travel to a seaside resort to relax on a British beach, while others fly off to more exotic locations. UK citizens make over 60 million trips abroad each year.

There are some common problems while preparing for and taking that holiday (or business trip), with a shift in emphasis and severity depending on where and when you go.

As with other books in the *Security Handbook* series, I use examples to illustrate the sort of problems you could encounter and suggest countermeasures that you can take to keep you and your family/group safe and healthy.

It would be easy to appear to be paranoid when reviewing what could happen, but it would be just as wrong to assume that nothing will go wrong, leaving you totally unprepared to deal with any incident that does occur.

If the unplanned-for incident is a simple insect bite, then perhaps the worst that could happen if you weren't ready to deal with it is probably some swelling, discomfort and irritation for a few days. On the other hand, if the incident was a deep cut that needed stitches, or a traffic accident involving a local bus and your rented motorcycle, failing to prepare for emergencies could be a fatal oversight.

How do you stop short of paranoia? That has to be your decision, as only you can decide when adequate planning and preparation slips into paranoia. Read through the book, learn from the warnings and anecdotes, then adopt any ideas that are appropriate to your holiday and travel plans, your experiences and your circumstances.

Look at what could or might happen. Look at the vulnerabilities, threats and risks to which you could be exposed, then look at what you can do to avoid them or reduce their impact. Consider taking appropriate countermeasures to remove or reduce each risk. A simple amendment to your holiday and travel plans could avoid a serious risk entirely.

Look at any risk and what the worst outcome could be, then decide what you want to do about it. The answer might be to pack an aspirin, or it could be to change your plans and go to a different country and resort altogether. For example:

- **Problem one** – an insect bite or sting. I have an allergic reaction to them, but if I take a tube of 'Sting-Away' I can soothe the area, suffer no more discomfort or get any secondary infection. (I made 'Sting-Away' up, so don't go out and try to buy it.) Reviewing the threat and the associated risk, I think my proposed countermeasure is justifiable and acceptable, so I will still go on holiday as planned but with a tube of Sting-Away.

- **Problem two** – a mad camel may kick me and break my collarbone. That injury needs hospital treatment, injections, an operation, a blood transfusion and medical repatriation. That exposes me to disease through tainted blood transfusion, infection from dirty medical instruments, or even blood poisoning resulting in death. My doctor tells me I can avoid all of the potential medical problems by taking a full medical kit, including sterile medical instruments, medicines, plasma, anaesthetics, needles and dressings. For even more protection, I could ask my local doctor to come on holiday with me to make sure that somebody with adequate medical skills is available to treat me. I can take out expensive medical insurance, and even wear body armour and a helmet every time I go near a camel. With all of those countermeasures in place, I am certain that I can avoid the camel injury and subsequent complications that could kill me.

Unfortunately, I think all of that would be far too intrusive and restricting. Those countermeasures are unacceptable to me. I want a holiday. I want to relax, not walk around in protective clothes with a medical team on standby. To fit in with my plans, likes and preferences I have decided to adopt a more sensible, acceptable and achievable countermeasure. Because mad kicking camels have apparently been declared a problem at my destination resort, I will simply make sure I avoid all camels during my stay – if I'm not within kicking range I cannot get hurt!

Preparation

For most people the excitement and pleasure of the holiday begins with the planning and preparation phase. Checking the brochure again for the fiftieth time, discussing romantic sunsets, buying a new swimming costume, selecting the sun tan lotion and skin moisturiser are all thoroughly enjoyable and certainly 'phase one' of the holiday itself.

You probably already consider it to some extent, but I want you to take a more detailed look at your safety and security when you are travelling.

When you go away you are leaving everything with which you are familiar. The more differences there are between home and your holiday destination the greater the risk to you. The more unfamiliar the weather, culture, people, laws, insects, animals, traditions and even landscape are, the greater the chance that you will become a victim of some mishap or crime.

Accepting that holiday destinations present unique threats, you should do everything you reasonably can to identify and avoid those threats. Sensible planning and preparation will relieve you of stress while actually on holiday, because you will know that you have done everything you can to stay safe. It doesn't end there though: while on holiday you have to maintain a level of awareness of your surroundings, so that you can identify and avoid any new threats – those mad kicking camels perhaps!

Through it all, your first objective has to be to relax and enjoy, while maintaining a level of awareness.

The following considerations should help you in planning your holiday, your departure, absence and return. Get them right, and your holiday will be a success, get it wrong and . . .

Leaving your home empty for a week or more while you are on holiday or on a business trip is a new threat that you have to overcome. You must make sure that the house is as secure as it can be for the duration of your holiday. If you have read and acted on the information contained in *The Home Security Handbook* your house should be secure because you will have identified and adopted any holiday-related countermeasures that you have decided are justifiable and appropriate.

Holiday Issues

You should address the following issues while planning and preparing for your holiday.

Remember List

Most people forget something when they go on holiday, but not many forget something important like their passport and tickets, or forget to turn off the bath tap. If you forget something, it is usually just an annoyance but it can have a greater impact.

As soon as you know you are going away on holiday or a business trip, start to compile a 'Remember List'. That is, a list of the things you have to do or take. They may not be as vital as your passport or driving licence, but forgetting them will be annoying. A few sample entries for your Remember List may be:

- Spectacles – your normal pair and perhaps a cheap spare pair.

- Prescription sunglasses (if you want to read on the beach).

- Address of your cousin Doris who lives out there, so you can visit her as promised.

- A videotape of the family Christmas to give to your cousin Doris.

- Your herbal tea, or you won't be able to get to sleep at night.

- Any prescribed medication you are taking with a prescription and note from the doctor.

You can also add other things to the list, which remind you what not to take. For example, you have to take your house key with you, but do you really need to take the whole bunch that you call your house keys? The bunch includes your Mum's back door key, three keys you use at work, that big key you never could figure out what door it fits and your old school locker key that you keep for luck! You don't need to take all of them, so do something about it before you go. What about your hanging baskets and the rest of the garden? Make a note to ask Mr Biggins to water the hanging basket, weed the garden and cut the lawn. (You will do his when they go away.) Use this list to capture everything that comes to mind and will contribute towards you having a really good holiday or worry-free business trip.

Remember List – countermeasures

✓ In the weeks before your holiday, keep a notepad with you. Make a note of anything that comes to mind, things to take, things to leave, things to do, etc. You never know how important the issue you think about may be, so you don't want to risk forgetting something that may be critical to your enjoyment of your holiday (such as holiday insurance).

✓ When preparing for the holiday, remember to actually look at, read and check the documents you are collecting. For example, read the holiday insurance to make sure it covers the right dates, etc.

Passport

Everyone needs travel documents for a long trip. Though passports are not required to travel within the UK, some documents may come in handy when planning and preparing for a holiday or foreign travel.

Check that your passport is valid and will be for the duration of the holiday. Check that there is enough space inside for any visa stamps that you will need. Immigration control may refuse entry if the passport expires during the planned stay, or if there is no space for visa stamps. Take a couple of spare passport photographs in case you need them.

Your passport is more than an official document. Your passport and what is written in it could get you killed. In a hostage situation terrorists often collect passports from their hostages, to see who they are holding. What information could a terrorist get from looking at your passport?

While you are abroad, dozens of people will see your passport. For example, airport, bank and hotel employees will all know your job, your title and the countries you have visited. These people almost certainly don't have any criminal or terrorist links, but it would only take one with those links to threaten your health, safety and security if your passport contains something of interest to terrorists.

- **Stamps and visas.** Apparently, the mere presence of an Israeli entry stamp or visa in a passport could be enough for a terrorist to pick out a passenger. They may feel that they have to kill a passenger just to prove to the authorities that they are serious and will carry out their threats. They need to pick on somebody, and they may base their selection on a tenuous link to their declared enemies, such as an innocent visa stamp in your passport. A new passport won't have any such stamp or visa in it, so there should be nothing to offend a terrorist or pick you out of the crowd.

- **Name and title.** Some people use titles in their passports, hoping for preferential treatment from airlines, or attempting to prove to the world that they are superior beings. Unfortunately, if a terrorist sees that he is holding 'Major General Wilfred Biggins' or 'Lord Biggins of Buglington' he could use a VIP passenger as leverage to make his demands. Being known to the world as plain old Bill Biggins may not get you into the VIP departure lounge, but it won't get you killed either.

- **Job.** What does your passport say about your occupation? Once again, 'senior civil servant' or 'nuclear physicist' may make you feel superior to the average airline passenger, but I would rather that my passport said 'office worker'. Anything that makes me 'one of the crowd' seems quite a good option to me.

- **Ransom.** The information above could make you a target for ransom demands in countries where kidnap and ransom is almost an accepted business. In some countries you have to surrender your passport to officials or to hotel management so that your presence can be registered. It is likely that at some stage employees could read your passport and tip off criminal gangs who would be quite pleased to take a major general, a lord and a nuclear physicist hostage. Not many people will be interested in Bill Biggins, office worker.

Documents – countermeasures

✓ Check your passport and the details held within it.

✓ Depending on what you find, consider replacing it. In a new passport consider removing titles and insert names. Put more innocent sounding employment details in your passport: 'Foreign Minister' may make you feel superior, but 'office manager' would be safer.

✓ **Tickets.** Have them ready for use, not left at home or in one of your five carefully packed and locked cases.

Travel insurance

You should have arranged appropriate travel insurance. You know what sort of holiday you will be taking, so you know what your holiday insurance should cover. Insurance against a range of problems is available – if you request it. If you take more than one holiday each year, annual travel insurance may be a better deal.

Travel insurance – countermeasures

✓ I think holiday insurance is a necessity, not a luxury. Your insurance should at least cover the usual things:

➢ **Your cancellation** – which will pay out if you lose money because you have to cancel the holiday due to illness or maybe if you are required to appear in court as a witness.

➢ **Their cancellation** – which will pay out if you lose the holiday and/or money due to the failure of the holiday company.

➢ **Delays** – which pays out if you suffer loss due to faulty aircraft or the illness of staff, etc. that causes your departure to be delayed.

➢ **Vehicle rental** – which will cover you for the cost of damage to the hire vehicle, damage to any other vehicle or property, legal claims against you, and medical and legal expenses of anyone involved or injured in any incident or accident.

➢ **Special risks** – which you may need if you intend to participate in some activities such as hang-gliding or parachute jumping.

> **Medical cover** – which will pay out to cover treatment, medicines, bandages and medical repatriation for you and all members of your group if required.

Read the small print

Always read the small print in your insurance. Some years ago when a trip went badly wrong I suffered problems with my holiday insurance. Thinking about going for a couple of weeks at some point in the future, my wife and I took a one-day 'Father Christmas' trip just to see what Lapland was like. We were due to fly out of Gatwick at five in the morning and due back at ten thirty that night. When we arrived, the terminal was deserted, but with only carry-on luggage we thought boarding would be quite speedy.

After we arrived and checked in, the ticket staff vanished. An hour later we were still waiting, and nobody knew what was going on. Much later they announced that a 'technical fault' was delaying the arrival of our aircraft, which eventually arrived over two hours after we should have taken off. We took off three hours late.

When we eventually arrived, the Lapland experience was curtailed and spoiled by stupid changes and a lack of co-ordination. Because we were late, our schedule was cut. The sightseeing coach trip was retained, even though in total darkness we could only see each other's astounded faces reflected in the windows. We drove for an hour through what may have been spectacular scenery, but in the darkness we saw almost nothing. Having left the coach trip in the schedule, the organisers dropped the anticipated snowmobile trip 'to save time'.

Next they rescheduled our shopping trip to the local town – forgetting one small detail. We had been delayed so long that by the time we got there all of the shops were shut. Dinner at a local hotel was a rushed snack, 'because we were too late for dinner', having stood around town outside the closed shops for an hour. We then had a very rushed 'hello Santa' for the kids (that was still very well received by lots of excited little faces – and my wife Rita the biggest kid of all), before we were shoved back onto the coach and taken back to the airport.

When we got back we complained to the holiday company but their response was more or less 'tough luck – claim on your travel insurance'. The insurance company refused to listen. They said we had taken out a standard holiday insurance policy, which only paid out if the delay was for more than 12 hours. We pointed out it was only a one day trip but they said it was the policyholder's responsibility to check to make sure that the protection was correct and adequate. They told us to go back to the company who sold us the insurance, because they had misrepresented the cover and/or sold us the wrong cover.

The holiday company denied all responsibility, claimed the changes to the schedule were reasonable, then refused to talk to us any more. A solicitor told me it would cost more than we would get back to take them to court.

So be warned! This taught me not to assume that the company or salesman knows best. I always check what I am being sold.

Insurance – countermeasures

✓ **Driving insurance.** Though most holiday insurance policies cover you for travelling by car to and from destinations, they sometimes only give minimal cover. Your travel agent should be able to advise on the level of cover you need. That should include injury to you, your passengers or anyone else involved in an accident with you. It should cover you for any damage caused to the vehicle you are driving, and any other vehicle or property involved. Finally, it should cover you for any legal action, medical costs and any awards made against you in court.

✓ NOTE: when arranging your car hire and driving insurance, ask if the insurance is for a specific make, model or size of vehicle. I often get offered a free upgrade to a better car. When taking out insurance, check to see that you will be covered for a free upgrade to a convertible or four-wheel-drive. You don't want to be exposed to legal action and compensation claims.

✓ **Health insurance.** You must take out health insurance to cover you for any medical treatment you require while away. Don't be tempted to lie. If you are suffering from a condition that has not been declared to the medical insurers, and then try to claim on that policy, your insurance company may declare your cover to be void. Be open and honest with them. Request medical insurance that covers everything up to and including specialist medical repatriation, hospitalisation, transfers, medicine, fees and any other potential costs. In some countries, the rates charged for treating something as simple as a rash can be extortionate. There are some risks for which you will need specialist insurance, if you can get cover at all. Cave-diving holidays, parachuting, hang-gliding, mountain-climbing and motor-racing were all excluded from my last holiday insurance.

✓ Itinerary. Make sure that you keep a copy of your itinerary easily accessible. You may need to refer to it to find the times and locations of transfer coaches, or contact details for tour representatives. Many tour companies hold you liable for being in the right place at the right time. If you fail to turn up for an airport transfer coach they simply assume you decided to take another route. They will probably not bother to come looking for you. If the transfer coach does accidentally leave you behind, even if the taxi driver doesn't speak English, at least with the itinerary handy you can point to your hotel name and address.

✓ If you are delayed by a broken-down coach or diverted aircraft, with the itinerary you can catch up with your tour or party, by going to meet them where they are scheduled to be.

✓ **Driving licence.** Most people want to hire a car or motorcycle when they go abroad to give them the mobility and freedom to explore. If you don't have your driving licence with you, they almost certainly won't let you drive. Make sure that your driving licence has been packed and is ready to go.

✓ If you do hire a vehicle, make sure that it is roadworthy. In many countries cars that would be on the scrap heap at home are still being used by tourists!

✓ **Emergency contact numbers.** Just in case anything happens, I take a list of emergency contact numbers, insurance policy numbers, plus the embassy and consulate numbers with me. I try to ensure that all members of the party carry a copy just in case we are separated. In an emergency it is best to have them all to hand – you don't want to try to explain to a foreign telephone operator that you want to speak to the British consulate or ask them to help you find an eye surgeon at 2am on a Sunday. Remember it is a holiday and having the contact details handy will give you the peace of mind to relax and enjoy it.

✓ **Medical history notes.** If you have a medical condition, I would suggest that you take an explanatory note from your doctor, if he has approved the trip. You might not be in a position to explain what your allergies are, what ailments you have suffered and what medication you are on, but a brief note from your family doctor could help doctors at your holiday destination to save your life. Take advice from your GP.

✓ **Medication letter.** If you are taking some form of medication, especially if it is critical medication, I would advise you to get a letter from your doctor stating the prescribed medication, its quantity and strength. Some countries are very suspicious of drug smugglers and treat them quite harshly. The legal system in some countries leaves a lot to be desired. I wouldn't want to be locked up in a rainforest jail because I couldn't get the police or customs staff to understand that the pills they found in my bag were legally prescribed to treat a medical condition. A letter could explain that, but if all members of the party had a copy of the emergency contact numbers, while I was in jail they could contact somebody who would be able to help.

Remember, if you require prescribed medication you should bring an adequate supply, still unopened and in the original packaging. That way, customs officers will know the medication is a commercial product.

In case of problems, you should take a note of the generic name of your medication, so that doctors or chemists abroad can identify it and treat you appropriately. One tip that was given to me by a diabetic friend was to pack the main supply of medication safely in your luggage but to carry a ready supply in carry-on bags. Then if there is a delay or your suitcases are lost you have some of your medication available while you look for your luggage or replacement supplies. He told me he now has to make special arrangements when flying. Because of the syringes, cabin staff take charge of his medication until the aircraft is at the destination airport.

✓ **Allergies.** If you have any allergies, for example serious reactions to food or some prescribed medication, you should wear a 'medical alert' bracelet and possibly carry a written explanation of your condition and the treatment to be used should you suffer an attack. Consider having notes translated into the local language.

A holiday can go wrong even when you have made every effort to make sure that everything is as it should be. If something goes wrong, there are some things you can do to maximise your chances of forcing the company to put things right, make sure that the problems do not occur again, and get yourself some compensation.

✓ Make sure that whoever is selling you your holiday insurance understands exactly what you are going to do while abroad. A friend went on a free-fall parachuting course in France, and found when he returned that his holiday insurance had excluded any injury suffered while flying, other than in the scheduled airline, and excluded any dangerous sports, including parachuting!

✓ Make sure that whoever sells you your insurance cover explains exactly what is covered, as well as explaining any exceptions and limits. If it sounds as if the limits and exceptions could be a problem to you, state your concern and ask about alternative cover.

✓ If you make a claim and it is rejected, consider going to the small-claims court to win compensation.

Don't give information away

Your house and property are secure and your car is locked in the garage. Now you are going away. Will you tell all of the local criminals that you won't be at home for two weeks, because you will be on the beach in Barbados or driving across America?

Well you say you won't, but are you *sure* you won't be telling them that? You are excited about your holiday and are happy to tell family and friends, neighbours and colleagues at work all about your imminent adventure. Can you trust all of them? Even if you can trust all of them, who might they mention your holiday plans to? How many people actually know anything about your holiday plans? Take a moment to consider the question and mentally add any names to the list below.

- You cancelled the milk, and because the milkman is talkative everyone at the milk depot knows where you are going and when you will be back.

- You told the newsagent and his staff, so he and fifteen paperboys and their families know, plus three people who were in the shop – and anyone else they told.

- The travel agent and staff know, of course, plus anyone they told and anyone else who was in the shop at the time.

- The bank employees where you got your foreign currency and traveller's cheques know.

- The doctor and his staff know, because you had to ask about and have your vaccinations.

- Everyone where you work knows, plus at least a few customers and suppliers.

- Everyone at the local pub and anyone they speak to know as well.

- Not forgetting everyone at the local taxi company, and they even know the precise date, time and flight numbers of your departure and return!

So, without too much trouble we have identified a minimum of one hundred people who know that you will be out of the country for two weeks starting on the 14th. Are you happy with that?

You aren't planning a military incursion into enemy territory, but it would be a shame if your home was burgled because you couldn't help showing off a little by telling Mrs Biggins about your holiday. I don't suggest that everyone is a criminal waiting for you to say when and where you are going on holiday, I am just illustrating the point that your holiday absence is not exactly a closely guarded secret.

When you speak to neighbours and friends you don't know who else is listening. Talk to someone on the bus and perhaps there is a prolific burglar sitting behind you. Hearing what you say, he gets off the bus and follows you home. Now he knows where you live and he knows that you will be away for two weeks starting on the 14th. He knows that you will be in Barbados and that you live in the really nice house he followed you to, so he thinks it will definitely be well worth him coming back on the 16th. Is that good?

When the taxi comes to collect you and take you to the airport, you quite happily say to this strange man, 'Take us to Terminal Four and then collect us again from the Vancouver flight that lands at Heathrow at 19:35 on the 29th.' Are you happy that you just told a stranger that your house is empty until then?

It is incredibly easy for information about your holiday absence to get into the wrong hands, but what can you do about it?

Information – countermeasures

✓ Limit the number of people who know about your holiday. There will be plenty of boasting time when you come back with stacks of holiday snaps and that straw donkey!

✓ If possible, get a relative to take you to the airport and collect you again on your return, then you won't have to tell any taxi drivers.

✓ If you have to take a taxi, don't tell the taxi company or driver how long you will be gone and consider using a different company to collect you from the airport on your return (that way nobody knows how long you will be gone).

✓ You could consider asking a relative to book the return taxi a day or so before your return so that the taxi staff have little warning about your empty property and little opportunity to do anything about it.

✓ It may be considered rude, but I tend not to talk to a taxi driver about anything other than the weather and traffic. He may be simply talkative, he may just be nosy, but he may be pumping me for details that I don't really want him to have.

✓ If you have to use the same company for the journey to the airport and your collection after your return flight, consider doing some acting. Without going over the top make them think somebody is still at home when you leave. For example, wait until the driver is moving and therefore can't pay too much attention to the house, then wave at your house and say something to him or your partner like, 'Look there's Colin, he said he would wave us off.' Hopefully you will have said and done enough to make the taxi driver think that there is somebody still in the house. Even if he was thinking of making a visit that night, he will hopefully think again.

✓ Don't put your home address on your outbound luggage tickets. They are an advert to anyone at the airport that you are going abroad, and any burglars could treat the departure lounge as a pick-and-mix burglary counter.

✓ Once again, the criminal can read you. Expensive luggage, booked on the scheduled flight to Barbados, home in the posh district of Commuterville – it won't take him long to spot the worthwhile targets.

✓ Have two luggage tickets, the outward bound ticket showing the holiday hotel address, then the return ticket with your home address, that you put on before going to the airport for the trip home. (I doubt if burglars have gone international yet, so anyone in the terminal in Barbados or wherever you are going won't be on the phone to his cousin Jimmy telling him to nip round to burgle your house.)

Holiday reps and tour guides

Some holidays have the benefit of a representative or tour guide employed by the holiday company. They are supposedly on hand to resolve any problems, and to make your holiday as enjoyable as it can be.

I say they are supposedly there, but it doesn't always work like that. I hate organised tours, partly because the reps don't actually do their job. Rather than make themselves available to resolve any problems or issues as they arise, they often demand that you attend them at a time and place to suit them.

On my one and only organised tour, the rep said he would be in reception between ten and eleven each morning. If we had any problems we were to wait for him there, though he said he might sometimes run late! His main interest was to sell us overpriced tours and extras for which he was paid a commission. He wasn't interested in listening to problems. As soon as he realised we didn't want to buy his tickets he left, ignoring the group and the problem we had with our accommodation.

Reps and tour guides – countermeasures

A holiday can go wrong even when you have made every effort to make sure that everything was as it should be. If something goes wrong, maximise your chances of forcing the company to make sure that the problem is solved or it does not occur again, as well as getting yourself some compensation.

✓ Always make sure that you understand exactly what is being offered, what the schedules are and what you are entitled to when organising and arranging a holiday.

✓ Make sure that you have a named contact point for subsequent questions. You don't want to speak to somebody different every time and spend half an hour explaining what you booked, what your question is, then waiting for an hour while they try to find out. Go straight to the person who booked your trip and who hopefully understands it.

✓ If there is a problem, speak to a representative of the company as soon as possible, explain what the problems are and ask what the rep is going to do to resolve those problems and when you can expect a result.

✓ Remember that the travel company representatives are supposed to be there to make your holiday enjoyable. In other words, they should fit in with you, not the other way round. I don't see why I should ruin a whole day of my (expensive) holiday just waiting for the opportunity to say there is a problem. Even if I did sit and wait for them, it could take the representative another day or two to resolve the problem, by which time my holiday is nearly over. I ask for a telephone number so that I can call when and if I have a problem. If they refuse, I complain to their head office.

✓ If a problem is not immediately resolved, start making a written record of what happens. Make a note of relevant times, dates and places. Take photographs if at all possible. Take videotape footage if somebody in the group has a camera. Lodge the complaint as soon as possible with local representatives, or if necessary fax to your travel agent in the UK (the hotel probably has a fax). Write down what the travel company representative or other officials say and do. Make it clear that if the problem is not resolved by a reasonable deadline (under eight hours on a one-week holiday and under 24 hours on a two-week holiday) you will press for significant compensation. Make it clear that you are willing to go through the courts and to publicise the case if necessary.

✓ If there is a problem that affects other travellers too, take their names and addresses. Explain to them that you will get a better response if you act together. Offer to take names, addresses, email addresses and phone numbers so that you can co-ordinate action against the travel company when you get home. The more people who join you, the stronger your case will be.

✓ Don't be afraid to seek publicity. Local and national papers will quite like a story about ruined holidays, crying children who didn't get to see Santa, and elderly or infirm travellers left out in the cold, etc. Make the most of what you have but stick with the truth when you use the media.

✓ Don't accept vouchers or discounts on future holidays as compensation for a ruined holiday. The company ruined one holiday, do you really want to give them a second chance? I always hold out for money, and aim to get a fair proportion of the cost of the holiday as compensation.

Protection – ATOL and ABTA

Two national schemes guarantee your holiday should travel agents or airlines that are members of the scheme cease trading. They are described below. If you book with companies who are members of these schemes your investment in your holiday is protected.

ATOL (Air Travel Organisers' Licensing scheme) is managed by the Civil Aviation Authority (CAA) and protects flights and air holidays that are sold in the UK through members.

The scheme protects you, stopping you from losing money or being stranded abroad if a tour operator ceases trading. To join the scheme, companies have to deposit a specified sum of money that will cover outstanding holidays and flights if they do stop trading.

If the company stops trading, anyone abroad can finish their holiday and get their flight back to the UK paid for out of the fund. Anyone who has not yet gone on their holiday should get their money back.

To qualify, when you pay any money for a holiday and flight the participating travel agents and holiday companies must give you an ATOL receipt. The receipt must give the name of the firm you have booked with and their ATOL registration number.

NOTE: In some cases, for example when no holiday is booked and you only pay for a scheduled flight and get the ticket within 24 hours, you will not be protected under ATOL even if you book through an ATOL member. For more information see www.atol.org.uk

ABTA (Association of British Travel Agents) is a scheme that protects holidays. Travel agents can join the scheme, but they must provide financial protection for their customers. Booking through an ABTA member means that if they cease trading while you are away on holiday, ABTA will guarantee payments so you can carry on with your holiday and return to the UK as though nothing had happened.

Anyone who has not yet started their holiday will get a full refund or possibly be helped to find an alternative holiday for the dates in question.

However, you must be careful, because if your holiday was booked at a non-ABTA travel agent, even though they actually booked the holiday and tickets through an ABTA member, your holiday is **not** protected by the ABTA scheme. If you want protection from ABTA, book direct through an actual ABTA member. For more information see www.abtanet.com

Protection – countermeasures

✓ Only buy from a recognised firm. If you buy tickets from an advert in the local paper, or pay by credit card through the internet, you often have little protection and some people don't get the tickets either.

✓ If you want protection you should make sure that your travel company is an ABTA or ATOL member. That way you know there is a guarantee of some protection.

Foreign currency conversion

When abroad you will use foreign currency in strange denominations, and just to confuse you a little more they sometimes even write the prices down differently as well. The result is that it is too easy to spend a lot more than we realised. Conversion rates and decimal places can make on-the-spot comparisons and calculations difficult.

When prices in some currencies are measured in millions, and there is confusion about the use of commas and decimal places, you can easily find you have spent a week's wages on a pair of cheap plastic sunglasses.

Before I go away, I research the currency and exchange rates. I make up a short comparison list that I carry and soon memorise to help me calculate what I am spending in 'real money'. For example, when you go to the market and see a nice beach towel it may sound like a bargain at the listed price of 91,500 Zorks. After all, in my imaginary country of Zorkland you get thousands of these Zorks for a pound, don't you? To check, I would use my comparison table to help me make a decision as to the cost and value.

Using my invented country of Zorkland as an example, where there are 1,395 Zorks to the pound, my currency comparison list would look like this.

ZORKLAND READY RECKONER
Created 17 Jan 20XX @ 1,395 Zorks to the Pound

POUND	Approx. ZORK
£1.00	1,400.00
£10.00	14,000.00
£20.00	28,000.00
£50.00	70,000.00
£100.00	140,000.00
Cup of tea	900.00
Can of fizzy drink	1,200.00
Meal for two	70,000.00
Taxi fare	7,000.00
Camera film	4,200.00

This gives me a 'feel' for the currency.

I know that £10 is about 14,000 Zorks!

I know that something priced at 42,230 Zorks will cost me the UK equivalent of about £30.

I know that a cup of tea should be about 900 Zorks, so by common sense comparison to UK prices, if somebody asks me for 18,000 Zorks for a glass of orange juice I can do a mental comparison without any mathematics and without my exchange ready reckoner. At 18,000 Zorks it seems to me that I am being asked to pay about twenty times the cost of a cup of tea for just one glass of orange juice. I wouldn't pay that in the UK and I won't pay that in Zorkland either.

Now we can go back to look at the beach towel, offered to us at 91,500 Zorks. Time to use our table and a little gentle mental arithmetic, which is even easier when looking at the table.

> £50 is about 70,000 Zorks, and the towel costs more than that so we already know it costs more than £50.
> £100 is about 140,000 Zorks, but the towel is less than that so we know it is less than £100.
> Without pulling out a calculator, or scribbling on the back of my hand with a ballpoint pen, the towel costs between £50 and £100. It is considerably closer to £50 than £100. So I guess it is about £65 – and at that price it is too expensive and I don't want it!
> Now just to confirm that decision, double check by working it backwards.

> If it is £65, that is £50 which is about 70,000 Zorks
> plus another £10 which is about 14,000 Zorks
> plus another £5 which is 7,000 Zorks
> which is a total of 91,000 Zorks

Which proves our method worked because using the conversion table to convert Zorks to pounds we got a total price in pounds. Then converting that 'estimated' price in pounds back into Zorks we arrive close enough to the original cost of the towel in Zorks that we can be sure our calculations are accurate.

(For anyone like me who just had to calculate it to see how accurate the 'guesstimate' was, 91,500 Zorks equals £65.59.)

Using this method, you have a simple foundation on which to build your understanding of the currency and the pricing system. At the start of the holiday you will use the checklist, but after a few days you will have become more familiar with the currency. You will begin to recognise prices, making mental comparisons and conversions that will allow you to recognise immediately that 1,234 Zorks for a chocolate bar or ice cream is about right.

Foreign currency – countermeasures

✓ Beware of foreign currency. Because you are unfamiliar with the denomination and value of the notes and coins it is easy to find that you have spent far too much money on a cheap item.

✓ Research the holiday, destination and currency, and draw up a simple comparison chart. Use this to fix the value of the currency and the price of a few key items in your mind so that you can quickly recognise reasonable and extortionate prices.

✓ Don't get so tied up in mathematics and conversion rates that you forget to barter. Traders in many countries expect buyers to barter and haggle over the price. They pitch the prices high, expecting to be beaten down a little. If you pay the asking price they think Christmas has come early!

Copy documents

Though I have all the relevant documents to hand I usually make a couple of copies. One copy I leave in the UK with a family member who is listed on my emergency contact list and another copy I keep on me while travelling and in my case while at the destination.

Some documents I always carry with me, such as emergency contact numbers and any important medical information. The copies which could be very useful if cases are lost, or passports, etc. are stolen include:

- Passports

- Tickets

- Travel insurance certificate

- Health insurance certificate

- Detailed itinerary

- Traveller's cheques numbers

- Driving licence

- Emergency contact numbers

- Medical history notes

- Medication letter.

Dental care

Think about your teeth if you are going to be away, especially if you are going to an exotic and remote location. Make an appointment to have your teeth checked before you go. You will get pretty hungry sitting high in the Andes, if because of severe toothache all you can suck on is a chocolate digestive biscuit.

Optical care

Similarly, you may want to make an appointment to get your eyes tested and seek professional advice, especially if you usually wear contact lenses. Get your eyes checked and consider taking at least one spare pair of glasses. (If you were feeling charitable you might even donate them to the local village doctor the day you leave.)

Guidebooks – local rules and laws

An important part of your preparation should be to read some information on your destination. Ask your travel company about leaflets and notes on local rules and laws. Buy a guidebook, look up the destination on the internet or consider contacting the country's embassy in the UK. Research will make you better prepared for your holiday. Research, planning and preparation will reduce risk.

You are expected to abide by their laws when you travel to another country. As a courtesy you should realise that you are a guest, albeit a paying guest, in their country and make sure that you know what their rules are. Ignore local laws, customs and traditions at your own risk.

It can be quite hard to be sure that you are abiding by the law of the land. I once went to Barbados and endured a rather spirited taxi ride from the airport, driving down the middle of the road. Collecting my hire car next day I decided to check to make absolutely sure which side of the road to drive on. When I asked the car hire guy, his laid-back response was, 'In the shade man, in the shade!'

Most important of all are laws and customs relating to drugs, alcohol, religion and national flags. I heard of one guy who was put in prison for two days because he sat on a beach towel which was printed with the country's national flag. It was innocent, but illegal.

Local rules and laws – countermeasures

✓ Research your destination, particularly any local rules and laws.

✓ Identify any laws that are likely to affect you. For example, laws against the possession and consumption of alcohol, or laws that prohibit women from driving cars or wearing short skirts, or laws that prohibit the possession or use of non-prescription and even some UK prescription drugs.

✓ When you have found out what the laws are, you must seriously consider whether you want to be subject to those laws. Don't go abroad and be surprised if you ignore alcohol laws and get arrested. A defence of 'It's OK to drink whisky at home' will not be accepted! If you cannot or will not follow the rules and laws in a country, don't go there or do be prepared to go to jail.

Photography

Many travellers like to take a video or a picture or two while they are on holiday. However, you must be careful when, what and where you take photographs. Even mobile phone cameras can cause problems.

What. In some countries the police and religious leaders object to having their pictures taken, especially if the photographer is a foreigner who is disrespectfully snapping anything that moves and treating them like a cheap tourist attraction.

When. In the wrong circumstances photography may be frowned upon, or in the worst-case scenario it could get you shot. Imagine innocently taking a picture when the local gangster chief is accepting or paying a bribe in the background (or any number of similar circumstances). When taking a photograph, look for the reactions of the people in the background. The more remote and exotic your destination, the more care you should take.

Where. Don't be stupid and casually get off an aircraft at a largely unknown destination and start snapping pictures for the album. Imagine going to a Greek air show, innocently taking pictures of a few outdated Greek aircraft and then being accused of spying! The combination of factors such as national pride, over-zealous officials, language problems, an archaic legal system and stupidity can lead to a holiday snapper appearing in court or the local jail.

Photography – countermeasures

✓ When using your camera remember that people may object to being photographed. Some people feel you are trivialising them. People may object for a variety of reasons.

✓ In some places your holiday snap photography may be viewed as espionage.

✓ Before taking any pictures, ask your tour guide or the subject for permission. Most people know what a camera is, so even if you don't speak each other's language miming taking a picture with empty hands usually gets the message across.

✓ If in doubt, leave the lens cover on and buy a postcard.

Plan for an acclimatisation period

Depending on your destination, you may have to plan a period of acclimatisation into your itinerary, even when travelling within the UK. Taking a walking tour in the Lake District you may need a day to acclimatise and get the muscles working. If you don't and overdo it on the first day you could spend the next week in bed wishing you had eased into it.

Similarly, when hitting the Caribbean after a UK winter of fog and rain, remember to wear a hat, a cotton top, apply copious amounts of sun block and ease yourself into the beach life (see sunburn and heat stroke, etc.).

A day or two of acclimatisation is worth your time. Better that than hit the beach on day one then be repatriated by medical evacuation with first-degree sunburn two days later.

Anyone intending to visit mountainous regions will certainly need longer than a day or two to acclimatise to the altitude and reduced oxygen intake.

Remember, if you are planning anything that will physically and mentally stretch you, speak to your doctor first and heed their advice.

First-aid material

A lot of us only speak English and that can be a problem if you are taken ill abroad. To treat upsets and insect bites I take a small first-aid kit with me. Just the standard things that you would find at home, but all very useful when you don't speak the language and don't know how to find the local chemist, let alone know what they call plasters. My doctor recommended that a first-aid kit should include:

- Two 5 ml syringes and a selection of needles in different sizes

- One dental needle

- One intravenous cannula

- Skin sutures with needles (i.e. stitches to sew up a wound)

- Two packets of skin closure strips (stick-on stitches)

- Two packets of sterile alcohol swabs to clean the skin

- A variety of good-quality sticking plaster dressings

- One large roll of surgical sticking tape

- Aspirin/Ibuprofen (painkillers)

- Anti-inflammatory cream/spray (for bites and burns)

- Anti-acid medicine (for upset stomachs)

- Antiseptic ointment

- Scissors

- Cotton-wool wipes.

NOTE: I have not included sun block and after-sun, etc. in the medical care kit. Also remember to check with the appropriate embassy that you are allowed to take all of the contents of the first-aid kit into the country.

Where medical facilities are very basic at best, in order to avoid being infected with any hypodermics or scalpels that have not been sterilised, take your kit when you need treatment. To avoid cross-infection from contaminated blood products in more remote areas, some experts advise that you take your own supply of blood plasma if you can, with a larger medical kit containing scalpels and other instruments.

I strongly disagree! As far as I am concerned, if medical services are that poor, and your destination is that remote, I suggest that travelling to that country represents an unacceptable risk to your life and health and you should simply not go there.

Illegal drugs

Illegal drugs are a global problem. A few countries seem to be ignoring it, but most impose strict penalties on anyone attempting to smuggle illegal drugs. To reinforce this, it is worth pointing out that more UK citizens are serving prison sentences in foreign jails for drug offences than for any other crime.

Many foreign countries have severe mandatory sentences, even for possession of a small amount of marijuana. A few tourists have been arrested for possessing prescription or over-the-counter drugs, such as tranquillisers and amphetamines or painkillers, which were purchased legally then taken into some Middle Eastern countries, where they are illegal.

If you have any questions or doubts about drug laws in your destination country you should check with their embassy before you go or better still don't buy, carry or rely on drugs in the first place. If you have to take and carry medication, you must check with the country's embassy before travelling.

Political situations abroad

From a variety of sources the UK Government receives information about the political and civil situation in countries around the world. From that the UK Government lists various countries which they advise UK citizens not to travel to at all, or only to travel to if they are on very important business. The threats in these countries are varied but real, so you should always check the lists and seek advice before planning any travel. The Foreign and Commonwealth Office website is www.fco.gov.uk

Vaccinations

When travelling to some countries you are advised to have inoculations against such diseases as diphtheria, hepatitis and typhoid. The pattern and period of inoculations vary, so you will have to seek the advice of your own doctor. He will also be able to advise you on the suitability of your destination bearing in mind your existing state of health.

Ask your doctor about supplies of prescription medicines to cover the holiday period and a letter explaining your medical condition, medication and the generic name of any medical supplies that you have to take with you. (You can then send the embassy of your chosen country a copy of that letter and list of medication if you need to, to get written permission to take it into their country).

You should also remember that some inoculations cause a reaction that could make you feel quite ill for a day or so. After others you will have to have a blood test to see if they have been effective. If not, you may need a booster.

Ask about appropriate vaccinations *at least* twelve weeks before you travel, though I would suggest that if you are thinking of going anywhere more exotic than Spain you should contact a doctor as soon as you can. Remember you will need to be tested to see if some vaccinations have worked, and others are given in a series with a waiting period of days or weeks in between. Leave yourself enough time to ensure that your vaccinations will be effective and that you have recovered from their effects.

Vaccinations – countermeasures

✓ Check carefully to see what vaccinations you need when travelling to a foreign country.

✓ Don't assume that the vaccinations you had when you went to your destination or a similar destination last year will still protect you.

✓ Give yourself plenty of time to research the vaccinations required, order the vaccine via your local doctor, then still have time to take multiple injections and tests over a period of time.

✓ Be prepared to feel unwell for a day or so. Some vaccinations can make you feel quite ill for a short period.

✓ Remember that there is no vaccination for some sexually transmitted diseases – abstain or take some condoms.

Cash/traveller's cheques

When you go abroad you will take some foreign currency and possibly traveller's cheques too. They should of course be secure.

Don't lull yourself into a false sense of security. I have heard of travellers being violently attacked for just a few pounds. In some countries the average weekly wage may be what you expect to spend at home on a snack. You may think of fifty pounds as 'pocket money', but to a native villager it may be more than their annual wage, and well worth attacking you for.

Cash/traveller's cheques – countermeasures

✓ Read the literature that comes with your traveller's cheques and take the security advice they give. Don't sign the cheques in advance.

Suitcase selection

Ever seen baggage handlers and automated baggage-handling systems working? As soon as they leave your careful hands suitcases are treated appallingly. Crushed and slammed around by machines, slapped by conveyor belts, thrown about by staff, jammed into baggage carts, towed through rain and snow, tossed onto slides, and if you're unlucky yours is the bottom case in a pile of twenty!

A suitcase has to be tough or the contents will not survive. If it breaks, don't expect much, if any, of the contents back again. A friend of mine was told his case had been lost. Two days later they called to say his case had been found 'damaged'. A week later a driver delivered his hard plastic case, which was in two pieces. With it were two plastic sacks of garments and 'holiday items', though none of it was his. He assumed that somebody somewhere had scooped 'about a suitcase-worth' of clothes and holiday items off a 'lost pile' and sent them on with what was left of his case and baggage labels!

Buy a case that is strong enough and makes it easy for you to pack, carry, manoeuvre and identify.

Suitcase selection – countermeasures

✓ Buy a case that is easy to identify. Ideally you want to identify your case from a distance. Selecting a bright and unusual colour will help. It is easier to spot a bright yellow case on the baggage carousel than to pick a navy blue case out of the 300 navy blue cases whirling around.

✓ If yours isn't the only bright yellow or cherry red case add some extra identification, anything that will make your case stand out as yours. For example:

➢ Stickers can make your case easy to spot. One neighbour worked for a toy company, and stuck toy stickers all over her cases, making them very easy to identify. Over time the stickers peeled off leaving nasty black sticky patches of grime, but she says that her cases are now the only yellow cases with nasty black sticky patches of grime on them!

➢ Luggage straps can help. They may be just bright colours or may have a name woven into the fabric of the strap. The straps I have seen are quite cheap and don't offer strength or security. If they stay on they make it a little easier to identify the cases.

➢ I have seen cases with painted diagonal stripes. The paint chips and wears off with use, but then I assume the owner simply applies a new coat of paint to the case and gives it time to dry.

➢ My wife Rita favours wool as an identifier. At first I was sceptical. Having seen very strong cases crushed and chewed up by the systems and staff at airports, I didn't think a few strands of wool would survive, but we tried it. She took a dozen strands of brightly coloured wool that were about six inches long, folded them in half and threaded them through the handle and tied them in a knot. That left each case displaying a scrawny red and yellow fringe around the handle. Four years later the wool is still there, and it is surprisingly easy to pick out our 'fringed' cases.

✓ Where possible buy cases with a hard shell. Soft cases offer less protection to the contents, and the soft fabric can be torn while in transit, exposing the contents to loss, dirt and weather.

✓ With hard-shell cases, look for a watertight seal. This is a rubberised gasket around the edges of the case, which when closed and locked forms a waterproof seal.

✓ The larger the case the more important it is that it has a built-in extendable handle and wheels so that it can be wheeled through the endless airport arrival and departure halls.

✓ Some hard cases can even be used as a temporary seat. Simply stand them down, retract the handle and they are strong enough to sit on while you await a delayed flight or work your way towards baggage check-in.

Packing

When packing, take the advice given to you by travel companies and airlines.

Packing 1 – countermeasures

✓ Only use your own cases and bags – so you know that nobody has sewed drugs or anything else into the lining.

✓ Always pack cases yourself and never leave them unattended.

✓ Seek and take the advice of travel companies and airlines when organising and doing your packing.

✓ Don't pack sharp bladed or pointed instruments in your hand luggage. They could all be seized and disposed of by the airline, no compensation is payable and, no matter what they are, if you want to take that flight the items will be removed and will not be returned to you.

✓ Airline rules require that electrical items packed in your luggage should not contain batteries. Batteries must be removed and packed separately. Items containing batteries will be spotted on x-ray equipment and the cases will be opened and the batteries removed. I have known airlines to call a passenger to a check-in desk and require them to open the case and remove batteries in front of a departure lounge full of nosy passengers.

✓ Make sure that your cases are secure and robust enough to take the damage they suffer in transit and at the hands of baggage-handling staff and machines.

✓ Make sure that the lids of any containers (such as shampoo or sun tan lotion) that you pack are securely fastened. If in doubt, discard the container or at least seal it in a plastic bag.

✓ Keep your bags with you at all times to prevent tampering and/or theft.

✓ Lastly, another reminder to have your tickets and passport, etc. available – don't pack them in your case!

Packing – what to wear and take

When you pack and prepare to travel, pay careful attention to the clothes you will wear and those you will need when you reach your destination, especially when flying. Leaving London in August you may be wearing a shirt and shorts, but when you land in northern Finland you will appreciate warm clothes and a coat when you step off the aircraft.

Take the same care when you fly back. Know what weather conditions you will be flying into and wear or carry suitable clothing for those conditions. Acclimatisation can produce strange results. My wife and I went to Canada where we drove through the Rocky Mountains one winter. It was spectacular and a holiday to be recommended. We had a four-wheel-drive car, did some snow-shoeing, hiking with a guide and on our last day went on a dog sled, 'mushing' through mountain passes at minus 41 degrees. The whole holiday was breathtaking in more ways than one.

We flew back into London and slipped on our winter coats when we landed, then quickly took them off again. Having acclimatised to an average of minus 30 degrees in the Rocky Mountains, at Heathrow we found it uncomfortably warm at just above freezing! Everyone thought we were mad for the next week or so, commenting on our light clothing and indifference to a little frost and ice. It took us well over a week to re-acclimatise to the UK winter.

Packing 2 – countermeasures

✓ Carry the clothes you will need when you arrive at your destination. You don't want to step off a plane from Florida into a UK winter and have to empty your cases to find a jumper to stop you freezing to death.

✓ Consider carrying a change of clothes for small kids and yourself in case the baby is sick on you during a flight.

✓ Consider having some books or puzzles in your hand luggage to keep small kids amused. Don't take anything noisy – let the other passengers have a little rest during the flight!

✓ Consider packing some boiled sweets to suck while taking off and landing. Sucking sweets helps to equalise the air pressure in the ears, sinus, etc., avoiding pain and discomfort.

Flight times

Flight times are given, but most airlines insist you arrive and check in at least two hours before the flight is due to take off. For some destinations, the check-in time is even further ahead of the flight.

Flight time – countermeasures

✓ On the day, confirm your flight time and the suggested check-in time. Incidents elsewhere may have forced the operators to change both. Make sure that you have the latest information.

✓ Check for delays and restrictions on your travel to the airport. A derailed train or a motorway accident could mean that you have to leave home an hour or more earlier to reach your destination.

✓ Despite all of the security, baggage does get damaged, lost and misrouted. Make sure that any critical items such as passports, money, medication, tickets and itinerary are not in a case that is checked in. You may not see that case again for a week or more. Keep these critical items with you.

3　Health

Throughout this book I tell you to seek expert advice if you are in any doubt about anything. Due to varying states of health, allergies, complications and circumstances, it is almost impossible to give general medical advice. In health matters, you should always seek expert medical assistance immediately. If you are caught in the jungle or on a mountain slope, miles from assistance, I offer some advice that could help to keep you alive. Before travelling, check with your doctor to make sure that the general advice given here is relevant to you and your medical condition and history.

When abroad, no matter where you are, you should be particularly careful with your health for a number of reasons.

- UK citizens are becoming increasingly adventurous, arranging to travel to ever more exotic and remote locations.

- Around the world there are any number of deadly diseases and conditions that can easily kill you or make you very ill.

- You can pick up infections that you can carry and pass on at home.

- There is a potential lack of decent, effective and available medical care at your holiday destination.

- Local medical costs can be exorbitant.

- Treatment may be refused unless you agree to pay medical fees in advance in cash, or unless you can prove that you have insurance that will cover those potentially huge medical fees.

About 50% of UK citizens have now abandoned the traditional package tour to a Spanish beach, preferring to arrange personalised holidays to increasingly exotic locations. UK tourists are now likely to be on a trek through the Himalayas, or on a jungle safari in search of rare orchids or animals. The following advice on holiday health will educate you and prepare you for the new health challenges that foreign holidays can bring.

This advice is designed to bring risks to your attention and to highlight hidden health dangers associated with travelling off the beaten track (or on that Mediterranean beach). I have included descriptions of common symptoms, to help you recognise the possible onset of a potentially fatal disease. I have also included potential countermeasures you might use to avoid contracting those diseases or to apply emergency treatment if necessary. Whatever you do, as soon as possible seek expert medical advice and treatment.

Water and Food

Many people suffer food poisoning while abroad. The problem isn't the water and food, it's the bugs and germs that are swimming in it, or climbing and breeding on it. Local people have usually built up a natural immunity to the infections, so they easily shrug off any bacteria and virus. A tourist can arrive in the country, take one sip of water and then be so ill from an infection that they spend the rest of their holiday in bed.

Holiday ailments like the infamous 'Delhi Belly' and 'Montezuma's Revenge' *are not inevitable*. If you follow some simple rules on hygiene, food and drink, you can greatly reduce the risk of suffering from these infections.

Be warned that apparently simple infections that cause diarrhoea and vomiting can lead to dehydration and ultimately to fatal complications. Young children and the elderly are particularly susceptible to dehydration.

You should be able to avoid the usual stomach upsets by taking some simple precautions.

Water and Food – countermeasures

✓ If travelling with young or frail people, consult your doctor before you go. Decide if the risks are acceptable and consider leaving young and the old and frail at home. If you take them, ask your doctor about taking re-hydration formula or anything else to help them recover if they fall ill.

✓ If any member of your group suffers from an infection, seek medical assistance immediately. These infections can easily become life-threatening.

✓ *Strictly* observe basic hygiene rules. Wash your hands when you have been to the toilet and before you eat or handle food. Make sure you use good-quality soap. Make sure that you dry your hands thoroughly afterwards using a clean towel.

✓ When you brush your teeth while abroad, don't trust the local water. Make sure that you use bottled or (cold) boiled water with your toothbrush.

✓ If self-catering, thoroughly wash all toilets, basins, kitchen work surfaces, plates, saucepans and utensils, using hot water and a bacteriological washing liquid or cleaner before you do anything else. Then thoroughly wash your hands again.

✓ Don't use a grimy wash cloth or tea towel. They are an efficient way of breeding and spreading germs.

✓ Any raw food is potentially contaminated. Don't buy raw food that is exposed to the touch in shops and markets. It is also exposed to flies and air-borne contaminants. Don't buy it, use it or eat it.

✓ Some raw foods such as oysters are especially prone to infection.

✓ Never eat salad ingredients that are unwashed or may have been washed in local water. If the water is contaminated, the food is contaminated too.

✓ If you want to risk eating salad, thoroughly wash it yourself, using clean boiled and cooled water or bottled water.

✓ Try to eat hot cooked meals where possible! Cooking makes the food hot, which kills most infections. Hot food means safe food – as long as it is fresh, hot and recently cooked.

✓ Don't forget that hot food served on dirty plates and with dirty cutlery, or drinks made with local water, can all infect you.

✓ How clean were the waiter's hands when he handed you that bread roll?

✓ Undercooked food is as dangerous and sometimes more dangerous than raw food.

✓ Avoid re-heated or warmed food. Re-heating food creates the perfect breeding ground for infections. Some hotels prepare food then leave it sitting around for hours, if not days, and then re-heat it. Others cook food and leave it on display in a restaurant or buffet in barely warm food containers – all of which introduces infection and increases the risk of diners becoming ill. Try to avoid standing food. Aim to eat freshly cooked hot food.

✓ If the conditions in the restaurant or dining room look less than clean, eat elsewhere.

✓ Some tropical fish contain high quantities of ciguatoxin, a harmful bio-toxin. Barracuda is apparently the worst, but it is also present in red snapper, grouper and amberjack. Unless they are tested, nobody knows how much ciguatoxin they contain, so be wary of exotic fish!

✓ If you are self-catering, be careful where you buy your food. They may claim it is pork, but it could be lizard or donkey! Worse, you don't know where that 'apparent' pork chop has been and how long it has been sitting there acting as an airfield for the local flies while it waits for you to buy it.

✓ If you buy fresh, try to buy things that you know are safe. Something that is wrapped by nature or a factory should be safe. A sack of local beans could be suspect. Baked beans in a can should be safe from contamination (assuming the can isn't dented, past its sell-by date, rusty or pierced). An undamaged banana, orange or other fruit that has to be peeled should be safe because it was wrapped by nature.

✓ Avoid washing anything that you eat whole, such as grapes! Try to avoid eating fruit that you can't peel, or wash using safe bottled water.

✓ Vegetables that need to be peeled and then cooked should be safe, because when the skin comes off most of the contaminants and potential infections are removed, and cooking kills almost anything else if you reach a high enough temperature.

✓ At a restaurant, don't be scared to ask to see the kitchens, especially if you will be eating there for the duration of your holiday. I have seen kitchens where I wanted to wipe my feet on the way *OUT* because they were so bad. Dirty walls and floors, windows open to flies, rodent droppings clearly visible, cockroaches wandering around. Pans, cookers and vents clogged with fat and grime, and cooked and raw food sharing the same cutting board. In one kitchen I saw a rat sitting behind a bin chewing on something! If it looks bad, avoid eating there and consider quietly warning others in your hotel about your concerns. Don't make a fuss. Some owners have been known to take a kitchen knife to a tourist who speaks out about a dirty kitchen. Report any concerns to your holiday company and get their response in writing.

✓ Even if you can't see into the kitchen, if the rest of the place is overrun with flies, the kitchen probably will be too. Find somewhere else to eat.

✓ Beware of rich foods, and exotic sauces and spices. They alone can be rich enough to upset a British stomach raised on burger and chips and an occasional roast potato or pork chop.

✓ Unscrupulous cooks can use spices to disguise the taste of slightly rancid food. Avoid spicy food unless you like it. If so, make doubly sure that the kitchens are clean.

✓ Some countries see the quality of their water as a status symbol, so they won't declare that it is unsafe to drink. It may be safe for the locals who have built up a working immunity to it, but it may not be safe for a tourist with no immunity.

✓ *Drink bottled water*, but make sure that the bottled water is safe. Criminals abroad know that we demand bottled water, so they are not slow in putting local tap or river water in bottles and selling it to us at a vast profit.

✓ Check bottled water is safe. Buy brands that you know and recognise. Check that the bottle lid is sealed and intact, then you are pretty sure that it has not been refilled with local water. Hold the bottle upside down and squeeze it gently, if it leaks it might have been tampered with. In any case, if water can get out through the cap, contaminants can get in, so don't buy it.

✓ Remember that water comes in other forms. Don't order a glass of water with your meal – ask for a sealed bottle so you know it is safe. If you want a whisky with a little water or a glass of orange squash, make sure it isn't local tap water they are using.

✓ Ice is water too, so avoid ice cubes or an ice lolly for you or the kids. They could be made with contaminated water.

✓ Similarly, avoid ice cream, yoghurts, etc. They could be swimming with harmful bacteria.

✓ Because they are made with boiling water, coffee and tea are usually safe, but consider avoiding local milk.

✓ Swimming pools are full of water. One survey showed over 25% of holiday pools used by British tourists abroad contained an unacceptably high level of bacterial infections. You only know it's infected when the whole family suffers from something nasty a few days after taking a swim. Avoid pools if you can. Make sure that the hotel or resort claims that their pool is clean and regularly tested and treated.

✓ On arrival, ask some of the guests who have been there for a while if they use the pool. If they say yes and they are OK, the water in the pool should be safe – for now anyway.

✓ Coastal seawater can also be heavily infected and/or contaminated. In rougher seas you are more likely to swallow some of the water with any infection and contamination it holds. (Also see warnings about strong currents, tides, sharks, jellyfish, etc. below.)

Diseases

For most people in the UK their biggest medical worry is whether they will catch a particularly debilitating dose of the flu each winter.

Washing your hands and maintaining standard domestic and kitchen cleanliness will reduce the chance of picking up a UK winter virus. If you are infected, you'll feel rough for a few days and then you will be back to normal, so the risks associated with becoming infected by most UK viruses are minimal.

Abroad, things are very different. Even just across the channel there are diseases that can easily kill. Tropical climates are particularly hazardous when discussing possible infections, but what are those infections?

To us, foreign diseases are just words you hear on the television news. We may vaguely recognise them as diseases but they aren't of any concern to us, until we go abroad.

Researching foreign diseases can be worrying, but I want you to worry! I want you to worry just enough to tear down your complacency and see how serious a threat these diseases could be to you and your family. Abroad you risk infection with some really serious and highly contagious diseases. I want you to be motivated to take steps to avoid infection. The diseases you may find in many holiday destinations include:

- Dengue fever (mosquito bite)

- Hepatitis (contaminated food or drink)

- Cholera (contaminated food or water)

- AIDS/HIV (sexual contact or bodily fluid transfer)

- Diphtheria (contact with infected person)

- Yellow Fever (mosquito bite)

You don't have to be a doctor to recognise most of them, but not knowing about them can lead to complacency. So the news says that 'Viral Hemorrhagic Fever' has broken out at my destination. I never heard of it, so should I worry? It's rare, isn't it? Something they catch in dirty villages – nothing for me to worry about, right?

You should worry about it because that term covers a range of similar conditions that you probably have heard of, including the more familiar Lassa fever, Marburg disease, and Rift Valley fever, and anyone can be infected.

At the same time the names of other infectious diseases scare us, but they may no longer be a threat. Smallpox is a killer, isn't it? Well it was. The World Health Organisation declared that smallpox has been eradicated.

But the plot thickens. The WHO now advises people *not* to take the smallpox vaccine. Apparently the minute risk of developing smallpox from the vaccination now presents a greater risk than not being vaccinated and risking contracting the disease (if it still exists).

Having warned you of the range of deadly tropical diseases that exist, I want to finally destroy any possible complacency that you may have about European diseases. Don't assume that all the really bad diseases only exist in tropical climates. Here are just two examples of European diseases.

Rabies

Rabies is almost always transmitted by an animal bite (unless the virus is somehow introduced into an open wound). The incubation period is between one and three months, but it can take several years for the virus to reach the brain and spinal cord, when symptoms appear.

All mammals are susceptible. The dog is the main carrier of the disease. There are two common types of rabies.

Furious rabies. These animals/victims are hostile to anything and everything, including inanimate objects. Infected animals usually produce lots of saliva. The movies show them foaming at the mouth. They don't, but they do dribble.

Dumb rabies. These animals /victims appear to be quiet, timid and shy. They often reject food and their lower jaw seems to be paralysed.

When abroad, you should play safe and avoid all animals. Anyone who thinks they have been exposed to rabies must:

• Remove any clothing that may still be contaminated with saliva from the biting animal, remembering to protect any wound from other infections such as flies and dirt.

• Immediately clean the wound and the surrounding area very thoroughly with soapy water. The more you wash the wound the smaller your chance of infection. Wipe outwards away from the wound – don't grind any saliva, infection and dirt into the wound.

• Apply a povidone-iodine solution if it is available.

• After thoroughly washing the wound with clean water, seek medical attention as soon as possible. Go to the nearest doctor or hospital immediately.

• Report all bites to the local authorities so that they can deal with the animal.

• As soon as you get back to the UK see your own doctor and report the circumstances of the incident, plus any treatment you had, then ask them to check you over.

Warning signs of rabies in animals. Animals with rabies may appear to act differently to normal healthy animals, and will behave differently depending on whether they have dumb or furious rabies. Some changes you may notice:

• Animals suffer behavioural changes when infected.

• Wild animals may be seen to be moving slowly or acting tame, or seem to be 'uninterested' in things and people around them.

• Infected animals may display signs of general sickness before other symptoms appear.

- A pet that is usually friendly may become aggressive and try to bite people or anything nearby.

- Infected animals often have problems swallowing.

- Depending on the type of infection they may produce a lot of saliva or can suffer partial paralysis.

- When an animal or human is infected and showing signs of the disease, it is too late – the result is always death.

Early symptoms of rabies in humans. The symptoms vary but they could include:

- Fever

- Headache

- Sore throat

- Feeling tired.

All of which could just be the early signs of flu – which is why it is important to seek medical advice and treatment after any bite or wound caused by an animal abroad.

Other symptoms of rabies in humans include:

- When the virus reaches the brain, the victim can become nervous, confused and upset.

- Pain or tingling at the site of the bite.

- Possible hallucinations.

- Hydrophobia – a fear of water.

- Paralysis in parts of the body.

As the disease advances, an infected person finally goes into a coma and dies.

There are vaccines, but the victim has to be treated as soon as possible. Without treatment, all victims will die.

Rabies – countermeasures

✓ Avoid animals when you go abroad – any of them could be infected.

✓ Use common sense and don't go anywhere near an animal that the locals are avoiding.

✓ Avoid any animal that seems to be aggressive or behaving oddly.

✓ Don't get bitten or scratched by any animal.

✓ Treat and cover all scratches and cuts, to prevent infection from entering an open wound.

✓ If bitten or scratched by an animal, seek medical help immediately.

Lyme disease

Lyme disease is found in temperate forested regions. It is not found in tropical climates.

Lyme disease is transmitted to humans through the bite of infected ticks, which are found in grass, bracken and bushes. The ticks jump onto people walking through the undergrowth and then work their way to a warm moist area. Once there they bite and treat you like a mobile snack bar. Actually the ticks don't just bite, they hold on to suck your blood over extended periods. By doing so they inject 'spirochetes' into you.

Anyone infected with Lyme disease can usually be cured by an appropriate course of antibiotic treatment. If in doubt, seek advice from your doctor or local hospital.

Warning signs of Lyme disease. Infected people display:

• A characteristic expanding rash at the site of the tick bite

• Fever

• Arthritis

• Neurological symptoms, for example facial paralysis.

Lyme disease – countermeasures

✓ Walkers should avoid walking in areas where ticks are known to be common – take local advice.

✓ Wearing long trousers that are tucked into socks, long-sleeved shirts, etc., offers some protection if you have to work or walk in an area where the ticks are present.

✓ Don't leave bare skin exposed or places where the ticks can get into your clothing. A shirt may be buttoned, but ticks can still get inside the shirt.

✓ Tick repellent used according to instructions on your skin and clothes should deter the ticks.

✓ Anyone walking in brush, bracken, etc., should regularly stop to check for and remove ticks. It is unlikely that infection will occur in the first 36 hours of tick attachment. Regularly removing them will drastically reduce the risk of infection.

✓ I am told that the way to remove ticks is to touch them with a burning cigarette – if you do, they let go. If you are a non-smoker, avoid trying to hold the tick to pull it off. Pinching the tick tends to squeeze it, injecting the contents of the tick through its own bite into your body. Instead, use the same method that is used to remove a bee sting. Put the thumbnail against the body above the tick. Scrape downwards through the tick so that your thumbnail acts as a blade pulling, scraping and removing the tick.

✓ If you discover that you have been providing lunch for any ticks, scrape them off, then take them with you in a sealed container to seek medical advice, or leave them on and get the doctor to remove them – assuming you can get an appointment quite quickly.

Mosquitoes and Malaria

Malaria is a highly debilitating and sometimes fatal parasitic disease, which is spread through the bite of an infected mosquito. Malaria is present in all tropical countries (and is creeping north into new areas). It comes in different forms, some of which are a lot more dangerous than others.

Local people often have a natural immunity to the effects of malaria, but tourists don't. About 2,000 UK residents contract malaria each year, and some of them die. If you are going to a tropical destination, ask your doctor for advice about anti-malaria treatments and measures.

If you are going to a high-risk area, your doctor can prescribe a course of the most appropriate medication, which has to be started at least a week before your trip.

Anyone making a last-minute booking is at greatest risk, because they may not have had time to see their doctor, or obtain the correct medication.

General mosquito, tick etc. – countermeasures

Though the medication is effective, you will still have to take precautions to avoid being bitten.

✓ Take any medication prescribed and always finish the course of medication. Don't assume that you can stop taking it because you are feeling OK or are back in the UK.

✓ Take and use effective insect-repellent creams.

✓ If you suffer from any fever and feel ill while abroad, or for up to three months after you come back from an infected area, see your doctor. Describe your symptoms and tell him you recently returned from an area infected with malaria.

If you are interested in researching any specific diseases, you may find the World Health Organisation website interesting at www.who.int/health_topics

Avoiding mosquito bites

First the bad news. You might just be unlucky, because some experts claim that mosquitoes are attracted by smell. If you are really unlucky your natural body odour might smell like a Sunday lunch to any passing mosquito.

Now the good news. More often than not it is a combination of the smell of your soap, aftershave, perfume, deodorant or skin cream that is attracting them.

Avoiding mosquitoes – countermeasures

There are three basic strategies.

Avoidance

✓ Don't give mosquitoes an opportunity to bite you by avoiding them in the first place.

> ➤ Places. The mosquito needs standing water to breed. A warm, humid, swampy area with plenty of pools or ditches full of stagnant water will provide an ideal breeding ground. When arranging your journey, avoid any area where conditions make it likely that the mosquito population will be high.

> ➤ **Location.** Most mosquito, tick and other insect-borne infections can be identified as being common in a given place. By avoiding travel to those places, a traveller can avoid exposure to the infection. Research and local advice should tell you the places to avoid. Generally, rural locations offer the greatest hazard.

> ➤ **Time.** The mosquito is particularly active during twilight at dawn and dusk and fairly active all night. If possible, plan your activities to avoid the times when the mosquito is most active.

> ➤ **Season.** To some extent some mosquito and other insect-borne infections are seasonal. By re-searching the destination and diseases, a traveller can avoid the times of year and seasons when infections are being carried by these insects.

> ➤ **Smell.** As mentioned above, whatever your combination of smells, if you are plagued by mosquitoes, you might try changing your smell. Use un-perfumed soap, or use a different brand of deodorant, your fabric softener, shampoo, hairspray, hair gel, skin cream, perfume or anything else you can think of that may change your smell. But remember your aim is to put the mosquito off, not the other people in the hotel or on the beach around you!

> ➤ **Speed.** Wind speed or your speed will defeat the mosquito. For example, when you are standing (safely and well back) on a cliff top enjoying a bracing wind, you will not suffer mosquito bites, because they couldn't cope with the wind strength. Similarly, if you have a convertible car with the hood down and are driving to a party through the smelliest swamp, you are safe from a mosquito, because they can't catch up with a car doing 50 miles per hour. (Is it safe to be doing 50 miles per hour through a swamp?)

Barriers

✓ Putting barriers between you and a mosquito will protect you.

✓ Before you go to bed:

➤ If fitted, close mosquito screens at all doors and windows before dusk. If no screens are present, close the doors and windows to stop more mosquitoes coming into the room.

➤ Spray the room with a mosquito killer, to kill any that got into the room when the doors and windows were open.

➤ Turn up the air conditioning if you have it. Apart from making you more comfortable, the cooler temperature seems to make mosquitoes less active and so less likely to bite.

➤ Make sure that beds are fitted with mosquito nets.

➤ Give a final spray of mosquito killer inside the net half an hour before you get into bed (giving the spray time to dissipate before you get in).

➤ When you get into bed, make sure that there are no live mosquitoes inside the net, and that the net is properly fitted and tucked in.

✓ Wear clothes that will cover as much bare skin as possible.

✓ Wear long sleeves and trousers to expose the minimal amount of skin to mosquitoes, especially in calm weather and at dawn and dusk when they are most active.

➤ Consider increasing your protection by tucking trousers into socks to prevent mosquitoes crawling inside your clothes.

➤ Think about wearing gloves and a hat too.

➤ A mosquito hat has mosquito netting attached. It is a wide-brimmed hat with a veil of mosquito-proof netting which keeps the mosquitoes off your face, ears and neck. It also prevents that annoying tickling and the whining noise when they cluster around your face.

➤ When wearing a mosquito hat consider tucking the netting into your shirt to prevent mosquitoes from getting underneath where they can bite.

➤ You can sit in a screened area, a sort of patio with walls and a roof of mosquito mesh screens all around you. Just like getting ready for bed, you will have to spray and kill any mosquitoes that are already inside. When the screened area is clear and the screens are shut, you have the advantages of sitting 'outside' while being protected from mosquitoes and other insects.

➤ Mosquitoes seem to be attracted to bright colours, just like a bee or wasp will fly around somebody in a bright yellow top. Avoid clothes made of bright-coloured material and some flower and leaf prints. Plain colours such as khaki, beige and olive seem to be safe to wear.

Treatments

✓ You can use chemical treatments to prevent bites.

➤ You could spray the surrounding area, killing any mosquitoes present.

➤ At the same time, drain or fill in any pools of stagnant water in the area to deny breeding grounds for new generations of mosquitoes.

➤ You could spray your house, mosquito net, patio, even clothing (depending on the spray being used – check the instructions) to deter them.

➤ You could apply special creams and sprays to yourself, concentrating on any exposed skin.

✓ When using chemicals, be warned that they are quite strong. Abroad, you may be using a product from a questionable source where quality control and safety may not be the highest consideration.

➤ Take local advice about which products work – but ask hotel staff, not the shopkeeper who wants to sell you the most expensive thing he has got.

➤ Always read the can, bottle or packet before buying and before use.

➤ Always read and strictly follow any instructions given.

➤ If there are no instructions, don't buy the product.

➤ Do not eat, drink or breathe mosquito poison or repellents and do not get them in your eyes or in open wounds.

➤ When using a new product, test it on a small area of fairly sensitive skin, such as the inside of your forearm, following the instructions on the packet. Wait to see if there is any reaction. If there is – don't use it. If not, try using it on all exposed skin.

➤ Only apply repellent on bare skin. Do not apply it to skin that will be covered with clothes. (Sometimes clothes rub and make the skin sore. If you have repellent on the skin and on your clothes, the rubbing action will grind the repellent chemicals into your sore skin.

➤ Be wary of applying repellent to your forehead. You don't want perspiration to carry it into your eyes.

➤ When you have applied the repellent, wash your hands thoroughly.

➤ Never touch your eyes or food until you have washed your hands thoroughly using soap and water and then fully dried them using a clean towel.

✓ Though some reports suggest that taking vitamin B1 will stop a mosquito from biting you, other reports claim vitamin B1 makes no difference. Your choice!

✓ Some people claim that smoking will deter mosquitoes. That may work on the smell principle, but I have seen no research to prove the theory.

✓ Finally, I am told that mosquitoes don't like Marmite. Apparently people who eat Marmite (the yeast-based savoury spread) seem to become 'unattractive' to mosquitoes!

Injuries and Illness

When abroad, be very wary of disease and injury. In extreme climatic conditions, a small scratch that you wouldn't give a second thought to in the UK could very quickly deteriorate to a state where it needs urgent medical attention and could even become life-threatening if left untreated.

Injury and illness – countermeasures

✓ Before you leave the UK make sure that you have had all of the vaccinations that are recommended for your holiday destination.

✓ When you pack, include a basic medical kit, so that you can clean and dress minor wounds to keep infection and infestation at bay.

✓ Before travelling to remote places, seek expert advice on the medical supplies to take.

✓ Take advice about local threats to your health, such as dangers from swimming in rivers and lakes, snakes, scorpions, wild animals, blood-sucking insects, etc.

✓ If you are injured, treat the wound immediately. A small cut in a hot climate can become infected.

✓ The same cut in a cold climate can be just as dangerous. You might not be able to feel the pain that tells you that you have been injured. A small cut in sub-zero temperatures can lead to the loss of a finger or a hand.

✓ If you are bitten, scratched, stung or even sunburned, seek medical advice and treatment. Be safe, not sorry.

If you do seek local advice, make a note of what they say when they treat you. Though they have treated you there may be complications or the treatment may be wrong or need to be continued at home. Get whoever treats you to write down what caused the injury, the diagnosis, the recommended treatment and any treatment given.

If you need to see your doctor back home, this should be enough information for him to understand what has been done, and decide what he should do. Just the name of the species of plant, snake or insect that caused the problem can be a great help.

Other Health Threats

Geological movements

Earthquakes are more common than most people think. When I was in San Francisco I was surprised to see that the daily newspaper carried a tally of the number of small shocks that had been recorded each day, and there were usually several.

Geological movements can include major earthquakes, volcanic eruptions and tidal waves.

Geological movements – countermeasures

✓ Research will tell you which areas are subject to these risks.

✓ When you book, ask your travel agent to inform you of any impending eruption or other disaster.

✓ Some areas in the world are known to be on continental fault lines, and so are more likely to suffer problems. It is up to you to decide if the risk is too great to take.

Weather

The more remote your location the more advice you should get. In the UK bad weather means you risk getting a little cold or wet. Abroad, bad weather can easily kill you, through extremes of heat and cold, avalanche, flood, mud slide, tornado, storm, and hailstones the size of tennis balls!

Thunderstorm/lightning
Thunderclouds are up to 10 miles high, and very cold at the top, allowing ice to form. In the turbulent airflow within those clouds, ice particles collide, separating their electrical charges. Positively charged ice crystals rise to the top of the cloud while negatively charged ice particles and hailstones drop to the middle and lower parts of the cloud. Because of that separation, a huge electrical differential develops inside thunderclouds.

The storm gathers a huge pool of positively charged particles as it moves over the ground. As the differences in charge continue to increase, positively charged particles rise up from taller objects on the ground, such as trees, houses and telephone poles, forming small upward-reaching electrical 'fingers' of charge. That means that electricity is forming in taller ground-based objects and reaching up towards the base of the thunderclouds. Those upward-reaching, invisible fingers of charge streaming off a tree, a chimney or your head if you are standing in a field are called 'leaders'.

A negatively charged area in the storm sends out a charge towards the ground, which is attracted to one of those 'leaders'. If they connect and make a circuit, the resulting discharge is what we see and call a lightning strike.

(In a storm, if your hair stands on end that is a sign of an imminent lightning strike on and then through you – so get down as flat as you can and hope a stronger and taller 'leader' will take any lightning strike that is coming.)

As the lightning channel heats quickly to 30,000 degrees, the expansion of heated air produces the noise we identify as thunder.

As light travels faster than sound, we see the flash first then hear the sound.

There are different types of lightning too! Negative lightning, from the base of the cloud, or positively charged lightning from the top of the cloud. Positive lightning is thought to be more dangerous, because it can strike as much as 5 or 10 miles away from the storm, in an area where people think they are safe. Positive lightning discharges also last longer, which means that they are more likely to cause fires.

- If lightning hits your car when you are inside it you will survive.

- If lightning hits you, even if you survive you will never fully recover.

- Consider the power, risk and danger of lightning, and think about what you would do if caught in a thunderstorm, on foot in an exposed place.
    - ➤ Each bolt of lightning can be over 5 miles long.
    - ➤ A lightning bolt can reach approximately 50,000 degrees Fahrenheit, and contain 100 million volts.
    - ➤ There are about 2,000 thunderstorms in progress around the world at any

given time. In those storms around 100 lightning bolts are discharged every second, which adds up to about eight million lightning bolts a day around the world.

➢ On average that lightning kills over 1,000 people each year, leaving thousands more injured and permanently disabled.

➢ On average, 20% of lightning strike victims die when the lightning strikes.

➢ At least 70% of survivors suffer serious long-term effects.

➢ There are up to 20 million thunderstorms each year, so you should be aware of the dangers and know how to protect yourself from a thunderstorm, wherever you are.

➢ American research has recorded 25 million lightning strikes (from the cloud to ground) every year in the USA. With that figure as a guide, the UK must have at least a quarter of a million lightning strikes each year.

Thunderstorm – countermeasures

✓ If you can hear thunder, you are probably close enough to the storm to be struck by lightning. If not you soon will be, so take shelter.

✓ As 'positive lightning' can strike from the top of a thundercloud and hit a target under blue sky up to 10 miles away, seek shelter whenever a storm is in the area.

✓ About 10% of lightning strikes occur in an area where there appear to be no clouds in the sky – that means to one side of the storm.

✓ Check for thunderstorms and aim to be inside a building or vehicle during any storm, particularly violent tropical thunderstorms. Never stand in the open during a thunderstorm.

✓ If you see billowing clouds with dark bases and the wind strength is increasing, you don't need a weather forecast to tell you that a thunderstorm could be forming, so get to safety.

✓ If lightning is forecast, seriously consider changing your plans, or have an alternative activity planned where you can take cover quickly. Then seek a building that will have walls all around you, not something like a carport which may not protect you. A cave would do in a rural area, or get into a vehicle (not a convertible) and wait until you can no longer hear or see the storm.

✓ A high proportion of lightning strike victims and witnesses report that there was no rain falling at the time. If you wait for the rain you are already too late.

✓ If you cannot get to cover, aim to be the lowest point in the area. You don't want those leaders (upward-reaching fingers of charge) attracting a strike to the top of your head. Move to lower ground if you can, and if necessary lay flat in a depression even though it is wet and muddy and cold. Remember that if your hair stands on end this indicates that a leader is running up through you and a lightning strike is not far away. Under these circumstances laying in the mud becomes quite an acceptable option!

✓ A lightning strike to a nearby object can send electricity through the ground and to you nearby. We all know not to shelter under a tree in a thunderstorm. If caught in the open, as a rough guide you should estimate the height of the tree, and stay three times that distance away from the base of the tree (or other tall object) to be safe from the radiating effects of a strike on it.

✓ Discard any metal objects, such as golf clubs, walking sticks or a metal-framed rucksack, fishing rods, tennis rackets and tools. Get off a bike or motorcycle. Don't lean on cars or metal fences and gates. Consider removing metal jewellery.

✓ Stay out of and away from water, because water is a very efficient conductor of electricity. Stay clear of beaches and get out of small boats and canoes. Don't get caught a long way from the shore in a small boat in a thunderstorm. If you are, lower any sails for safety because of gusting winds, move to the middle of the boat and lay flat. Stay as far away from any metal fixtures and fittings as you can. Be wary of metal fittings on any safety lines, life belts, etc. you may be wearing.

✓ Even people in the water, swimming and scuba-diving aren't safe. Swimmers can suffer injury through lightning strike.

✓ Give first aid after a strike and call for medical assistance as soon as you can. If the victim has stopped breathing, begin mouth to mouth. If the heart has stopped beating, a trained person should give cardiopulmonary resuscitation (CPR). If the struck person has a pulse and is breathing, address any other injuries.

✓ Beware of additional lightning strikes – lightning does strike twice in the same place!

✓ NOTE: After a strike, the human body drains the electricity, so you cannot get a shock by touching a victim and it is therefore safe to offer assistance (assuming there are no other risks around).

✓ The victim will have burns in two places. There is usually an entry wound/burn and an exit wound/burn. For example, a victim may have been holding a metal umbrella, and the lightning entered through their right hand, travelled down through their body and exited through their left foot into the earth. There will be a burn wound at the entry and exit points. Being struck by lightning can also cause nervous system damage, broken bones, and loss of hearing or eyesight.

Moving water and vehicles

Another danger that is unfamiliar to most UK residents is mixing vehicles with moving water, particularly streams and rivers that cross roads and floodwaters on roads.

Moving water has immense power. It can destroy houses, rip down bridges and move huge boulders. Don't make the mistake of assuming that it is safe to walk or drive through a few inches of moving water.

- Because floods are uncommon in the UK, we are unfamiliar with the dangers of moving water. A few inches of fast-flowing water can kill you.

- Off-road-driving instructors say that before driving into any water, in even the biggest and meanest four-wheel-drive vehicle, the driver should check for depth, flow and obstructions by prodding with a long stick. (They also need to see if there is somewhere to drive out of the water on the far bank.)

- Any water may be deeper than it appears.

- Water may be flowing faster than it appears.

- The power of flowing water is immense. Less than two feet of water can wash away almost any vehicle. If the circumstances are right, a small family car can be washed off the road by just six inches of moving water.

- If you or you and your car are washed into deeper water, you are at the mercy of cold, fast currents and floating debris. DON'T RISK IT.

- If faced with flowing water and floods, get out and get to dry land and high ground as soon as you can. Don't try to save the vehicle. Don't risk your life for a metal box with a wheel on each corner.

- STAY OUT OF MOVING WATER.

Excess heat

Some countries can be so hot and humid that it can affect your well-being, comfort and health in several ways. Obviously the energy sapping heat and humidity of tropical jungles will shock your system so you need a few days to acclimatise.

Even the moderate heat and humidity of a Caribbean island can shock the system of UK citizens more used to chilly winds and drizzle.

Excess heat – countermeasures

✓ Take your time getting used to the climate.

✓ Pace yourself until you have acclimatised.

✓ Drink plenty of water (not alcohol).

✓ Don't forget that when perspiring you need to replenish your body salts, so don't forget to eat some salty foods to balance the loss or drink something specially formulated to rebalance the body chemistry.

Strong sunshine

Our UK skin is generally not used to coping with a 12-hour daily dose of extremely high UV rating sunshine.

What is the UV rating that people talk about when discussing sunburn and the strength of the sun?

The sun emits three different types of ultraviolet (UV) radiation, which all damage the skin and can damage the eyes too. The three types are:

• UVA

• UVB

• UVC.

UVA radiation penetrates deep into your skin, and causes damage such as apparent ageing, wrinkles and discoloration.

UVB causes what is commonly known as sunburn. Surface blood vessels expand and leak fluids, producing the identifiable redness and pain of sunburn. Any sunburn can cause permanent and irreversible skin damage. UVB is associated with the most harmful effects of UV radiation, including ageing, wrinkles, cancer, cataracts, snow blindness, etc.

UVC should be absorbed and blocked by the ozone layer in the atmosphere. Global pollution and the depletion of the ozone layer have reduced the filtering effect of the atmosphere, so we are in ever-greater danger of exposure to UVC radiation.

In most people, when their skin is exposed to sunshine (UV radiation) their skin reacts to protect itself by producing melanin pigmentation, which darkens and protects the skin. That darkening is often called a 'suntan'.

The melanin absorbs UV radiation, protecting skin cells from UV damage – for a while!

Experts say that fair-skinned people should gradually expose their skin to sunshine in stages for up to 7 days before their melanin production has reached a maximum. Unfortunately very fair-skinned people take longer, while darker-skinned people take a shorter time, so no fixed rule can be given.

Cumulative Danger. UV radiation has a cumulative effect. The more often you burn the worse the damage. If you burn often enough and badly enough, especially during childhood, your chances of developing skin cancer increase significantly.

Sunburn

The strength of the sun varies according to a number of factors. They are:

- **Latitude.** Equatorial regions have stronger sunshine.
- **Altitude.** The higher you are, the less ozone and atmosphere there is to protect you from solar radiation.

- **Season.** Days are longer in summer so you are exposed to more sunshine.

- **Time of day.** The sun is stronger from 10am to 2pm, when it is at its height.

- **Reflection.** Sun reflects off water, glass, white surfaces and hard surfaces, possibly concentrating radiation on you – even if you are sitting under an umbrella.

The best way to protect yourself from the sun is to move into the shade, remembering that you will still be susceptible to reflected radiation unless you go into a building with walls all around you.

The shade from balconies, umbrellas and porches offers some protection, but beware. Don't become complacent. You are still susceptible to solar radiation unless there are walls all around you.

Sunburn – countermeasures

General precautions
YOU must consider your personal skin colour, tolerance of sunshine, the location and climate you are in, the season, time of day and all of the other factors that determine whether you will burn or not. YOU have to make the decisions to protect yourself from sunburn.

✓ Stay out of the sun during the hottest part of the day, usually between 10am when it starts getting hotter, reaching a peak at about noon, and falling off after 2pm. If you have fair hair or red hair and light skin or have just arrived at a tropical destination, you may want to expand that danger period to 9am–3pm.

✓ Remember that you are still receiving UV radiation when sitting in the shade. Light and radiation reflect and bounce off the sea, the beach and buildings, which means you are still burning while sitting under an umbrella or in a beachside bar.

✓ UV radiation is reflected by different surfaces, which may even amplify the effects of UV exposure. As an example, snow reflects about 90% of UV radiation (which causes snow blindness). Beach sand reflects only about 20% of UV radiation. Remember that some things absorb UV radiation. Glass absorbs almost all UV radiation so sitting behind glass is quite safe.

✓ When it is daylight the sun is up there somewhere, even if it is overcast or cloudy. It may seem dull but the sun is still shining and UV radiation is still burning through those clouds and reaching you.

✓ Plan your activities to avoid the strongest sunshine, taking into account location, season, the time of day, weather conditions and the task to be done.

✓ Buy and wear a broad-brimmed hat to protect your head and the back of your neck from the sun.

✓ Cover your skin with loose and lightweight clothing, long-sleeved shirts and trousers. Any covering will offer some protection from the sun. Loose lightweight clothes will protect you without making you too hot.

✓ Be aware that some clothes are designed to allow UVB to pass through so that the wearer can still 'get a tan'.

✓ Open-mesh fabrics and any clothing with a loose weave will tend to allow some radiation to pass through, so you will still burn. Try any new clothing before you rely on it to protect you for longer periods.

✓ Buy a good-quality sun cream, with a high protection factor. About half an hour before exposure to the sun, apply it to all exposed skin, not forgetting ears, nose, back of the neck and elbows. Any exposed skin is likely to burn.

✓ Anyone participating in outdoor activities (surfing, swimming or other sports) should be aware that sunscreen is likely to be washed off, worn off or be affected by perspiration. Be particularly careful about re-applying the sunscreen to maintain good protection.

✓ After swimming, jet-skiing, surfing, etc., you should get out of the sun or dry off with a towel. Full sun on wet skin will burn the skin in a very short while.

✓ Mountaineers and glider pilots or others who reach higher altitudes must realise that the level of solar radiation present increases with altitude. The higher you climb the stronger the radiation and the quicker you will burn. Protect particularly the back of the neck and the nose.

✓ If you begin to feel any effects of the sun, your skin is telling you to go into the shade and away from any UV radiation. By the time you start to feel uncomfortable, your skin has already been 'damaged'.

✓ Adults should make sure that children wear suitable clothing and that they keep this on while playing. An unsupervised child in a park or on a beach can quickly shed a hat and other clothes as they play.

✓ Children have particularly sensitive skin. Remember the effects of solar radiation are cumulative. You should frequently apply high protection factor sunscreen to them, and plan to take them to indoor activities on high sun strength days.

✓ Babies under a year old should be kept out of and protected from direct and reflected sunlight and radiation.

✓ People who are on certain medication such as diuretics, and people with some skin conditions such as eczema and psoriasis (which in non-medical terms means you have a weak skin), need to take extra care to avoid the effects of UV radiation.

✓ As a final thought, remember that a 'tan' is just a visible symptom of damaged skin. Healthy skin is the colour of your skin 'where the sun doesn't shine'. The bigger the difference between your 'pink bits' and your tanned skin, the greater the damage your skin has already sustained.

Sunburn treatment

Just like a burn from scalding water or fire, sunburn can be serious, though it develops gradually. It can range from slightly coloured skin to severe pain with blisters and swelling. Treating sunburn is common sense, with a golden rule of 'seek medical assistance if at all in doubt'.

Sunburn treatment – countermeasures

✓ First, remove the patient from the sun and take them to a clean cool place.

✓ For mild sunburn, take the heat out of the skin. Take a cold or cool shower. If a cold bath or shower is not possible, put a clean, cold, wet cloth over the affected areas, and allow a fan to blow air over the cloth to evaporate the water and cool the patient.

✓ If necessary, the patient can be given Ibuprofen or other over-the-counter painkillers, as long as they are not allergic to them or taking any other medication at the same time. If in doubt, seek medical advice.

✓ Commercial products are widely available to treat sunburned skin. Look for calamine lotion and aloe vera. Whatever treatment you use, never use anything that feels greasy, because grease traps heat, reflecting heat back into your skin and making the burn worse.

✓ If blistering develops, the skin will probably break, leaving a wound through which infection could enter the body.

  ➢ Keep sunburned skin clean.

  ➢ Avoid any hot baths and showers – the heat will add to the damage and discomfort.

  ➢ Avoid infection by making sure that anyone treating the sunburn patient thoroughly washes their hands.

  ➢ If blisters do form, never burst them deliberately.

➢ Following the instructions on the packet or advice given, you may apply antibacterial cream to the area.

✓ Severe sunburn can be accompanied by dehydration. If there are any complications or you have any cause to be concerned, seek medical advice immediately.

✓ After being burned, learn your lesson. Remember that the effects of solar radiation are cumulative so take sensible precautions in future.

✓ Think about other members of your family or group. If you have been burned, elderly, young or light-skinned members of the group may be hiding sunburn because they are embarrassed to admit it.

UV scale

The UV scale indicates the expected level of UV radiation. The scale runs from 1 to 20. Television, radio and newspaper weather forecasts include the expected level of UV radiation for that day.

Tables attempting to indicate the level of danger from UV radiation offer only a rough guide, because so many factors can affect the level of damage that UV radiation can do to your skin.

For example, altitude, cloud cover, level of previous exposure, wet or dry skin, and whether or not a sunscreen product is being used can all affect you.

For that reason treat tables as a rough guideline, issued with a strong health warning. Anyone can suffer sunburn in under 30 minutes, depending on skin type, UV rating, activities, locations, etc.

When there is a forecast UV Scale of 10 or above, everyone should avoid exposure to the sun where they can. See table on page 72.

Moles

Hundreds of people in the UK die each year from sun-related cancer. If you have a 'mole' that is

• of irregular shape

Skin type	Danger level
Fair skin that does not tan	Up to UV Scale 1–2 should be safe if you limit your exposure. Slowly get used to exposure. Stay out of the sun from 9am to 3pm. Use high-factor sun lotions. Wear a hat. Wear long sleeves and trousers to protect your skin. Get into protected shade if you start to feel uncomfortable. **Above UV 2 stay out of the sun.**
Fair skin that does tan	Up to UV Scale 3–4 should be safe if you limit your exposure. Slowly get used to exposure. Stay out of the sun from 10am to 2pm. Use high-factor sun lotions. Wear a hat. Wear long sleeves and trousers to protect your skin. Get into protected shade if you start to feel uncomfortable. **Above UV 4 stay out of the sun.**
Brown skin	Up to Scale 6 should be safe if you limit your exposure. Slowly get used to exposure. Stay out of the sun from 10am to 2pm. Use high-factor sun lotions. Wear a hat. Wear long sleeves and trousers to protect your skin. Get into protected shade if you start to feel ncomfortable. **Above UV 7 stay out of the sun.**
Black skin	Up to UV Scale 7 should be safe if you limit your exposure. Slowly get used to exposure. Stay out of the sun from 10am to 2pm. Use high-factor sun lotions. Wear a hat. Wear long sleeves and trousers to protect your skin. Get into protected shade if you start to feel uncomfortable. **Above UV 7 stay out of the sun.**

- has a dark centre

- bleeds

- is growing in size

- is changing shape

- itches

or in any way causes you concern, see your doctor **immediately.**

Sunstroke and heat stroke

Sunstroke and heat stroke can kill. They occur when the natural body temperature regulating system fails because of extended exposure to high environmental temperatures.

Heat stroke is often combined with periods of high physical exertion. The patient experiences a sharp increase in body temperature and an associated fever, which can cause permanent damage to internal organs, resulting in death if not treated immediately.

Heat stroke is often seen when somebody who is not acclimatised enters a particularly hot or humid environment, or performs strenuous physical activity in a hot and humid environment. Young children and the elderly are at most risk, though in the right circumstances anyone can become a victim.

These are the symptoms to look out for:

- The skin seems red, feels dry and very hot.

- The patient doesn't seem to be able to sweat.

- Their pulse is strong and fast.

- Possible hyperventilation.

- Check the eyes. Do the pupils appear small?

- The patient seems to be developing a very high fever.

- The patient may appear disoriented or mentally confused.

73

- In advanced stages – unconsciousness with possible convulsions.

- Ultimately – death.

Treatment

If you suspect that somebody is suffering from sunstroke or heat stroke, you should take steps to offer immediate first aid, but your main aim should be to seek professional medical help as soon as possible.

Initial treatment should include:

- Take the patient out of the sun to a cooler place as soon as possible.

- Loosen their clothing or take it off for maximum cooling out of the sunlight.

- If possible, immerse the patient in cool water, a bath, a shower, or even a nearby stream or lake as long as it is safe. Don't risk drowning them, or risk the victim being washed downstream on a strong current.

- If you can't immerse them in water, cool them by spraying them with water and consider turning on any electric fans that may be available for maximum evaporation and cooling.

- If available, use cold compresses, such as ice wrapped in a tea towel applied to the head and neck area, as well as the armpits and groin for maximum cooling effect – but don't overdo it.

- While doing this, summon professional medical assistance. Carry on with the above treatment until the ambulance or doctor arrives.

- Do NOT give any medication to lower a fever. It will not be effective and may cause further harm and complications.

- Avoid giving the patient water or anything else by mouth until the condition has been stabilised or until medical staff instruct you to give something to the patient.

Sunstroke and heat stroke – countermeasures

✓ Stay out of the sun.

✓ If you are not used to the heat and humidity, avoid any activity that requires you to work hard or play active sports in the sun and heat.

✓ Be particularly careful with young or elderly people in a hot and sunny environment. Don't underestimate the cumulative heat that can be experienced when walking in a canyon for example. The rock walls can reflect and retain the heat and turn a canyon into a natural oven.

Dehydration

Dehydration is a real threat, which is more common than people realise. It can accompany heat-related illnesses such as sunstroke or heat stroke, as well as being a complication of prolonged attacks of diarrhoea, vomiting or fever. Young children and people over the age of 60 are particularly susceptible to dehydration.

Everybody loses bodily water during the day, through sweat, tears and using the toilet. Normally that water is replaced by eating and drinking. If anyone has to work hard, hike, climb or play sports in a very hot or humid place they can easily upset the balance between water intake and water losses.

As you lose water you also lose essential body salts such as sodium, potassium, calcium bicarbonate and phosphate. Losing that water and those salts will upset your body chemistry, which results in a condition that is commonly called dehydration.

Common symptoms of dehydration
Symptoms vary from patient to patient due to changes in body size, age, health, fitness, local temperature, local humidity and whatever the patient is doing at the time. Generally symptoms may include:

- Thirst – because your body knows it needs more water and is trying to make you drink some.

- Increased heart rate and breathing rate as the body works harder to recover.

- Dizziness and confusion. The patient may say they feel light-headed.

- The patient doesn't want to urinate as frequently as they usually do, partly because the body is trying to preserve fluids and partly because the flow of fluids through their system is drying up.

- Dry mouth and nasal linings, because the body is pulling moisture back into the core to sustain life.

- The patient feels tired and their skin is dry.

Children and babies may display additional symptoms, mostly due to having smaller bodies and smaller reserves of water to use to maintain life. For example:

- An early symptom could be a dry mouth and tongue.

- If they cry but no tears are visible.

- Small babies stop wetting their nappy.

- The loss of moisture shows on the body and face of a baby or child. They have sunken eyes, cheeks and stomach.

- A child may appear to be unusually irritable, angry or tired and listless.

- A little test that parents can do on small children is to gently pinch the skin. When gently pinched, normal skin is moist and elastic, and when released it will flatten out and return to normal, showing no sign where it was pinched. Dehydrated skin will stay pinched and wrinkled like a bed sheet, plastic or paper, and it will be obvious that the skin is not as normal.

Dehydration prevention – countermeasures

Adults should be sensible enough to recognise when conditions can cause dehydration. If you are not used to hot, humid, sunny conditions but have to work, walk or play hard, beware.

Adults should extend their care of children and the elderly when conditions are likely to promote dehydration.

✓ Try to stay out of the sun and heat.

✓ Reduce your activity to a sensible and sustainable level, or undertake activities earlier or later in the day when it is not so hot.

✓ Drink plenty of water. Make yourself drink it even though you don't feel thirsty. Take regular small drinks to be sure that you are taking in more water than you are losing. Remember, by the time you feel thirsty you are already a little dehydrated. If you are very thirsty you are definitely dehydrated!

✓ You can drink some sports drinks, which are formulated to help your body maintain its electrolyte (chemical) balance, but they can be quite expensive and are not widely available.

✓ If you feel or see any of the symptoms listed above, assume that you are losing the battle against dehydration and take immediate steps to prevent further loss.

Dehydration treatment – countermeasures

✓ Watch for the warning signs of dehydration. The conditions that cause dehydration are plain to see. Don't become dehydrated because of stupidity.

✓ Early dehydration can usually be treated at home after seeking advice from a doctor, but always consult a doctor when dehydration is suspected, especially with children.

✓ Early dehydration can be treated by drinking water. More severe cases will need formulated drinks that restore body salts as well. If available, sports drinks may be recommended because they are formulated to restore the balance of salts and electrolytes.

✓ In more severe cases a patient will have to be hospitalised. Remember dehydration can kill or cause organ failure and damage. If in doubt, get in the cool and seek medical advice.

Dazzle

The dangers of being dazzled by the sun shouldn't be overlooked. At home if we get sunshine for three days in a row it gets national news coverage!

Abroad the bright sun could dazzle you and cause an accident. When driving on unfamiliar roads or walking on cliff-top paths, climbing up and down steps in unfamiliar towns or negotiating boarding ramps onto ferries and docks you could have an accident. Expect bright sunshine and be prepared for it.

Dazzle – countermeasures

✓ Early morning sun and late afternoon sun coming from low on the horizon might dazzle you.

✓ Wear a good pair of sunglasses.

■ ■

✓ The sun can dazzle you at any time of the day, by reflecting off cars and windows. When you drive up a steep hill you may find yourself looking directly into the sun.

✓ If dazzled while driving, slow down carefully. Remember that drivers behind might already be dazzled, so they won't see your brake lights and won't stop when you do.

Hypothermia

You may have selected a holiday destination at the other end of the climatic range where cold becomes a threat. In those conditions loss of body heat can lead to hypothermia.

Hypothermia is defined as a state where the core body temperature falls to below 35 degrees Celsius. If the body temperature drops another three degrees to 32 Celsius, the patient is in a state of reduced consciousness. At or below 30 degrees Celsius the heart stops and death occurs.

Be warned. The two-degree difference between 32 and 30 degrees Celsius is DEATH.

The body loses heat in several ways.

- **Radiation.** That is, the body acts like a radiator, a heat source trying to warm the area around it. Radiation heat loss is greater from exposed skin, the head, and anywhere that might be covered by wet clothes.

- **Conduction.** That is, through direct contact with something cold. If you touch a cold metal bench your body heat quickly transfers to the metal bench. NOTE: You lose up to 25 times more heat in water or wearing wet clothes than you would if you were dry.

- **Convection.** That is, where heat is lost to moving air or water. For example, riding a bike your skin heats the air in contact with your skin, then as you cycle the wind blows that warmed air away. Cold air takes its place and you warm that, until you stop cycling. There is a similar effect in flowing water.

- **Evaporation.** That is, where energy in the form of heat is lost when water evaporates. Sweat is a good example of this. When you are too hot you sweat, the sweat evaporates and cools the skin.

- **Respiration.** That is, where you lose heat by breathing. Everybody has noticed their breath coming out as steam on a cold day. The steam is warm moist air coming out of your lungs and condensing, a clear indication that you are losing body heat by breathing.

Remember the five methods of body heat loss above. To survive in a cold environment, stop or reduce as many as you can.

Losing body heat by losing body fluids, in sweat or breathing will also affect the fluid levels, salts and electrolytes in the body, which can lead to dehydration even in a cold climate. Dehydration is a dangerous and unwanted complication of hypothermia!

Who is at risk?

- Babies are at risk because they cannot do anything to protect themselves, or let anyone know that they are cold.

- Older people are possibly inactive, not able to seek shelter, or not able to participate in activities that would warm them.

- At home the elderly may also be possibly less well off, which means that they may not be able to afford to keep warm.

- Anyone who has a disability or is already suffering from an illness is also more susceptible to hypothermia.

- It has also been found that people who take some drugs are less able to regulate their own body temperature. Some prescription and illegal drugs have this effect.

Signs of hypothermia

- There will be a cold environment.

- Muscle stiffness noticeable in the neck, arms and legs.

- Possible gentle trembling that may be confined to one side of the body or one arm or leg.

- Shivering is the process the body uses to keep warm. If shivering stops, the patient may have warmed up, OR they may be even colder and in the early stages of hypothermia.

- Their face could appear to be puffy or swollen.

- The patient's co-ordination may be deteriorating. They sometimes find it hard to walk and they easily lose their balance.

- Breathing and heart rate slow as hypothermia progresses.

- The skin looks pale (because all blood supplies have withdrawn from surface skin to protect vital organs), but there may be large pink or blue spots of skin. The skin feels very cold, even where it is not exposed to the air. (Check for this by touching under their clothing on the stomach, lower back, arms, legs, etc.).

- As the condition gets worse, the patient begins to lose consciousness. An indication of which is that they often lose the ability to reason and communicate – but that doesn't always happen. Test this by asking simple questions, such as what is the date, what is twelve divided by four, etc.

- As hypothermia gets worse, the patient becomes more confused. They may forget the name of close family members and friends, or not be able to remember the town they live in.

- The patient can become listless, though some patients become aggressive or argumentative.

The Umbles
'Umbles' is a simple term to remind you of these symptoms. The 'umbles' are stumbles, mumbles, fumbles and grumbles.

In very cold conditions, expect hypothermia to be a present and real risk and take steps to find shelter.

Hypothermia – countermeasures

The advice is different if the victim is on land or in the water. If you believe that somebody is suffering from hypothermia, seek shelter and urgent medical advice and assistance.

On land

✓ Let somebody know where you are going and when you will be back.

✓ Arrange for them to check on your return and raise the alarm if you do not return when you should.

✓ Carry a whistle to signal rescuers or people around you.

✓ Carry a signal mirror or flares to signal aircraft in more remote areas.

✓ In the wilderness, try to make a signal that is visible from the air, for example by laying branches in a cross, or by making a smoky fire that can be seen from a distance.

✓ Find or make shelter as soon as you can. Dig a snow hole (a cave in a bank of snow – but don't get buried or cause an avalanche). Build a shelter from any materials you can find. Get in and get out of the wind but keep an air hole open (don't suffocate).

At Home

✓ Anyone who lives alone or in remote areas should agree to mutual checks with several other residents. Call each other every day and make sure that each of you is alert, responding, answering questions correctly and seems healthy.

✓ Wear multiple layers of loose clothing. The insulation effect of multiple layers increases your body heat retention.

✓ If you feel cold, wear a scarf and hat even indoors. A lot of heat is lost through the head, so cover it in extreme conditions.

✓ Put extra blankets on the bed at night. In really cold weather you can suffer from hypothermia while sleeping. Consider sharing a bed!

✓ Eat a sensible balanced diet. Your food is the fuel that keeps your body running.

✓ Make sure that you drink enough fluids. Warm drinks help to maintain your temperature and prevent hypothermia.

✓ Avoid alcohol! It is a stimulant, but though you might think of it as a 'bracer', the net effect is that alcohol will make you lose body heat and accelerate the onset of hypothermia. Fall down drunk, and you could be on your way to the undertaker!

✓ Make sure that you get enough rest and sleep. Lack of sleep makes you more susceptible to hypothermia.

✓ Stay dry. Wet clothes lose their insulating value. If you get wet from perspiration, rain or snow, change into dry clothes as soon as you can.

On the water
Take sensible precautions, such as:

✓ Knowing the limitations of your boat.

✓ Knowing your personal limitations in skill and ability as well as strength.

✓ Having the right equipment on board.

✓ Having a radio so that you can pick up weather reports and summon assistance.

✓ Taking shelter if a storm is approaching.

If you still get into trouble:

✓ Summon assistance immediately you start having problems. Don't wait until you are desperate.

✓ Stay out of the water for as long as possible. Water conducts heat away from the body at least 25 times faster than air.

✓ Make sure you wear a lifejacket and that it is properly fitted and secured.

✓ When in the water don't remove any clothing. Even wet clothes and shoes offer a little insulation when you are in cold water.

✓ Don't try to swim to shore. In cold water even the strongest swimmer is unlikely to be able to swim more than half a mile. Swimming quickly drains your energy, increases your heat loss and accelerates the onset of hypothermia. Even if you get to shore you may be in no condition to walk several miles in soaked clothing to find help.

✓ If you often sail in cold waters, buy and use a 'survival suit' for everyone on the boat.

✓ Make sure that you have and use good-quality life jackets and rafts.

✓ When abandoning a boat, take food, water, radio, signal devices and a prepared survival kit with you.

✓ Don't leave the boat until you have to. If you have to abandon your boat, stay near it. Rescuers will be able to spot a big sinking or burning boat easier than they will spot you alone. Any search for you will start with your boat.

✓ If you have to get into the water, reduce the surface area you are presenting. Make every effort to cover and protect those areas where heat loss will be greatest.

> ➢ Cover the head and neck area. Some survival suits come with a full-face hood. If yours has one, use it.

> ➢ Hold your arms into your sides to protect the armpits.

> ➢ Hold your legs together and raise them to a sitting position to reduce heat loss from the groin.

✓ If you are in a group:

> ➢ Keep the group together near the boat. A group will be easier to spot than individuals.

➢ The group will be able to maintain good spirits. Survival experts say that a positive mental attitude is a major contributor to survival.

➢ Consider tying yourselves together to stop people drifting away if they fall asleep or become unconscious.

➢ Huddle together, sharing body heat, and reducing the surface area of skin that is exposed to the cold water.

➢ Keep children in the centre of the group where they will be best protected.

General Advice

✓ Always let somebody know where you are going and when you will be back.

✓ Arrange for them to check to make sure you returned as planned. If you don't, they should raise the alarm and tell the authorities where you were going and how.

✓ Try to make a signal that is visible from the air. For example, release dye into the water or spread a sail on the water.

NEVER

✓ Never try to give a hypothermia victim food or drink.

✓ Never try to artificially warm a hypothermia victim. For example, DO NOT wrap them in working electric blankets, DO NOT put them near to a blazing fire, DO NOT put them into a warm or hot bath or shower.

✓ Though it is a standard first-aid treatment, DO NOT raise the patient's feet. That will force cold blood from the limbs to flow back into the body core, worsening the patient's condition.

✓ DO NOT move the patient unless you absolutely have to. In advanced hypothermia the patient's heart will be weak and dragging them around might kill them.

Frostbite

Frostbite is the name used to describe human skin and flesh when it freezes.

If the subject is careless about clothing and shelter, when the temperature hits freezing (zero degrees Celsius) human skin and flesh can freeze, especially if the subject is wet or wearing wet clothes. If the temperature falls below minus 5

■ ■

degrees and wind chill is a factor, frostbite becomes a real problem. Below minus 10 with wind chill and/or wet clothes, frostbite is a major risk. Blood flow slows, ice crystals form within blood and tissues, then the ice expands and damages the tissues. When thawed, the tissue damage may get worse.

Frostbite makes the skin numb. It appears to be grey and waxy in colour, is cold to the touch and may feel stiff and 'wooden'.

Frostbite is usually restricted to skin and surface tissue but it can reach deeper tissues. In severe cases it can even affect muscle and bone. In these cases permanent damage is almost inevitable.

Frostbite – countermeasures

✓ Carefully move the victim to shelter to protect them from the wind and cold.

✓ Summon medical assistance, describe the symptoms and effects and seek advice as to what you should do.

✓ Remove wet and tight clothing.

✓ Cover the victim in multiple layers of dry blankets.

✓ Attempt to warm affected areas by gentle skin-to-skin contact. For example, a conscious victim can hold their frostbitten fingers in their groin or armpit.

✓ Only on the advice of a doctor, should you consider immersing frozen areas in warm water. If you do, you should control the water temperature because the victim won't be able to feel it and is in danger of burning the affected area. They won't realise how hot the water is.

✓ When medical assistance arrives, take the victim to hospital as soon as possible.

✓ DO NOT try to thaw areas that are frozen.

✓ DO NOT make a victim walk on frozen feet.

✓ DO NOT warm frozen flesh on or near naked flames.

✓ DO NOT rub frostbitten skin with snow.

Eye Damage
Cold weather can also affect the eyes.

✓ Eyelashes freezing together. Cup your hand over your eye. The combined heat of your hand and eye will melt the ice so that you can open your eyes. This is a warning sign that you should be seeking shelter!

✓ Freezing of the cornea, which can happen when a patient is struggling through strong cold winds and forcing their eyes open so that they can see where they are going. If it happens, cup the hands over the eye until the natural warmth thaws the cornea. If a cornea has been frozen, if possible wear a patch over the affected eye and seek urgent medical attention.

✓ Snow blindness. A condition where the dazzle and UV radiation reflected by the snow can injure the eye.

  ➢ It generally takes about 12 hours to develop.

  ➢ The eye feels dry and irritated. Patients report that their eye feels as though it is full of grit or sand.

  ➢ Moving the eye around causes extreme pain.

  ➢ Eyelids may be red and swollen.

  ➢ Tears often flow freely.

  ➢ Exposure to sunlight hurts the eyes.

✓ Treatment for snow blindness:

  ➢ Do not rub the eyes.

  ➢ Apply cold compresses to the eyes.

  ➢ Keep the patient in a dark environment.

  ➢ Seek urgent medical advice.

✓ Prevention of snow blindness:

  ➢ Wear good sunglasses or goggles.

  ➢ Though the lenses of sunglasses or goggles protect the eyes from the front, there may be gaps at the side. Make sure any sunglasses or goggles used have 'side shields' to fully protect the eyes.

  ➢ Remember to wear sunglasses or goggles even if the sun is obscured behind clouds.

Altitude sickness

Altitude sickness occurs at altitude, where 'altitude' is usually defined as anything higher than 2,500 metres (8,000 feet). Anyone who plans to travel to higher altitudes should understand the danger, symptoms and treatment of altitude sickness.

You don't have to be a mountaineer to experience high altitudes.

• Jet aircraft always have a pressurised cabin, but though some light aircraft are capable of flying at over 8,000 feet, their cabins are not pressurised.

• A few roads approach or climb through altitudes where altitude sickness could be experienced.

• Hikers and walkers may well find themselves at dangerous altitudes when walking in some mountain ranges and through high passes.

• The highest mountain in Britain is Ben Nevis in Scotland, but that is only 1,344 metres tall (4,409 feet). Compare that to major cities in some countries which are at extreme altitude:

  ➢ Cuzco in Peru is at 3,000 metres (11,000 feet)

  ➢ La Paz in Bolivia is at 3,400 metres (11,300 feet)

  ➢ Lhasa in Tibet is at 3,749 metres (12,500 feet)

Most people assume that there is less oxygen at altitude, but at any altitude the proportion of oxygen in the air is quite constant at about 21%. The reduced air pressure at altitude means that the air is thinner, so when you take a 'normal' breath, each 'lung full' contains less oxygen. Over 8,000 feet you get significantly less oxygen per breath than you do when breathing the 'thicker' air at lower altitudes.

To compensate for the reduced air density and hence reduced oxygen, your breathing rate will automatically increase to take on an adequate supply of oxygen. In these conditions many people suffer from a potentially serious side effect of high altitude and low air pressure, which causes fluid to leak from the capillary blood vessels.

That fluid can then build up in the lungs or the brain causing complications as described below. If sufferers do not receive treatment *immediately* they will die.

Patients suffering from and having treatment for diseases such as congestive heart failure, angina, sickle cell disease, asthma, etc. should avoid higher altitudes. If in doubt, seek advice from your doctor before travelling to high altitudes. As a general rule, talk to your doctor before travelling anywhere off the beaten track.

Apart from low air pressure and reduced oxygen, other factors often contribute to the onset of altitude sickness. For example:

- Lack of acclimatisation.

- Over-exertion and rapid ascent.

- Possible dehydration.

- Possible hypothermia.

- Existing medical problems.

Statistically, few people have ventured to higher altitudes, but from the evidence available there appears to be no known group or factors that make a person susceptible to altitude sickness. Age, sex, and physical condition seem to matter less than acclimatisation.

Different classifications
Altitude sickness is usually described in three different forms. They are:

- **AMS**. Acute Mountain Sickness is the most common form of altitude sickness. It can be experienced at altitudes as low as 1,200 metres (4,000 feet) but is more common when patients quickly climb to altitudes of 2,700 metres (9,000 feet). Symptoms are noticed some hours after the ascent, and have been compared to a hangover.
  ➢ Headache
  ➢ Loss of appetite
  ➢ Nausea and sometimes vomiting
  ➢ Mild symptoms that feel like hangover/not feeling well
  ➢ Fatigue and tiredness
  ➢ Shortness of breath
  ➢ Sleep disturbance
  ➢ Dizziness.

Severe cases may also suffer from breathlessness and chest tightness (which are signs of HAPE), or confusion, lethargy and unsteady walking (which are signs of HACE).

- **HAPE.** High Altitude Pulmonary Edema can be described in simple terms as water in the lungs. If the capillary blood vessels leak fluid, it can collect in the lungs and cause severe breathing problems. The symptoms may not be noticed until a day or two after a fast ascent. Symptoms include:
  - ➢ Being very tired, reporting unusual levels of fatigue while walking
  - ➢ Any exertion causing increased breathlessness
  - ➢ Breathlessness does not subside with rest
  - ➢ Increasingly short of breath even when resting
  - ➢ Severe cough that may be dry or productive
  - ➢ High pulse rate, i.e. 110
  - ➢ Possible blueness of face, lip, fingernails, which is a sign of a failure to absorb oxygen and/or the failure of oxygen to circulate in the blood.

- **HACE.** High Altitude Cerebral Edema can be described in simple terms as water in the head or water on the brain. Symptoms include:
  - ➢ Feeling very tired, reporting unusual fatigue while walking
  - ➢ Severe headache
  - ➢ Vomiting
  - ➢ The patient walks as though they are drunk
  - ➢ The patient displays mental confusion
  - ➢ The patient is often irritable and wants to be left alone
  - ➢ Eventually – unconsciousness, coma and death.

Treatment
Because the symptoms of altitude sickness develop gradually, a sensible traveller will be aware of the dangers and will be able to return to lower altitudes to reduce the impact and allow the patient to recover.

If you are at altitude and experience any of the above symptoms you should assume that it is altitude sickness and act accordingly by returning to lower altitudes immediately.

- **Descend.** There is only one foolproof treatment, and that is to return to a lower altitude. If the patient has only just begun to experience the symptoms, recovery should be quite fast, usually within a few hours. Once symptoms begin, you should not climb to higher altitudes under any circumstances.

  For AMS and HAPE descending 1,000 metres (3,280 feet) is usually effective in reducing symptoms and will allow the patient to recover. Patients with suspected HACE should descend at least 2,000 metres (6,561 feet). If the symptoms persist, descend even further and urgently seek medical advice.

- **Gamow Bag.** Some expeditions carry a Gamow Bag for the treatment of altitude sickness, and they are very effective. The patient is placed inside the bag, which is then sealed and inflated using a simple pump. It works by increasing the air pressure inside the bag, which simulates the atmosphere of a lower altitude – two pounds of pressure per square inch inside the bag (which is easily achieved with a hand pump) simulates a descent of 1,500 metres (6,000 feet).

- **Oxygen.** Giving the patient oxygen can give temporary relief to the effects of lack of oxygen but the underlying problem of the altitude and thin air is still present – avoid climbing any further, be sensible and go down.

- **Medication.** There are a range of medicines that can help with altitude sickness, by increasing your tolerance to high altitude and treating the symptoms. All of these medications are considered to be quite strong, so they should not be treated lightly, and should only be administered by somebody with medical training, or at least only administered on the radio or telephone advice of a doctor. I would suggest that if you are ill enough to need medication you have ignored the warning signs and should have turned back a couple of days before!

Altitude sickness – countermeasures

Other than by previous experience, there is no way to predict how any individual will react to high altitudes. Generally, the best prevention is common sense, preparation, acclimatisation and more acclimatisation.

✓ Take exercise before you go to increase your general level of fitness and the ability of your lungs to cope with the strain of altitude.

✓ Stop smoking.

✓ Select a sensible route.

✓ Plan for a gradual ascent. Pace yourself, do not try to climb too high too fast.

✓ Take a few days to acclimatise at your starting point.

✓ Drink more fluids than usual when travelling and at altitude.

✓ Allow extra rest days at intermediate altitudes. As a general rule plan to stay one extra day and night after climbing 1000 metres (3,280 feet).

✓ When travelling avoid alcohol or other stimulants.

✓ Avoid using sleeping pills or any medication designed to relax you or help you to sleep.

✓ Never travel alone.

✓ Don't try to carry too much.

✓ Keep an eye on each other. If anyone suffers any symptoms, go back down.

Acclimatisation

The human body is remarkably resilient. Within a few days we can acclimatise to most conditions. You may have noticed when you go on holiday that a destination that feels cold or hot on arrival quite quickly starts to feel 'normal'. We can acclimatise to environmental changes but that acclimatisation usually takes from one to a more usual four days.

You must understand that acclimatisation is a progressive process, which has to be completed in stages. For example, if you walk to 3,048 metres (10,000 feet) then stay there several days you will have acclimatised to that height. If you now walk higher up the mountain and reach 3,658 metres (12,000 feet), you will have to stop to acclimatise to the new altitude and environment.

As you acclimatise to altitude, your body will naturally make changes to compensate for the changes around you so that you can function at reduced air pressure with reduced oxygen. The altitude changes are:

• You will breathe deeper, taking more air in with each breath.

- The blood pressure in your lungs will increase, making more efficient use of areas of your lungs that are not used normally.

- You will automatically produce more red blood cells, which carry oxygen around the body.

- Chemical changes take place within your body so that it can more efficiently release and use oxygen.

Acclimitisation – countermeasures

In the absence of any other guidance, the basic rules below will help a healthy adult to achieve the safest and most efficient acclimatisation.

✓ Make your way slowly to altitude, travelling from sea level by car if possible to 3,000 metres (10,000 feet), then slowly walk to higher altitudes, taking your time and stopping to acclimatise when you need to.

✓ Avoid flying or driving direct to altitudes of over 3,000 metres (10,000 feet). The body will require a longer time to recover from the transition from sea level, and will take longer to acclimatise.

✓ When travelling to altitudes above 3,000 metres (10,000 feet), don't climb more than 300 metres (1,000 feet) per day.

✓ Aim to ascend by an average of 300 metres (1,000 feet) per day.

✓ Take at least one full rest day (and night) for every 900 meters (3,000 feet) you ascend.

✓ If you begin to show symptoms of altitude sickness, descend.

✓ If symptoms persist or increase, descend further and seek urgent medical assistance.

✓ In a group (you should never be travelling alone), remember that different people will acclimatise at different rates. Just because a group leader feels well enough to go on after half a day, it doesn't mean that the rest of the group has acclimatised yet.

✓ American research shows that people travelling in a group are actually *more likely* to die of altitude sickness and complications than single travellers (probably because people who travel in a group don't want to hold up the group or don't want to appear weak, so they agree to carry on when they are not really ready). When travelling in a group, make sure that everybody is ready and agrees to move. Keep a close eye on all group members.

✓ Climbing to altitude and then waiting to acclimatise often leaves people dehydrated. Aim to drink at least five or six pints of water each day.

✓ Avoid alcohol.

✓ Do not take drugs (other than prescribed medication – having checked with your doctor that you would be safe to climb to altitude with your condition).

✓ Do not smoke. Before travelling you should have given up smoking to allow your lungs to be as efficient as they can be.

✓ Seek advice as to what foods to take and eat while ascending, staying at altitude and descending.

✓ Where possible, even if given medical permission to climb to altitude, it is recommended that pregnant women should stay at or below 3,658 metres (12,000 feet).

✓ Be warned that children are as susceptible to altitude sickness as adults, but they may not tell adults in the group that they are feeling unwell and have been known to hide symptoms. Watch them very closely for any signs of altitude sickness.

Motion sickness/travel sickness

Known as sea sickness, car sickness and air sickness, motion sickness is caused by a bodily reaction to a mismatch of sensory information.

Under normal conditions, your senses feed information to your brain, telling you what is happening to your body. At the same time your eyes are feeding your brain information about what is happening to the world around you. The design of the human senses has evolved over millions of years, and in all of that time the world has stood still. People, animals and clouds move, but the world just stands there!

Usually the information from your senses and your eyes matches. When sitting on a park bench you know you are stationary and there are trees and rubbish bins around you that are also stationary. The information matches, so your brain is happy and you feel well.

The problem comes when your brain receives conflicting information. For example, if you are sitting on a bench but that bench is on a ship, your senses tell your brain that you are sitting still on that bench. Unfortunately your eyes and balance mechanism are telling a different story. You can feel the movement as the ship rises and falls, rolls and pitches. Your eyes are deceived as well. As you steam past a cliff or lighthouse, your eyes are telling your brain that you are actually moving forward quite fast. Result, confused senses inducing sickness – 'motion sickness'.

In short, the signs and symptoms of motion sickness occur when sensory information about your position in or movement through space is contradictory or contrary between different senses in relation to prior experience. Symptoms include:

- Yawning (early symptom)
- Dizziness
- Drowsiness
- Clammy skin
- Cold sweats
- Restlessness
- Possible cold hands and feet
- Nausea
- Vomiting.

Travel sickness is common among passengers in cars and ships, or on trains and aircraft. The common name is 'sea sickness' because it is most often experienced on water. At least 90% of sea passengers initially feel the symptoms of 'sea sickness' but only about 45% of people experience 'car sickness'.

Motion Sickness – countermeasures

✓ Widely available medication can reduce or remove susceptibility to motion sickness. Seek advice and medication from your pharmacist or doctor.

✓ Get a good night's sleep the day before you travel.

✓ Some people report that acupuncture has helped them. There are commercially available 'acupressure' wristbands that are reported to press on the correct acupuncture points to suppress motion sickness.

✓ Some people report that hypnotism has helped them.

✓ Select a seat at a point that will have the least movement. To explain that, imagine that your ship is a seesaw. If you sit at either end when the seesaw is in use, you will travel up and down several feet, but if you sit in the middle you will hardly feel any movement at all. Select a seat or position on any transport which is the equivalent of the centre of the seesaw.

➤ At the exact centre of a ship (where the rolling and pitching will be least noticeable).

➤ In the front seat of a car.

➤ Seats between (not over) front and back wheels in buses and coaches.

➤ Over the wings in an aircraft.

✓ Sit still. The more head movement you generate the more you intensify the mixed messages being sent to your brain.

✓ Try to sleep if you can. If you are asleep most of the senses shut down so mixed messages are reduced.

✓ Don't try to read a book. You will usually feel better if you focus on a distant object. (The further the object is away, the smaller any movement appears to be.)

✓ In aircraft, avoid looking at the in-seat television screens.

✓ Eating can affect your response to motion.

➤ Don't eat rich food before your journey.

➤ Avoid any foods that are high in fat.

➤ Don't eat dairy products before or during the journey.

➤ Don't drink alcohol before or during the journey.

➤ Avoid coffee and tea before and during a journey.

➤ Don't smoke just before or during the journey.

✓ Try to eat something light before travelling. Fruit is best, particularly oranges (because if you are ill they taste the same on the way up as they did on the way down).

✓ Get as much fresh air as you can.

✓ Avoid strong smells such as diesel on a ship, or strong tobacco, strong perfume, aftershave, etc.

✓ On a ship move away from areas where there is heavy vibration from engines or propellers.

✓ In a car, if small children are strapped into child seats, raise them up enough so that they can see out of the windows and therefore focus on distant objects.

Jetlag

We know that the human body is remarkably resilient and will usually adapt to any new circumstances within a few days, but the 'within a few days' causes us the problems.

We each have a quite sophisticated internal biological clock, which tells our bodies what they should be doing, for example getting ready to get up, eat or sleep.

When it is noon on one side of the earth, on the other side it is midnight, with a range of different time zones in between. If you travel slowly around the world, your body has time to adjust to the slightly different time zones, but when you travel by jet aircraft, your body has a shock. Your biological clock says it is 10am UK time, but when you get off the aircraft the world around you suddenly demands that you comply with the local timeframe!

The physical and mental affects of this confusion are called jetlag. The effects of jetlag vary for a variety of reasons:

- Some people are not susceptible to jetlag. Their body clock seems to be able to cope with being 're-set' after flights to different time zones.

- Some people seem to be able to cope with travelling east better than they cope when travelling west, and vice versa.

- For some people the effects seem to be minimised if they depart and arrive in daylight or depart and arrive in darkness. The time doesn't seem so relevant as long as the broad conditions of day and night are constant.

- Some people seem to be able to maintain a steady body clock time, and ignore the local time around them. For example, I am told that some airline pilots stay on UK time for the duration of their trip, ignoring the fact that their body says it is noon but it is dark outside.

Symptoms
As explained above, the symptoms of jetlag vary but can include:

- General fatigue that may last for a few days after arrival

- A loss of the ability to concentrate

- A feeling that you have no energy, no drive

- An inability to sleep at night

- General feeling that you are not quite right

- Headaches

- In some cases you can become short-tempered and intolerant

- Dehydration and constipation

- Swollen legs and feet.

Jetlag and air travel health – countermeasures

✓ Have a few good nights' sleep before your flight. Being tired before you travel exaggerates the effects of jetlag in many people.

✓ If you suffer from motion sickness, consider taking commercially available medication and following the advice above.

✓ When I book a flight I try to arrive at my destination early afternoon. That means I can collect my baggage, transfer to the hotel, book in and unpack, explore a little, wind down a little and go to bed. I am usually tired from the journey so I sleep, then when I wake up, be it 5am or 10am, I start the new day with my biological clock synchronised with local time.

✓ The air quality in most aircraft is dry, stale and poorly filtered (so germs from other passengers are generously circulated around the aircraft). You are therefore likely to suffer from headaches, dry skin and a dry throat. On top of that, with the germs circulating it is the ideal environment to contract a cold, flu or other virus. Drink as much water as you can to counteract dehydration and resist the virus-loaded air.

✓ If you have special dietary requirements, most airlines claim to offer a service that will cater to your needs. If you contact them far enough in advance to explain your requirements you could try to request a special meal. In my experience, even on scheduled flights at least 50% of the time cabin staff just shrug and deny all knowledge of special meals.

✓ Don't forget eye care. Dehydration, dry air and generally poor air quality are not conducive to the wearing of contact lenses. Consider wearing a pair of cheap spectacles for the flight and recovery period after the flight.

✓ Combat dehydration by drinking more water than you think you need.

✓ Most airlines are now 100% non-smoking. If you are a smoker, given the choice don't smoke in-flight and avoid smoking before the flight as well.

✓ When taking off, suck a sweet or suck your teeth to balance the air pressure in your inner ears and sinus with the pressure in the aircraft. Some reports claim if you travel while suffering from a cold or flu, the pressure changes in a passenger airline can cause permanent ear and sinus damage. With severe or prolonged congestion, seek medical advice before flying.

✓ Depending on the length of the flight, and your ability to sleep in strange places with strangers moving around and the in-flight film playing, you may want to take a few things with you in your carry-on luggage.

   ➢ My wife always takes a pack of moist wipes, the sort they use when changing babies. They are good for wiping your hands, or any other exposed skin. They refresh and moisturise. A cool moist wipe on the forehead is surprisingly refreshing.

   ➢ Consider taking earplugs to cut out the aircraft noise so that you can get some sleep. (Travel shops sell earplugs.)

   ➢ Consider taking an inflatable neck pillow and something to cover your eyes to shut out the light inside the aircraft, to make sleeping easier and more comfortable.

   ➢ On a flight of more than three hours, I take a small toothbrush and toothpaste. When I can't get a small tube of toothpaste, I take a tube that has just enough left for me to clean my teeth a few times. Rinsing my face and cleaning my teeth before descent and arrival always makes me feel 100% better.

   ➢ Some people take and use moisturising hand creams and moisturising lipstick.

✓ Plan to wear something light and loose for the flight. You will almost certainly be stuck in economy-class seats for many hours. Don't aggravate the situation by wearing tight and restrictive clothes to further strangle your internal organs.

✓ Similarly, wear loose slip-on shoes if you can. Your feet will swell during the flight so unless you want to constantly loosen the laces, wear slip-on shoes that will allow for the slight swelling.

✓ Stale air could also make you tired and irritable. Use any air vent over your seat to get as much as you can of what passes for fresh air on most airlines. If you think the air is still stale, ask the cabin staff if they can crank up the ventilation to freshen the air.

✓ Alcohol tends to dehydrate, causing problems with headaches. Drinking alcohol on a flight increases your chances of dehydrating and increases the effects of jetlag. Avoid alcohol before or during a flight.

✓ All stimulants tend to dehydrate the human body, and the cheap tea and coffee brewed by the gallon and served by airlines is no different. If possible, avoid tea and coffee before, during and immediately after a flight.

✓ While flying your digestive system is under stress, due to the air pressure changes and being squashed into narrow seats with little leg room. The effect is that, combined with dehydration, you are at a high risk of becoming constipated. Avoid rich, sweet, fatty and salty foods before, during and immediately after a flight.

✓ If flying in and out of third-world countries, remember the risks associated with contaminated shellfish, food prepared and washed in questionable conditions, etc. You avoided food poisoning while you were there, so don't relax and come back with food poisoning from their sometimes suspect, cheap, mass-produced aircraft meals.

✓ Exercise will help to keep your body operating properly during the flight. Sitting squashed into economy-class seats, your body is in distress and not operating properly. If you take every opportunity to stretch your legs, or take gentle exercise in an area where it does not obstruct or interfere with crew or other passengers, you will help to keep your body functioning during the flight. Some researchers claim that exercising as soon as possible after arrival speeds up the acclimatisation process. (Also see section on deep vein thrombosis on p.138.)

✓ Now airlines insist that passengers check in hours before a flight, the problems are multiplied and extended. You check in and then have to sit and wait in the terminal for two or more hours, extending the time that your body is under stress. You are under stress, listening for announcements, keeping an eye on your carry-on luggage, trying not to lose the rest of your family or group, and often desperately looking for somewhere to sit down. Added to that is the problem of food and drink. Many airport outlets serve the same inedible concoctions that the airlines will serve up during the flight. I personally won't eat anything I can't peel or open from a sealed container at any airport.

➢ When going to the airport, take a supply of safe food and drink. Why pay inflated airport prices for something that could make you feel ill? Take something of what you like to keep yourself going during the inevitable delays.

➢ Don't take fruit and other food onto the aircraft unless you plan to eat it during the flight. Most countries will not allow fruit and meat and other foodstuffs to be 'imported' so don't make problems for yourself.

➢ You will almost certainly have to wait for your flight, so be prepared. Find a comfortable spot where you can listen to announcements and see departure boards.

➢ Get a comfortable seat out of the sun and away from a main access route, otherwise people will constantly be tripping over you and bumping into you.

➢ Take something to read if you can, but at least every half an hour get up and stretch your legs.

➢ If somebody else can keep an eye on the bags, take a walk around the terminal. You will be stuck in economy class soon enough, so you should take the opportunity to get some reasonable exercise when you can.

> When your flight is called, walk to the departure gate, and walk to the baggage hall when you get to the other end in order to get your blood pumping. Don't use lifts, escalators or moving walkways unless you have to.

✓ In the week running up to a flight, some people try to adjust their sleep patterns to suit their destination time zone. For example, they go to bed an hour earlier or later every couple of days so that the difference between their biological clock and their destination time zone is smaller and therefore easier to cope with.

Drowning

Drowning is a real risk. The statistics make it important enough to include a cautionary note.

Statistics

Though it is difficult to collect accurate figures from third-world and communist countries, it is estimated that:

- Each year at least 150,000 people die from recreational drowning around the world.

- For every death from drowning there are 500 'non-fatal submersions' – that is, people who nearly drown.

- In at least 50% of non-fatal submersions of children, those who require resuscitation suffer brain damage due to lack of oxygen.

- Lack of oxygen causes brain and tissue damage after about 4 minutes.

- Drowning is the second most common cause of death for children under 15.

- Nearly 20% of children who drown are in the presence of parents, lifeguards or other adults who are distracted at the time.

- Statistically, any given swimming pool is at least ten times more likely to be involved in the death of a child under four than any given car.

- The highest drowning rate per 1,000 population is shared by children under five and young people between the ages of 15 and 24.

- Of the children under six who drown, 70% will have been in the care of at least one parent and 75% will have only been missing for 5 minutes when they are found.

- 92% of children who get into difficulties survive if they are found and retrieved within 2 minutes of the incident.

- A child can drown in just 2 inches of water.

- 10% of all submersions occur in toilets, pools, buckets, baths and other domestic water containers.

- Contrary to popular belief, people don't usually shout and scream when they are drowning – they are too busy fighting for breath. Most people drown quietly.

Water-based activities – threats

You don't have to travel very far in any direction in any country to find water. Holiday destinations are often constructed on or near water, and also provide water as an amenity to attract guests. Holiday water attractions include:

- Lakes/Rivers/Streams/Reservoirs/Flooded Quarries/Oceans etc.

- On fresh water – Sailing/Speed boats/Canoes/Water Skiing/Rafting etc.

- In fresh water – Swimming/Diving/Fishing etc.

- On the sea – Jet Skis/Sailboards/Windsurfing/Surf Boards/Fishing etc.

- In the sea – Scuba Diving/Snorkelling/Spear Fishing etc.

- At purpose built water parks the whole point of their existence is to attract people to play in the water!

Why do people drown?

People drown for any number of reasons. More often than not children drown because they are exploring and don't recognise or understand the danger associated with water. Reasons for drowning include:
- Not being able to swim, but still going into the water.

- Leg cramp or cramp after eating too much food or rich heavy food.

- Loss of consciousness due to injury, e.g. swimmers hit by boat or jet ski, diving into unknown and untested shallow water, hitting the bottom or an unknown underwater obstruction.

- Getting out of your depth, in water that is too deep or too rough.

- Medical condition such as a stroke or heart attack.

- Falling through ice and being trapped.

- Not wearing a life jacket for water sports.

- Drinking alcohol, which leads to risk-taking, bravado and possible death.

- Overloading boats with cargo or passengers, making them sink.

- Falling victim to unknown currents and rip tides.

- Being cut off by incoming tides.

- Water being colder than the swimmer thought – as found in deep quarries – leading to muscle cramps, hypothermia and death by drowning.

- Swimming where boats, jet skis and ships are manoeuvring, then being involved in a collision or injured by propellers.

- Disabling action of sea creatures such as jellyfish.

Drowning – countermeasures

General advice

✓ Make absolutely sure that children are strictly supervised at all times when around water.

  ➤ The person supervising children around water must be a strong swimmer.

  ➤ The supervisor must be an adult, never allow older children to supervise younger children.

  ➤ Supervisors will need to take a break. They cannot maintain concentration on more than two children for more than 2 hours. If you need a break, insist that the children come in for a break too, and make sure that they all come in and stay there. Lock the door if you have to!

  ➤ The supervisor should have a phone at the pool, and should never go inside to answer the phone or the front door bell, make a drink, collect food or anything else.

✓ Teach your children to learn to swim or stay away from the water. At least if you know how to swim you stand a chance of reaching the shore.

✓ Make sure that all pools are protected by locked doors, fences at least 5 feet high, locked gates, and where possible alarms. Make sure that neighbour's pools are fenced, locked and secured as well.

✓ Make sure that fences, gates and door locks are child-proof.

✓ Keep the area around water free of furniture, shrubs and sheds or other obstructions. You should have a clear view of the water so that you can see what is happening at all times, not just when you are supervising children. For example, a child visiting your neighbours may stray onto your property to see the water. It will therefore be safer if anyone in your house has a clear view of the water and anyone who may be around it.

✓ Consider making a monthly safety inspection of your pool.

   ➤ Check any barrier or fence surrounding it for good repair, locks, gaps children can squeeze through, places they could climb over, etc.

   ➤ Are gates locked? Is the key kept safely? Can children get to the key? Check that rescue equipment is available around the water, e.g. life belts, ropes, and long poles with hooks or loops on the end. Rescuers can use the long pole to reach anyone in difficulties without having to jump in themselves. (It is easier to see the victim while standing up on the pool edge or riverbank than it is when you are in the water too.)

   ➤ If you have an outside hot tub, is it kept covered and locked when not actually in use?

   ➤ If you have a pool at home, of if you have children, take a first-aid course so you know what to do if somebody is pulled from the water.

✓ Teach children that water can be very dangerous. Never let them treat areas near water as play areas. Keep toys off pool surrounds, riverbanks and the areas surrounding lakes and streams.

✓ Never swim alone and never leave a child alone near water, swimming pools or any container of water.

✓ When in a group near water, just as you would designate a driver who would not drink alcohol at a party, consider designating a lifeguard who will concentrate on keeping an eye on everyone around and in the water. You could take it in turns to be the lifeguard as long as you can swim and haven't been drinking.

✓ Never leave a baby or very young child in water. A baby can drown in a baby bath while you answer the phone or the front door.

✓ Teach children to swim as soon as you can. Local authorities and education authorities can often advise on reasonably priced or subsidised lessons.

✓ Before diving into any water, everyone should check the depth and check for obstructions.

✓ Refuse to use a pool where the water is dirty or cloudy. Children have drowned in dirty pools because nobody could see that they were in difficulties.

✓ At home, treat the bathroom with as much care as you would treat a swimming pool, a child can drown just as easily in a bath.

✓ Remember that any container of water is dangerous. Empty and cover or turn over any tubs, pots, buckets, barrels, etc. that may hold water.

✓ If a child goes missing, it is vital that you should **check any water sources first**, whether it is a bath, pool, stream or bucket. Remember, with drowning you only have 4 minutes to make the rescue.

Adult safety

✓ Never swim

> ➤ Alone.

> ➤ After a heavy meal.

> ➤ In unknown waters.

> ➤ After using drugs or alcohol (alcohol and drugs are a contributory cause of nearly all recorded drowning accidents in Europe).

> ➤ In deep or cold water.

> ➤ When there is a fast current or tide.

> ➤ You should also avoid using hot tubs after using drugs or alcohol. The water is warm and relaxing. If you fall asleep you may not wake up!

✓ If you can't swim, and can't avoid the water, wear a good-quality lifejacket that has been fitted correctly.

✓ Avoid fishing alone. There will be nobody to help you if you get into difficulties.

✓ Before jumping or diving into the water, always check for:

> ➤ Other swimmers in the water.

> ➤ Boats or other river users.

> ➤ Depth. To dive safely water should be at least 9 feet deep.

> ➤ Obstructions on and around the bank, in or under the water.

> ➤ Currents and tides.

> ➤ Broken glass, fishing line, old bikes and other hazards.

✓ Don't overload boats with cargo or passengers and remember that the safe load will vary depending on the water conditions.

✓ If using boats, jet skis or other craft, make sure that you have been taught how to handle them safely and that you know the laws and rules for their use.

✓ Do not use drugs or alcohol and then try to swim. Both will have an adverse effect on judgement and co-ordination.

✓ Try to use supervised areas, particularly when swimming in the sea. Beaches where lifeguards are patrolling are usually clearly marked.

✓ If warning flags are flying, don't try to swim.

✓ Stay away from ships, docks, piers and other structures when swimming. There may be spinning propellers, obstructions or rusty metal that can cut or trap you.

✓ Don't swim too far out to sea. If you want to swim a long distance, swim up and down along the shore, close enough to get to land if there is a problem.

✓ If caught in a fast tide, never ever try to swim against the tide. Float with the tide and try to swim in to safety at an angle of 45 degrees to the shore, aiming for a point where waves are breaking on the beach. (Where you can see waves breaking on the beach is where waves are flowing in towards the beach.)

✓ Only use jet skis, surfboards, wind-surfers, etc. if you are a strong swimmer, and always wear a lifejacket.

✓ Only participate in surfing, scuba-diving, snorkelling, water-skiing and other ocean activities if you have had professional instruction and your equipment has been thoroughly checked and approved by a qualified person.

✓ Don't participate in any water-based activity alone. Always make sure that you are with somebody so that you can watch and help each other if there is a problem.

✓ If diving or venturing to deeper water on surfboards, etc., consider wearing a wetsuit to protect you from the cold water.

✓ If you are going to take a river or white-water trip on any craft, make sure that the operator is experienced and qualified. Make sure that you wear a lifejacket, safety helmet and any other safety equipment provided. If no safety equipment is provided, don't go!

✓ Beware of rogue waves that are bigger and stronger than the average wave. They could wash you off a sea wall or rocky outcrop, or capsize your boat.

✓ Beware of high tidal ranges and very high spring tides. Know the tidal times and ranges at your resort. Don't get cut off by the tide.

Drowning – first-aid

This is the advice I was given on my first-aid course a few years ago. If you live or play near water, attend first-aid training to learn the latest advice and techniques.

✓ Send somebody to call for help and medical assistance at the first sign of trouble, but make sure that you ask them to come back to report to you what they have done, so you know what is happening.

✓ Make a note of the time. You should report to paramedics or doctors how long the patient was under water and/or when the heart stopped, etc.

✓ Be ready to hand over the care of the victim to anyone with more skill or experience than you have.

✓ In cold water a pulse may be hard to find. Take your time to look for one. You shouldn't start cardiopulmonary resuscitation (CPR) unless the heart has actually stopped.

✓ Clear the patient's mouth to remove any seaweed or other obstructions.

✓ Start artificial respiration as soon as it is possible. On gently sloping beaches it may take you 2 or 3 minutes to carry a victim clear of the water because you have to wade in a long way. In those circumstances, stop in shallow water and give them a few breaths. Support the patient out of the water behind the head, bend the head back, gently pinch the nose and breathe into the patient's mouth. Watch the chest rise with each breath as you blow. Help should soon be with you to take the patient to the beach.

✓ When clear of the water, turn the victim face down on the sand with their head to one side and arms stretched above the head. Infants or children could be held upside down for a short period. Raise the middle part of the body with your hands round the belly. This is to cause any water to drain out of the mouth and throat – this is an extension of clearing seaweed, etc. from the mouth. Drowning people suffocate, they very rarely breathe much water into their lungs.

✓ Give CPR until medical help arrives, or until you are relieved by somebody else who is qualified.

✓ If medical help has not arrived, in case they are having trouble finding you, send runners to the nearest road or access point to attract the attention of the ambulance crew or lifeguards. Tell them to stay there and guide the medical help back directly to the patient.

✓ When there is time, if the patient is cold, remove cold wet clothes and cover the patient with several layers of blankets, etc. to warm them, as long as this does not interfere with CPR.

Medication

If you are taken ill abroad, be wary of medication. In many countries, powerful medication, which is only available on prescription in the UK, is available over the counter at popular holiday destinations.

The brand names often differ from the products that you may know, and the quality of the product and the strength and dosage can also vary. You cannot be sure of what you are getting, or what the effects may be.

Medication – countermeasures

✓ If you are already suffering from a condition that may require treatment or medication while abroad, get your doctor to write it down so that you can take a note with you listing:

> ➢ The name of your condition.

> ➢ The generic name (and the brand name) of the medication prescribed.

> ➢ What strength and dosage of the medication has been prescribed.

> ➢ Any other medication you may be taking, e.g. blood pressure pills.

> ➢ Any other complication and/or conditions, allergies, etc. from which you suffer and which may be relevant in your treatment.

✓ Make sure that you have sufficient supply of medication for the duration of your holiday, and a week or so afterwards. (The extra week allows for travel delays, and time to get an appointment and repeat prescription when you get home.)

✓ Make absolutely sure that it will be legal for you to carry any medication through customs as you travel from country to country.

✓ Be very, very careful with self-prescribed medication that can be purchased without prescription in many countries. In some countries the 'chemist' is just a shopkeeper selling 'potions'. He is not a trained pharmacist, so his advice is often sales talk, not a medical opinion or professional consultation.

✓ If you are prescribed or take medication while abroad, keep the packaging or bottle, instructions and label so that you can tell and show customs and your doctor what you were given and took.

Include health care in your plans

Having read this section, you are now more aware of the threats to your health, and how those threat levels usually increase significantly when on holiday.

If you didn't previously know the range of holiday health threats that you face, you do now. Knowing what threats and risks you may encounter is one thing, doing something about them is another. You can quite easily wash your hands before eating and avoid risky foods and dirty restaurants. You can even wash and treat a mosquito bite when you know that the bite can become so infected that it will require medical treatment.

The big question is, when you or a member of your party needs urgent medical assistance and you are the first person at the scene, would you know what to do?

Forget holidays, what about everyday life? If your daughter, father, sister or a close friend collapsed in front of you, other than calling for an ambulance would you know what to do?

First-aid – countermeasures

✓ Take a first-aid course. The Red Cross, St John's Ambulance and other organisations offer first-aid courses.

✓ If nothing else, learn CPR – the kiss of life.

You may come up with some general health and safety questions relevant to your holiday. For example, you might now decide to check to see what safety and first-aid equipment has been installed on the canal boat you are thinking of hiring next summer, or you may want to ask about the presence of lifeguards at your holiday hotel pool. Make sure that you have asked your doctor about any proposed unusual activity such as bungee jumping and climbing to extreme altitudes.

When you are happy that you have made all the medical and health preparations that you can, pack this book. This may be the only guide to symptoms available to you in an emergency at a remote spot.

You should also remember that the locals probably know best. They live with the conditions all year, so they probably have more experience with local illnesses, bites, stings and diseases than most UK doctors.

Be safe, not sorry.

4 Travel Out

With your preparations completed, you are ready to travel and that brings a whole new list of issues for you to consider. Some relate to security, some relate to health and some potentially relate to the difference between being alive or dead.

Home Security

Most people go away for a few weeks on holiday each year. When you are away, and your house is unattended, it is vulnerable. In the excitement of planning your holiday remember that there are some basic precautions you should take.

Deliveries

In everything you do, remember that you are planning to be away between given dates. Packages waiting on doorsteps are tempting to a casual thief, as well as advertising to a whole range of people that you are not at home and may not be around for a few days.

Deliveries – countermeasures

✓ Avoid ordering anything that will be delivered while you are away.

✓ If you have to order something for delivery while you are away, ask for it to be delivered to a relation or trustworthy neighbour.

✓ If you do have something delivered to a relative or neighbour, don't damage your security by telling the company that you can't have it delivered to your home address because you will be abroad from the 2nd to the 23rd of the month!

✓ Make sure that you give the lawn and hedge an extra trim the day before you go on holiday. Pull out the weeds and water the garden thoroughly if you have to. That will delay the onset of an unkempt and unattended appearance that may tell criminals you are away.

✓ Try to arrange for a relation or trusted neighbour to come to the house each day to check for mail or other items delivered and left on the doorstep or filling the letterbox.

Leaving notes

No matter what the excuse, never ever leave a note on the door. Notes such as 'Milkman – we are on holiday – no milk until 18th August' or perhaps 'On holiday until 18th August ALL deliveries to Number 7 please' are a gift to criminals. Remember, even a note saying 'Gone to shops, back in five minutes' may be enough to tempt a burglar.

Leaving notes – countermeasures

✓ Arrange matters so that a note will not be necessary, by making sure that deliveries are all made before you go on holiday.

✓ If you know and trust the milkman, tell him that you don't want any milk until the 18th August, but don't ever leave a note advertising that fact to everyone.

✓ If you don't know or trust the milkman, consider NOT cancelling the milk. It will cost you a few pounds but you could arrange for a relative to collect your daily milk delivery and use it while you are away, so the milkman will be none the wiser.

✓ If possible, arrange for a trusted relative to collect mail, etc. so that notes are not necessary.

Junk mail and circulars

Your letterbox and front step are important areas in maintaining your security. For a few weeks before your departure keep an eye on what is delivered. Not just the usual post and milk. It is the 'unwanted deliveries' that could be a problem. Free newspapers, circulars, flyers and pizza advertisements are often just dumped on the doorstep. Unfortunately, these are the deliveries that can cause you problems.

If not collected and disposed of, within a few days they could overflow your letterbox and doorstep, cascading out to blow around the garden for all to see. That is a very clear indication to everyone that you are not at home. By the time the doorstep is stacked up with this rubbish you clearly haven't been there for some days, which will attract the attention of the local criminals.

Make sure that though you have carefully managed and cancelled all deliveries, these free deliveries don't spoil all your good work. Where possible get some-body to check the property each day, and if possible spend a few hours there, to make the place look 'lived in'. Remember to ask them to make absolutely sure that they secure the house when they leave though!

Junk mail and circulars – countermeasures

✓ Try to make sure that your mail is cleared each day while you are away. If a few bulky circulars are forced through your letterbox, they can block future deliveries. The postman should take new deliveries back to the sorting office to await collection when you return, but people delivering free newspapers and junk mail circulars will almost certainly simply dump new deliveries at and around the front door and doorstep.

✓ A visiting relative can clear the letterbox each day. (Consider removing any mail basket for the duration of your stay, particularly if you receive a lot of mail, then the letterbox will not become jammed with letters!)

✓ I did see a house that had a special delivery slot for circulars and any free newspapers. Actually it was a large box with a wide access slot, sited near the front door. The owner told me that inside the box was a plastic crate. A couple of times a week he would take the crate out of the 'circulars mail box', taking each item out and throwing it into his recycling bin. He only checked it in case some genuine post had been put there in error.

✓ If you want to try to stop or at least reduce the amount of unsolicited advertising you receive by mail, fax and telephone, visit the following specific sites to register your details. It will take a few months to work and isn't guaranteed to stop all junk mail, but it helps.

➢ www.fpsonline.org.uk Register your number and state that you do not want unsolicited fax advertising material.

➢ www.mpsonline.org.uk Register your address and state that you do not want unsolicited mail advertising material.

➢ www.tpsonline.org.uk Register your number and state that you do not want unsolicited telephone advertising material.

Central heating

If you are going on a winter holiday you may have to leave your heating on, so that the water pipes are protected from frost damage. A low setting will not use too much fuel, but it will prevent the pipes from freezing and keep the house safe and comfortable for your return.

Central heating – countermeasures

✓ Make sure that your central heating system has been properly serviced and maintained. If it is, you can be pretty sure that it will not cause a fire or leak and flood your house while you are away.

✓ If going away in winter, you should consider leaving your central heating on at a low level to prevent the pipes from freezing. This will also keep the house dry and fairly warm for your return.

✓ If the central heating is on, you have another reason to get a trusted relative or very close and trusted friend to check the property daily!

Lights on timers

While away, try to make the house look as occupied and lived in as possible. Any action you can take to make it appear as though somebody is around will be an extra deterrent to a criminal who could be considering attacking your house.

A number of manufacturers supply electrical timers. They plug into an electrical socket and you can plug a light or other device into them. The timers then work off the electricity and at set times programmed by you they will switch the device plugged into them on and off. So you can make a light come on and go off at times you have set.

The better electrical timers have a battery backup function. Without the battery, in a power cut the timer could lose its programmed operation and stop working, or carry on working with a clock that was running a few hours late. That could make lights go off and on in the early hours of the morning, which would attract the attention of criminals rather than put them off.

Lights on timers – countermeasures

✓ Make sure that you only buy safe and approved electrical timers – something that will not cause a fire while they are unattended.

✓ Use timers sparingly. Don't make your house look like seaside illuminations with all sorts of things switching on and off at different times.

✓ Make sure that you have some non-ceiling lights that can be operated by the timers, such as table lamps.

✓ The timer light will look better if you can get a relative to go to your house and draw the curtains in the evening and open them again in the morning – which is when they come to collect the milk, gather up the post and check that the central heating is behaving itself.

✓ Use timers strategically, and make sure that you plan their use. I suggest that their use should reflect your lifestyle patterns. For example, if you wake up at six each morning, have a bedroom light that comes on at six. If you sit in the lounge from five until ten each evening then go to bed, use timers to switch the lounge lights on at five and switch them off at ten. At the same time the bedroom timer light comes on at ten to ten and goes off at quarter past ten. This should give the indication of the normal pattern of use, so to a casual observer there is no indication that you are away. Depending on your window dressing you may have to ask the relative or neighbour who is checking for junk mail to make their visit in the early evening when they can close the curtains, then come back in the morning to open them again.

Radio talk stations

Just as the timer lights give the illusion of occupancy, leaving a radio on could help your illusion, depending on how you use it. I put a radio onto one of the timer switches, and arrange for the radio to be tuned to a talk station. Music stations are OK, but an intruder won't believe current pop stars are staying at your house if he hears their music. On the other hand, if you tune the radio to a talk station, all he will be able to hear from the outside is muffled voices, from which he cannot be sure if there are actually people in the house talking.

The basic security of your house and the added uncertainty of the muffled voices should be enough to make him look for an easier and safer target down the road.

Radio talk stations – countermeasures

✓ Buy a timer switch to operate the radio.

✓ Tune the radio to a station that you know will be all talk.

✓ News and current affairs discussion channels are acceptable, because the participants are usually fairly unknown. A channel with a well-known and recognisable celebrity talking won't fool the criminals.

✓ Tune the radio accurately. A crackling, badly tuned, hissing station will not fool anyone.

✓ Set the volume to a subdued conversational level. Don't be tempted to turn it up so that the criminals 'will definitely be able to hear it'. If it is too loud they will know what it is.

The garden

Don't forget that your garden can tell tales on you too. An uncut and overgrown lawn is very obvious to anyone passing by. Wilting hanging baskets or weed-infested flowerbeds give the criminals more indications that nobody is home. If you usually trim the hedge every Sunday and then suddenly it is left to grow for two weeks in August, it will be noticed.

The garden-based evidence alone can point to a family on holiday. Add the extra information about the lack of activity in the house, the milkman doesn't stop there any more, there aren't any kids playing in the garden, and you begin to see that it is quite difficult to hide your absence from anyone who regularly passes by. It might take them ten days to notice, but eventually the evidence builds up to the inescapable conclusion that you are away and the house is empty.

Garden – countermeasures

✓ Water the hanging baskets and borders so that they don't wilt and die, drawing attention to the empty house.

✓ Cut the lawn, trim the hedge and weed the borders.

✓ Possibly arrange for a relative to enter the house and make it look lived in for a few hours every now and then. My neighbour asks me to go into her house a couple of times a week to tend to the post and house plants, then watch television for a few hours, so that people can see life and activity.

✓ If you have children, you may ask your relation to move things around when they are there. That can be done while watering the garden or mowing the grass to make it look innocent but the idea is to move children's bikes, toys etc. If the kid's bikes and toys stay in one place for a week or two it will be noticed. Move things and the house and garden look normal and in use.

✓ Make sure that sheds are locked, cars are in the garage with secondary security devices fitted and that the garage itself is secured.

✓ Make sure that all ladders, tools and any equipment that could be stolen or used to break into your home are securely locked away.

Dustbin/rubbish collection

When making your arrangements, don't forget the dustman. Here is another task for that visiting relative or friendly neighbour. In the first week you will have rubbish in your bin that you don't want to leave to decompose and rot for the time you are away. Neither do you want a passing criminal to notice and investigate why all the neighbours in the street have put their dustbins out – but not you!

Arrange for somebody to put the dustbin out and take it in when it has been emptied. In the first week all will then appear to be normal to the passing burglar. In the second and any subsequent weeks, ask the visitor to bring a few bags of rubbish, put them in your bin and put it out for collection as normal. **115**

This should maintain another little bit of the illusion that somebody is still at home and that the house is not empty.

Remember these things may be minor, but every single action helps to build on the illusion that you are still at home.

Dustbin – countermeasures

✓ If at all possible, make things appear as normal as they can be to passing criminals, including putting the bin out and taking it in as usual.

✓ You should have arranged for somebody to visit your house every day to take junk mail off the step, look after the garden and generally make the house appear to be in use. They should also put the dustbin out the first week. In subsequent weeks they should put junk mail and rubbish into the bin and put it out for the dustman.

✓ Ideally they must have time to spend an hour or so at the house, following the normal pattern of the homeowner. The dustbin should be put out and taken in following the same pattern as normal. If it is usually put out the night before, then do the same while the homeowner is away. If the bin is usually emptied and taken in about mid-afternoon, then as far as is possible that should be kept up. You are trying to maintain a normal appearance! If a harassed relative races up in his car and screeches to a halt minutes before the dustman arrives, waits for the dustman, then races off back to work in a cloud of tyre smoke when the bin has been emptied, it will have totally the opposite effect to the one you are planning. That sort of behaviour will draw attention to your house. Just like milk piled up on a doorstep, or mail overflowing from a letterbox, a dustbin left out overnight is a clear sign that nobody is home. A burglar will soon notice that and take action to investigate further.

House sitter/pets

Pets have to be considered when taking a holiday, and while some people are happy to bear the cost of putting their dog or cat in a boarding kennel, others arrange for a house sitter to take care of the house and their pets. This has the double benefit of keeping the house lived in and secure, as well as keeping the pets at home in familiar surroundings.

Boarding and kennel rates of £9 to £12 per day for a large dog and £6 per day for a cat are not uncommon and certainly not the most expensive. Individually they don't seem too high, but when some kennels charge extra for insurance, heated accommodation and special diets the price soon adds up. The cost of boarding a family dog or cat while you are away on a holiday could quite easily reach £250.

When the cost can be as high or higher than that, inviting somebody to stay at your house begins to make sense. You will however have to ensure that they are trustworthy and will maintain your security standards while you are away. It is pointless making your house secure, if for two weeks of the year your nephew Trevor Biggins leaves doors and windows open, holds open house parties and can't quite get the hang of not leaving the keys in your car!

House sitter – countermeasures

✓ If you are wealthy and have a lot of valuable possessions, your house will be a lot more secure when you are away on holiday or business trips if somebody is living in your house.

✓ It is possible to hire somebody as a house sitter, but you will have to be very sure of their credentials before you hand over the keys. More often a homeowner will arrange for a relative to stay in the house and look after it. A relative is a known quantity so should be easier to select, easier to arrange and more trustworthy than a stranger.

✓ If the homeowners have any pets, bringing in a house sitter could make sound financial sense. Apart from saving hundreds of pounds in pet boarding fees, you get the extra security of somebody living in the house. (An additional benefit is that the pets are happier because they get to stay at home.)

✓ If you do organise a house sitter, you must be very certain that the sitter is honest and trustworthy, and that they are as careful with home security as you would be.

Create an illusion of activity

There are some things that can be done to add to the illusion of life and activity at your empty home. I have given a couple of examples below. Knowing your own home, family and personal circumstances, see if you can add a few illusions of your own.

Illusion of activity – countermeasures

✓ Depending on your relationship with your neighbour, you could invite them to occasionally park a car in your drive or outside your house to increase the illusion that there is activity in, around and associated with your empty house.

✓ If safe and appropriate, you could ask a neighbour to allow their children to play in your garden occasionally. You might wish to ask a visiting gardener, or the relative who is collecting your milk and checking for unwanted mail and circulars, to bring their children with them to boost the illusion of occupancy.

✓ Remember that carefully rationed acting will help as well! When the man who looks after your garden is leaving, he could stand at the gate and pretend to be holding a *short* conversation with 'you'. For example, he could pretend to be answering a question and call something like 'OK, I'll check to see if I can get a couple of those roses, see you next week' towards the back of the house. If the acting is low key and only tried once a week it should help.

Careful collection

Think security in everything you do. Don't make a big thing out of leaving for the airport. It is pointless taking all of these security steps to make people think you are still at home, if you make so much noise and fuss about leaving that half the county can't help knowing that you have gone to the airport with three large suitcases. If Uncle George is taking you to the airport, get him to reverse up to the house and slip the cases into the boot. If you are going in a taxi, try to arrange for a time when there won't be a big audience watching you. If everyone drives past your house on the way to work between 8 and 9 in the morning, try to arrange for the taxi to collect you before 8 or after 9. That way fewer people will see you leave with your obvious holiday cases.

Long holidays and business trips

There are ways of covering up a holiday that lasts a couple of weeks, but longer holidays and long business trips present some unique problems and are harder to hide.

As a police officer I was called to a house that had been burgled and heavily vandalised. It was a detached house set in a large garden, and the owners were on a six-month business trip to the USA. They had taken some holiday countermeasures to disguise their absence but that wasn't enough. Unfortunately they hadn't identified the new problems presented by an extended absence. When they had been gone a couple of months, louts noticed that the house was clearly unoccupied, broke in, stole some property and then stayed to trash the place. Toilets and basins were broken, taps were left on, paint thrown around and doors ripped off their hinges. The television was smashed and china and glassware was broken and thrown all over the house. The final bill for damage and loss ran into thousands of pounds.

Standing on the road outside the house the signs and evidence that it was empty were clear and easy to see. For example:

- Tall weeds had grown up through the drive and around gates. It was obvious that nobody was using the drive. Car wheels and people's feet weren't knocking weeds down and killing them. Gates were not being opened, sweeping weeds aside.

- It was late spring going into early summer. Bushes in the front garden had grown quickly, partly blocking the front path, the lounge windows and the front door step.

- Ivy that was growing up the side of the house had started growing across the living room window, a blatant sign that nobody was caring for the house.

- A telephone directory had been delivered and left on the front door step, but spring rain had partly turned it into paper mulch.

- The front windows, front door and doorstep were all dirty and dusty. Even an untrained eye could clearly see that footprints in the dirt on the front step showed where a male (postman) had stood on the step then left. The footprints clearly showed that nobody had come out of the house.

Overall the impression was of an unloved and unused house. It didn't take a master detective to read the clues. Even the local louts couldn't fail to notice – and unfortunately for the homeowner, they didn't.

Long holidays and business trips – countermeasures

If you are going to be away for a long time, remember the lessons that can be learned from the case above. Spend some time identifying the new vulnerabilities to which you are exposed by being absent from your home for more than a couple of weeks. When you have identified them, define and introduce countermeasures to them. For example:

✓ If you are going away for more than three weeks, you MUST have somebody trustworthy looking after your house.

✓ Check your house insurance. Some policies are void if the house is empty for more than a specified number of weeks. You could find on return from an extended absence that your house has been destroyed and the insurance company refuses to pay out because the house has been left empty.

✓ Plan ahead and think of the seasons. Take time to consider the things that will happen while you are away and take steps to overcome any problems. For example:

➢ **In spring.** Remember that plants put on a spurt of growth. In winter nothing much will happen in your garden, but during a three-week absence in a good spring, your garden can become a jungle. Hedges, ivy, lawns, even weeds suddenly appear and demonstrate the lack of a controlling presence. Make sure that somebody is keeping an eye on the garden and trimming back energetic plants where needed.

➢ **In summer.** Many plants put on a growth spurt, drought kills them, wasps and other pests build nests and take properties over. Whoever is looking after the house and garden should take whatever steps are necessary to keep everything in order. That may mean watering the lawn, or arranging for a wasp nest to be removed from the porch!

➢ **In autumn.** Falling leaves are the main problem. In itself this is not a major disaster, unless your garden is usually immaculate, then rafts of decaying leaves can display your absence. Add a little wind and the leaves can blow together to collect in sheltered corners which gives two problems. A stray bonfire night rocket can set fire to leaves collected against your shed or garage and put it at risk from fire. The same leaves can blow up against the back door, or collect on the front step, another clear sign that there is nobody home. Whoever is watching your house should rake them up, and put them on the compost pile. They should certainly be looking for anything that is a clear sign of the absence of residents, such as making sure leaves don't collect on the front door step.

➢ **In winter.** Frost and snow clearly shows that there is no activity in a house. Activity leaves clearly visible tracks in heavy frost or snow, for example footprints, garage doors and gates being opened or closed, and car tyre tracks.

✓ If your house is the only one with none of these signs, it will be noticed. If you are going on an extended holiday or business trip, you may have left your car in the garage. If the person checking your house is insured for it they could use your car to leave appropriate tracks and turn the engine over now and then.

✓ Alternatively, you could ask a neighbour to park their car in your drive so that there are signs of activity. After fresh snow, they could walk up and down the path a few times, break a path to the shed, make tracks out to the greenhouse, consider sweeping or shovelling snow off the drive and definitely clear any off the front door step.

✓ Make sure that somebody opens and closes the gates, shed and garage doors. The opening action sweeps leaves and snow off the path, showing that the doors and gates are in use.

✓ The person looking after the house should consider sweeping the path and drive. It will take some time but will show activity and occupation in a number of ways.

✓ The person looking after the house should keep an eye on the condition of windows and the front door and door step. They need to be swept, dusted and occasionally washed. Dirty doors and windows make the premises look vacant. Remember that there is no crime in walking up to a front door to ring the bell. A passing criminal could see a house that doesn't seem to be occupied, and all they have to do to check is to walk up and ring the front door bell. If nobody answers, they make a note to come back when it is dark. If somebody answers, they make their excuses and leave.

✓ In the summer and autumn, the person looking after your house should be asked to check any fruit or vegetables growing in the garden. Ripening and uncollected fruit could be noticed. Tell them to collect and take tomatoes, fruit and vegetables growing in the garden.

✓ At Christmas if you are away, you might ask them to put up a few decorations that are visible through the front window. Nothing elaborate is needed. Just enough to show to anyone who looks that the phantom occupants are there and getting into the festive spirit by putting decorations up. Just as importantly, they must be taken down at the right time too!

✓ Increasingly properties need protection on Halloween. The once innocent American child's pastime of 'trick or treating' has been increasingly used by louts to demand money or goods under threat of retribution. Their approach is more akin to blackmail and threats than childish fun. Any householder who does not answer their door and give food, money, drinks, etc. is likely to suffer from blatant criminal acts. I have seen windows broken, cars vandalised, expensive shrubs broken off, paint thrown over a front door and fireworks pushed through letterboxes. If you plan to be away during Halloween it may be prudent to ask somebody to stay in the house and distribute a few pounds worth of chocolate and fizzy drink cans to avoid trouble.

✓ You should also plan to avoid known local problems. Many areas suffer annual problems from a variety of large gatherings, be they pop festivals, race meetings or other events that attract large numbers of people. If there is such an event in your area, if you can't plan your absence to be at home to protect your property at that time, you should certainly arrange for somebody to stay in the property over that period to protect it.

Locking up

For your peace of mind more than anything else, define a routine for closing the house while you are away. You already know that you have to cancel the milk, cut the grass, arrange for deliveries to be made before you go, etc., but look beyond that.

You don't want to get to the airport or be sitting in the Andes Mountains worrying about household security. Think of the stress you would suffer if you couldn't quite remember if you had turned off the kitchen tap when you had a glass of water before you left, or if anyone ever actually shut the back door when Uncle George arrived to take you to the airport.

Define a procedure, list or method that will take you from room to room, to secure the house, switch on the electric timers that will operate lights and the radio, close the bedroom windows, lock the side gate, etc.

If you do that, and then follow that procedure or list in good time before your transport arrives, you should be able to avoid those nagging worries and enjoy your holiday.

Locking up – countermeasures

✓ Pay particular attention to securing the house when you are leaving for more than a few hours, particularly when going on holiday.

✓ If a relation will be visiting the house and they will actually have access to the building, make sure that they know how to secure the house properly. Show them how to lock up, especially if there is a knack to locking the patio door!

✓ Be careful with your cases and bags, especially any bag that has your tickets, passports and money in it. It is not unusual for travellers to arrive at the airport and only notice that a bag is missing when they go to check in for the flight. Only then do they realise that they left that bag on the bus, on the train or maybe it was stolen when that group of people started fighting at the bus station!

✓ When you get to the airport, for a fee some airports will shrink-wrap your luggage in clear plastic. This helps protect your luggage from damage, water and theft!

Public Transport

Public transport includes using commercial public service to undertake a journey. This includes:

* Train

* Underground

* Bus

* Tram/Trolley

* Ferry

Risk Levels

For every thousand journeys made, there are far more accidents and injuries suffered by private motorists than by public transport passengers. This means that in the UK, statistically, travelling by public transport is a hundred times safer than using your own car.

Trains

Other than terrorist attacks, the main risks associated with trains are accident, assault and theft, but these can be discussed in a variety of ways.

Terrorist attacks

It is worth remembering that public transport systems are by far the safest way to travel, even if you include the risk of terrorist attacks. Considering the number of rail journeys taken each day, the likelihood of anyone being involved in an incident is minute, even if you travel in a city targeted by terrorists.

However, this doesn't mean that there is nothing you need to do to protect yourself. See the terrorism chapter for advice and discussion of terrorism countermeasures.

Accident

Though rail travel is heavily regulated, in recent years there have been a number of high-profile accidents and very old rolling stock is only just being phased out on some lines.

If there is a rail accident, you can be fairly sure that it will be serious. When a couple of hundred tons of train runs off the line or hits a broken rail, the tightly packed travellers inside are bound to suffer serious injury and possibly die.

Rail travellers are also susceptible to injury or death caused by train versus vehicle collisions and derailments. By the very nature of cross-country rail travel, the locations of railway accidents can often be inaccessible to emergency services, so the subsequent delay in rendering assistance usually leads to more fatalities than would have occurred if help could have got to the scene quicker and easier.

Accidents – countermeasures

✓ Always sit down when travelling by train, and where possible sit with your back to the front of the train at the rear of the carriage at the back of the train. If the train does run into an obstruction all passengers and goods will tend to be thrown forwards as it breaks or stops suddenly due to the impact. If that happens when you are standing up, you will be tossed around like a rag doll. If you are sitting facing the engine, you will be thrown forward out of your seat. If you are sitting with your back to the front of the train, the impact will have the effect of pushing you deeper into your seat. If you are at the rear of the carriage in an accident most flying luggage, etc. should be behind you.

✓ The dynamics of motion mean that any object thrown at the train, along with any shattered glass, will enter the train and tend to fly towards the back, giving risk of injury to those facing the front. Passengers seated with their back to the front of the train will be protected by their seat backs.

✓ Maintain an awareness of what is happening to the train. In many rail accidents surviving passengers have reported that the train seemed to be out of control, or was 'shaking or rattling' more than usual. If these are potential warning signs of impending disaster, be aware of them. Due to the state of some of the tracks, not every jolt or rattle will mean that you are about to be involved in an accident. However, if you are on a train and feel something, there is nothing to stop you from bracing yourself against a seat or bulkhead just in case. Move away from windows and doors and adopt a position that will help you survive any accident. If the moment passes then go about your business. If there is an accident, a second or two of forethought and effort could have saved your life.

Robbery and assault

Criminal gangs have been known to attack rail services. They board the train as passengers, and then when the train is between stations and the passengers are helpless, the gang members run through the train assaulting and robbing passengers at will. When the train pulls into the next station down the line the gang members get off and are gone before anyone can report the crime.

There is also a risk of robbery and assault on platforms and in railway subways, generally later at night. Passengers are also at risk of crimes to their person or to their vehicle in railway station car parks.

Statistically a traveller is unlikely to be the victim of an assault when travelling by train, and women are apparently even less likely to be assaulted when travelling by train than men, but that is no reason to relax and let your guard down. There are criminals out there, don't make life easy for them. Every single thing you can do to protect yourself makes you that much less likely to become the target of criminal activity.

Robbery and assault – countermeasures

✓ Sitting in the carriage nearest to the driver/guard/inspector offers a little more protection, because they are the representative of authority on a train. A single criminal is likely to look for carriages as far away as possible from these railway employees, to reduce the chances of detection.

✓ In all cases, if confronted by violence and aggression remember that nothing is worth risking your life for. Never try to fight robbers, never try to argue with them. They could have been drinking or may be on drugs. If they have, the chances are that they are acting on instinct and are oblivious to the consequences. You can replace a watch and other possessions. There is no point in getting killed or crippled for the sake of a few pounds and the odd credit card. Don't fight back. Switch to information-gathering mode and remember as much detail as you can. Look at things the robbers touch so you can tell the police where fingerprints might be found. Listen for names, look for tattoos, notice anything unusual and report it to the police. The more evidence they have the greater the chances of the robbers being caught.

✓ Never display valuables in a careless manner. Avoid wearing very expensive jewellery or carelessly waving a wallet or purse stuffed with cash. When paying for tickets or otherwise using cash in public places, be discreet. I like to keep a few pounds out of my wallet and put it ready in my pocket, so that I can buy a ticket or pay for a drink or newspaper without showing criminals that I am a worthy target for their attention.

✓ Keep your luggage nearby where you can see it. Lock your cases and bags. Don't leave anything valuable in the outer pockets of bags and cases because they cannot be locked. Take extra care of handbags, rucksacks and briefcases that are too easy for a criminal to take as he walks past.

✓ In any attack or assault, shout and scream. Get away from the attacker and head for safety, but remember to stay away from the edge of the platform or carriage doors. Make as much noise as you can to attract attention to get help and scare the attacker off.

✓ When leaving a station, remember to take into consideration the time of day. The path through the park that you used last summer when you visited Aunt Mary may have been safe in mid-afternoon on a summer day, but will it still be and feel as safe in the dark on a winter night? Never use dark, unlit and deserted paths. If in doubt, take the long way round or take a taxi.

✓ While travelling, be aware of CCTV cameras, manned points and push-button enquiry systems. Try to stay in view of the cameras, stand near a member of staff or, if none is present, stand near a push-button enquiry point.

Pickpockets

Pickpockets usually operate in gangs and in crowds. Busy railway stations and carriages give them an excuse to jostle and push up against people. Seasoned commuters are so used to crowded conditions that they rarely take any notice of somebody bumping into them on a busy platform and pickpockets play on that. Though the movies often show pickpockets dipping into pockets and removing wallets, pickpockets today usually target bags worn on the back or over the shoulder. Because they are out of sight of the owner they are particularly vulnerable.

Pickpockets – countermeasures

✓ Don't give pickpockets a gift – secure your valuables. Make sure bags are zipped and secured. Make sure that your valuables are not stored in those convenient, easy-to-open little pockets. In a crowd, carry your rucksack or bag in front of you or held down by the straps. You will notice if a pickpocket starts feeling around the rucksack.

✓ Tourists in particular should take care. They are generally relaxed and enjoying their holiday, often carrying valuable documents such as passports, quite large sums of money, credit cards, expensive cameras and other items that are interesting to a thief.

✓ Carry purses, chequebooks and credit cards in internal secured pockets. Wrap a wide rubber band around a wallet or purse, which means it won't easily slide in and out of a pocket or bag. That means that if a pickpocket tries to take it you should feel them pulling to get it out of your pocket as the elastic band snags and catches on the material or bag.

✓ Be suspicious of anyone who seems to be edging unnecessarily closer to you. The train may be crowded and with standing room only, but do they need to come and stand out of your line of sight on the side where you are holding your handbag or rucksack?

✓ While travelling, if you see a theft or any suspicious activity, draw it to the attention of a member of staff as soon as possible.

Children

Travelling while struggling with several suitcases is a nightmare, but travelling with cases *and* children is worse. At least if you put a briefcase down it should stay where it is. Children can often be curious and adventurous. Many a parent has stopped to show their tickets, then found a child has wandered off while they were talking to the ticket inspector.

The worry of lost luggage, missed connections, delays and cancellations seems immaterial when you consider lost children, dangerous high-speed trains and electrified tracks – not to mention kidnap or worse!

Because the outcome could be particularly traumatic, I have included a few specific tips for travelling with children.

Children – countermeasures

✓ Do not try to make a journey with more children and bags than you can safely cope with. If you have a lot of children, get another adult to help you get them all safely to your destination.

✓ Make sure that all of your children know how dangerous railways, trains, stations and strangers can be. Don't scare them, but explain the dangers of fast-moving trains, carriage doors being opened, baggage carts driving around, crowds of strangers, etc.

✓ Consider giving each child a brightly coloured plastic wristband with your phone number on it, or pinning a card inside the coat of each child, where the card contains details such as your mobile phone number and proposed rail route. For example, a card may include your mobile phone number, your name, and the fact that you are taking the 10:56 from Waterloo, changing at Reading then onto the 12:34 to Exeter. In that way, staff or police will be able to trace you and your route and should know where you will be (other than at the nearest place you can report a missing child).

✓ The usual lessons for children about talking to or going off with strangers should be reinforced.

✓ Give them a few lessons such as how to use escalators, moving walkways, long staircases, high-capacity lifts, etc. Stress that they should always stay with the group, away from the platform edge, and shout for attention immediately if there is any problem.

General train – countermeasures

There are a few things that you can do to try to reduce the impact of crime or accident on you and your family while travelling by train.

✓ I used to commute with a small leather briefcase. I kept that case on my lap at all times.

   ➤ It stopped my case being stolen.

   ➤ It stopped me forgetting it when I got off.

➤ It stopped passengers getting on and off from carelessly gouging my knees with cases, bags and buggies.

➤ I had it in mind that if there was an accident I could raise the case in front of me to protect myself from flying glass or luggage.

✓ When travelling by train, don't give away personal information.

➤ Don't carry a suitcase with your full name and home address clearly visible, advertising to criminals that you are not at home.

➤ Don't hold mobile phone conversations and forget that twenty people around you can hear what you are saying, including any personal information you tell the person on the other end of the phone, such as mobile phone numbers, medical conditions, etc.

➤ If reading company documents, private letters and cards, or looking at information on a laptop computer or hand-held device, remember and realise that the people around you can see the text too.

✓ If in doubt, allow an overcrowded service to pass by and wait for the next train. I would rather travel on a later train in comfort than stand nose to armpit all the way to my destination.

✓ If at all possible pre-plan your journey, especially if you are travelling to a town or station that you have never used before. Consider calling that station and asking for advice. Tell them what train you will arrive on, and where you want to go. They should be able to tell you how to get there even if it means transferring to another train on a different platform. Remember some of the bigger stations have a maze of subways, bridges, exits and entrances, some linking to bus or tube stations, some giving direct access to streets and pedestrian precincts. If station staff can tell you to 'use the steps in the middle of the platform, turn right at the top, leave the station by the south exit and turn left to the taxi rank', you will be more confident, comfortable and therefore less likely to be targeted by criminals.

✓ Be comfortable when travelling. Stiletto heels and tight skirts may be highly fashionable, but they make coping with escalators, and climbing into and getting out of carriages difficult if not impossible. Add a large case and 2 minutes to make your connection because a service is running late and you will really wish you had chosen to wear jeans and trainers!

Underground Trains

The main risks associated with underground trains are similar to those for surface trains. They are accident, assault, theft and terrorist attacks, so the train advice given above is applicable to underground trains too. However, there are a few specific problems that might be encountered on the underground services.

Accident

While rail accidents tend to be serious, underground accidents are infinitely worse, because the site of the accident is often so inaccessible. Fire or other incidents on a train in the tunnels is almost guaranteed to lead to fatalities. The tunnels and escalators act like chimneys drawing heat, smoke and flames to upper levels. Trains pushing fresh air through the tunnels constantly feed oxygen into the base of the fire, while emergency crews have difficulty approaching the fire because they have to come down through the very flames and smoke they have been sent to extinguish. Passenger unfamiliarity with the tunnels, poor signposting and lack of staff will all tend to make a tube fire infinitely worse than a surface fire, because there is no simple emergency exit door you can open to leave the scene and reach cold fresh air.

Newer trains have a functional public address system and some are fitted with electronic displays through which the driver or guard can pass information to passengers. Ordinarily these systems are used to announce the arrival at a given station, or declare that an escalator is out of use, but in an emergency they can quickly and efficiently pass on life-saving information to passengers.

Robbery

Criminal gangs have also been known to attack underground services. As with surface trains, they can run through the train assaulting and robbing passengers at will. When the train pulls into the next station the gang members get off and are gone in a maze of tunnels and different lines before anyone can report the crime. Though police are targeting these criminals and CCTV coverage is improving, there are limited resources. Pickpockets also operate on the crowded commuter services, freely helping themselves to wallets and purses in over-crowded carriages.

Platform falls

There is also a risk associated with falling off the platform in front of a train, or onto the live electric rail. When stations become dangerously overcrowded, staff will close them. Closing the station stops more people coming onto the crowded platform, but that still leaves the early arrivals on dangerously overcrowded platforms.

It would be easy for somebody at the back of a platform to trip and push into somebody, initiating a wave of movement and pressure that could push somebody at the front of the platform off the edge and onto the track. Unfortunately it has been known for drunks, people in a drugged state or the mentally ill to deliberately push people onto the track.

General underground – countermeasures

When travelling by underground trains your health and safety are in the hands of the employees of the railway companies. Adopt the same countermeasures that you would use for surface trains and add a few specific to the underground.

✓ If an underground service is packed to the point where people are pinned to the carriage doors by the crush inside, don't even try to get on. I will always travel over ground if given any choice because I think that buses are cheap and a lot more civilised than underground trains.

✓ Check the distance from your starting point to your destination station. Though the distance between two points on an underground map looks like a long way they are in fact often within easy walking distance.

✓ If at all possible, keep well away from the platform edge. If you tripped you could fall onto the track, if somebody else trips they could push you onto the track, and there is always the possibility that somebody could push you onto the track deliberately. If the platform is so crowded that the only free space is on the platform edge, leave the station and find another way to get to your destination.

✓ Always try to be aware of signposts. Know where the nearest exit is, and know where the exit to an alternative line is. If there is an announcement telling you to head for an exit or a different line, try to make sure you can immediately start moving in that direction without having to stop and look around to see where you should be going.

Buses and Coaches

The main risks associated with bus travel are accident, assault and theft, and possible terrorist attacks.

Accident

Though there is a range of legislation and regulations associated with the standard and quality of the maintenance of public service vehicles, mistakes are made. The simple dynamics of an accident are that the occupants of the largest vehicle involved in an accident are better protected and suffer fewer injuries than people in a smaller vehicle. As buses and coaches are so big, they tend to suffer least in accidents with cars and vans. However, in an accident involving a lorry, the bus or coach will come off worst.

Protection. Modern cars are designed to have a rigid passenger compartment, which is engineered to protect the driver and passengers. Buses and coaches were engineered with commercial principles in mind.

Light construction meant that there was less weight to carry around and so a vehicle used less fuel. Larger window areas allowed the passengers to have a better view during the trip and so attracted more passengers.

All of these matters legitimately maximised profits, but weakened the structure, leaving passengers open to death and serious injury resulting from even minor accidents. Modern coaches use modern materials and engineering to combine strength with good passenger views.

Seat belts. Older coaches do not have passenger seat belts. Major accidents have resulted in a review of coach and bus safety, but the improvements are only now appearing. New-generation buses and coaches have safety cages, reinforced body frames and seat belts, but thousands of older-generation buses and coaches are still on the road and will be for years to come.

Upper deck dangers. Double-deck buses have been known to leave their designated route then try to pass under low bridges or drive under low trees, with devastating and potentially fatal results to top-deck passengers.

Robbery. Criminals have been known to target bus passengers and crews. They often operate in gangs who board a bus at a carefully selected stop and intimidate the crew and passengers. They steal everything they can and then jump off the bus at the next junction or stop. Criminals have been known to resort to unnecessary violence, for example stabbing passengers who were no threat to them.

Traffic risk. Passengers on the old open platform double-deck buses have been known to jump off the bus between stops and be hit by a car.

Bus and coach – countermeasures

The countermeasures to avoid risks associated with bus travel are simple and cost nothing.

✓ Before booking a seat for a bus or coach journey I enquire about the age of their fleet, company safety records, if seat belts are fitted and if the driver knows the route. If the company is unwilling to answer those questions, I assume they have something to hide and I will not travel with them. If they answer and the fleet is quite new and seat belts are fitted I will consider booking seats with that company.

✓ Where I am being asked to approve a children's school trip, I will do so only if I get satisfactory answers to my questions. If I don't get an answer, or if there are any safety problems, I refuse to approve the trip and urge other parents to do the same. Schools should ONLY ever use the best and safest coach and bus companies. Insist that the school or coach company confirms in writing that:

> ➢ Seat belts are fitted.

> ➢ An experienced driver who knows the route will be driving.

> ➢ Passengers will be supervised by at least one adult, who is not the driver.

✓ I make a point of never travelling on the upper deck. Roadworks, road closures due to flooding or accidents, and drivers unfamiliar with routes mean that off-route diversions are likely. That means that upper-deck passengers are more likely to be faced with unexpected and unnoticed low bridges and low branches.

✓ On single crewed buses, the only crewman is the driver-operator who has to be on the lower deck. Many buses now have an attack alarm system installed so that the driver can quickly summon assistance. Criminals tend to go to the upper deck where they can work unseen by the driver. For that reason, you may choose to travel on the lower deck, which will put you as far away from the criminals as you can get. If they do come to the lower deck, they are in running mode and the temptation of an open door and escape is usually greater than the temptation to stay and rob or assault lower-deck passengers.

✓ To avoid accidents associated with falls on buses, or accidents while getting on or off buses, use your common sense. If you can, sit down when on a bus. If you have to stand, use the handrails that are provided to steady yourself. If you want to get off a bus, ring the bell, then wait for the bus to stop before you stand – especially if you are elderly, injured or infirm. Finally, only ever get on or off a bus at an approved bus stop. In that way you will never be exposed to other vehicles.

✓ Don't use remote bus stops if you can avoid it, especially after dark. You don't want to be standing alone at night on some country road, waiting and hoping for a bus to come.

Tram/trolley

The tram and trolley bus system is making an urban comeback. As a cost-effective method of moving people it has been rediscovered, along with environmental benefits. Tram systems are often electrically operated, reducing or eliminating noxious fumes and emissions. However, they also bring their own unique hazards. The main risk associated with tram travel is accidental collision.

Accidental collision. Trams and trolleys usually operate on a rail system, similar to those used by trains. Unlike trains, the tram rails are laid in and along and beside public roads. The risk and threat comes from several different sources.

Trams cannot swerve to avoid an accident. Most car drivers don't realise how much they drift from lane to lane, and how much other car drivers accommodate their bad habit by avoiding them. When a car or van driver drifts into the path of a tram, a collision is almost inevitable because the tram driver simply cannot swerve to avoid them.

Finally, because trams and vehicles co-exist on city streets, it is not unknown for tram passengers to be knocked down by other vehicles when they are attempting to board or leave trams.

Tram/trolley – countermeasures

Countermeasures that will help you avoid injury involving trams and trolleybuses are easy to specify but hard to enact.

✓ When driving in an area where trams and trolleybuses are operating, you must be particularly careful of your lane discipline. Maintain total positional awareness at all times so that you can safely negotiate traffic and trams. (Positional awareness and lane discipline are skills you should work on when driving in traffic anyway.)

✓ You should also realise that trams can run quite silently, so motorcyclists, cyclists and pedestrians must use their eyes to make sure that they do not stray into the path of a tram.

✓ When driving in an area where trams are operating, or when using a tram or trolleybus, passengers should take exceptional care when boarding or alighting. Remind yourself constantly that traffic is often flowing all around a tram, which makes stepping off or running to get on a tram a particularly hazardous operation. Before you get off a tram, and when you are thinking of going to get on one, force yourself to think about the traffic hazards.

Ferry

Few people travel by ferry now, and even fewer do so regularly. That makes a ferry particularly dangerous because the chances are that on any given day most of the passengers will be unfamiliar with the ferry's operation. The main risks associated with ferry travel are accident and subsequent drowning.

Accident. Ferries operate over substantial bodies of water, where the presence of deep water, currents and tides are major hazards. Passengers and vehicles boarding a ferry will have to negotiate the hazards associated with docks and jetties. Lack of familiarity with the whole process, location and operation make it even more dangerous for the average person. Being directed along docks and down metal ramps into the vehicle deck of a ferry can be scary in itself. Though they usually erect safety barriers to prevent it, human error and a confused driver can easily see a car take a plunge into deep water.

Then there is the risk that the ferry itself could be involved in a fire or other accident. Ferries have been holed and sunk, and have capsized after collisions and car-deck flooding. Even though there will be no trouble for a thousand trips, you have to be ready for that one time when there is a disaster. By remaining alert and being familiar with emergency equipment and procedures you could turn a potential disaster into a mere problem, as well as saving your life and the lives of other passengers.

Protection. UK ferries operate within strict rules. They are required to carry lifejackets, rafts, fire-fighting equipment, etc. All members of the crew should also be familiar with the use and deployment of all safety equipment and should take problems seriously and professionally.

Abroad it is very different. If I boarded a ferry where there were problems, for example if crew members couldn't speak English, or they appeared to be less than competent or ignoring their duties, I would leave the ferry and report my observations to the authorities.

Ferry – countermeasures

In any unfamiliar environment take extra care to make sure that you do what is expected and required of you.

✓ When in any unfamiliar or potentially hazardous location, you should make strenuous efforts to follow all of the rules and regulations that are imposed for safety and management purposes.

✓ Identify and comply with all signs, e.g. no smoking, keep left, no entry, etc.

✓ If booking ahead there is no need to be paranoid about these matters, but while asking about availability and fares there is nothing to stop you asking about safety matters. If more people do ask about life belts and rafts, operators will realise that safety is a significant concern to a growing number of people.

✓ On boarding a ferry, see what your impression is of the operation. If the captain is drunk and the crew are sitting playing cards, or if the boarding ramp seems to be held together with string, get off and report it.

✓ If the crew and boat appear to be in order, I usually seek out the emergency equipment. If I have time to kill while crossing the water, I may as well spend it looking for the life belts or lifeboats. I'd rather kill time when I first use a ferry, than kill myself because I didn't know where the life belts were in an emergency.

Transport: Safety Demonstrations and Cards

Be aware that when you travel you are in unfamiliar surroundings and your unfamiliarity with those surroundings makes them that much more dangerous to you. If you know a venue and know your way around it, you will be more comfortable, more confident, happier and safer. You will know where the toilets are, where the lifts are and more importantly where the exits, ramps and stairs are. At the same venue, a stranger will be lost, they will have to follow the crowd or aim for different signposted facilities. Their unfamiliarity with it makes the venue that much less safe for the stranger.

Be alert to unfamiliar dangers such as escalators and moving walkways. Don't trip over carelessly placed luggage. Look out for hazards such as ride-on motorised cleaning machines or luggage trains that may be moving around in a large terminal or port.

If there are safety notices, take the time to read them. Take the opportunity to double check your tickets and travel documents while in the queue, be informed and be safe. Don't flash that wad of cash or traveller's cheques – your fellow travellers or others around you may be criminals.

When you eventually board your aircraft or ship or train, listen to the safety announcements. Watch the safety video, the demonstrations of available exits and any demonstrations of such things as lifejackets. Ignoring them could kill you!

Not too many years ago a small airliner crashed into the sea, broke up and sank. Passengers had been advised during their pre-flight safety briefing that in the event of a water landing they should put their lifejackets on but not inflate them until they were in the water and well clear of the plane. This message was repeated when the emergency was declared, but a lot of passengers took one look at the water beneath them and inflated their lifejackets while still strapped in their seats. When the aircraft began sinking, fewer than half of the passengers managed to get out even though it was so close they could almost have walked to shore. They drowned because they inflated their lifejackets and were so cumbersome that they were unable to escape from the sinking aircraft. Those who made it outside and inflated their lifejackets as instructed were rescued.

Safety demonstrations – countermeasures

✓ Always familiarise yourself with the position of your seat, and the location of the nearest and alternative exits.

✓ Always listen to and understand any safety advice given. If you don't understand – ask!

✓ If you are sitting in a seat at an exit door, make sure that you read and understand the instructions. You may be required to open the door in an emergency.

✓ If you think there is a problem, like flames coming from the engine on the left wing or smoke coming from the toilet, quietly and urgently bring it to the attention of a member of staff.

✓ If there is an incident, obey any instructions the staff or members of the crew give to you. Act immediately and don't try to take any valuables, bags or luggage with you if and when ordered to exit.

✓ By all means assist other members of your family or party, but don't needlessly disrupt any evacuation.

Deep Vein Thrombosis (DVT)

It is now accepted that inactivity in cramped seating conditions on long-haul flights can cause blood clots to form, which can lead to the death of an airline passenger. If research shows that blood clots can form on long-haul flights, do smaller clots form on shorter flights or even when sitting in a car or bus for long journeys?

The human body was not designed to sit in cramped conditions for hours at a time, and certainly not designed to sit in a pressurised aluminium tube at 35,000 feet while being starved of oxygen and fed mass-produced food and quantities of alcohol.

Airlines should make their passenger environment healthier with more leg room, more air and less alcohol.

Definitions

First a few facts and definitions. Depending on which statistics you refer to, it is estimated that anywhere from 2% to 7% of ALL air passengers develop some form of blood clots during flights, though most clots dissipate without causing complications.

A blood clot in the leg is called deep vein thrombosis and is often shortened to DVT.

As they form in the veins and arteries, blood clots can move around the body with the blood flow. If a clot reaches or forms in the lungs it is called a pulmonary embolism, and can cause pain, fainting and even death.

Blood clots in the heart can lead to heart failure and death.

The root cause is a lack of exercise and movement, which allows your blood to stagnate, forming clots. To counteract that, you should exercise when you can.

Risk

Though everyone is at risk, it has been seen that various factors are a useful guide to your risk of suffering from DVT. For example, being unusually tall, short or fat will increase your risk of suffering from blood clots. The risk increases if you are pregnant, have heart disease, or are taking hormones in HRT or birth-control pill format, so you should talk to your doctor before flying (or travelling a long way by car or coach). The highest risk group are those who have had a stroke, a major operation or are known to have blood-clotting problems. Anyone in this group should always talk to their doctor before flying.

Symptoms

Even though a clot has formed during a flight, there may be no symptoms until a day or several days later.

Early symptoms can be mistaken as cramp! The symptoms of DVT are described below. You may suffer several or all of these symptoms. If you suffer from any of these symptoms after a flight or long journey during which you were unable to move, you should seek medical advice.

- Pain in affected area.

- Swelling, tenderness and visible redness in affected area.

- Shortness of breath and a rapid heart beat.

- Possible joint pain and/or chest pain.

- Enlarged and protruding veins.

- Leg pains while standing still or walking.

- Leg pains which ease when the legs are raised.

Deep vein thrombosis – countermeasures

✓ Take any opportunity to exercise before you get onto the aircraft. You will be stuck in your seat for several hours during the flight, so don't add to the problems by sitting motionless in the terminal lounge for hours before the flight.

✓ When you can, get up and walk around the cabin. Stand at the back of the cabin and do some gentle exercises, knee bends and stretches as long as you don't interfere with the crew or other passengers.

✓ Wear tighter long socks or stockings that will tend to prevent your blood from settling into your lower legs. I have even seen special 'aircraft passengers support socks' advertised. They are designed for airline passengers to wear during flights, helping their circulation and avoiding DVT.

✓ While in your seat, try not to sit in one position without moving. Adjust your seating position between exercise sessions. I call what I do 'seat exercises', but you may better understand when you know that my wife calls it 'fidgeting'! Any movement generates muscular activity, which promotes blood circulation. While sitting and reading or watching the in-flight movie I move my legs and arms, rocking my feet back and forth and raising them up on the toes then back on the heels. Any little leg, feet and ankle movements have to help – unless your wife tells you to stop fidgeting, of course!

✓ When you arrive at your destination you should exercise gently. Don't use the moving walkway unless you have to, and walk to the baggage claim area and immigration control. Use the stairs instead of the lift. When you get to your hotel or back home, take a gentle walk. All of this will warm up muscles and boost your circulation, losing the stiffness and sore muscles associated with long-haul flights.

✓ Where possible:

  ➢ Take preventative measures.

  ➢ Get up and move around the aircraft cabin during a flight, stop the car and get out for a walk when driving long distances, or walk up and down the coach on long journeys.

  ➢ Exercise gently when you arrive at your destination by car.

  ➢ Watch for symptoms for at least a week after a journey.

➢ If in any doubt, seek medical advice, and make sure that you tell them that you recently made a long flight or drove a long way.

➢ If your doctor tells you it is just cramp, he could be right. BUT if it doesn't feel right and seems to be getting worse, seek alternative medical advice and stress the fact that you made a long flight and are worried about DVT.

Alcohol

Drink and travel do not mix. Though a little nerve-steadier may be beneficial in some cases, the consumption of alcohol in any quantity puts you at risk.

Alcoholic drinks tend to dehydrate you. Add that to the dehydrating effects of air travel and you have a problem.

Dehydration will give you a headache, make you feel ill and irritable, and the ultimate symptom is death. That is an unlikely eventuality when travelling, but feeling unwell will not make the journey pleasant.

Add to that the reduced co-ordination and subsequently limited ability to escape in an emergency and consuming alcohol becomes a pastime that sensible travellers avoid.

Drink – countermeasures

✓ Flying will dehydrate you, so drink a lot of water.

✓ Alcohol will also tend to dehydrate you, compounding the dehydrating effect of flying.

✓ Dehydration leaves you irritable, which could lead to conflict. Mix that with alcohol and you are left with the possibility of drunken brawls on aircraft. Avoid alcohol on aircraft.

Valuables

Usually when going on holiday we carry more valuables than we ever would normally. Apart from UK currency, holiday currency, traveller's cheques, credit cards, holiday tickets and vouchers, we also take expensive cameras and other holiday electronics.

Some suitcases are lost, damaged, misrouted or simply broken into and rifled by dishonest and poorly supervised baggage staff. I would suggest that you shouldn't trust your valuables to a case that will be stored in the hold. I prefer to retain all of my valuables in my carry-on baggage. That way I can keep an eye on them, but it also means that I have to remain particularly vigilant because that one bag contains everything essential to my holiday.

When we travel, everyone in the family knows which one is 'The Bag' and we have a system to keep an eye on it. I always carry it, but when I am going to the toilet or want to sleep on a long-haul flight another member of the family will take over as watcher of 'The Bag' and make sure that it is not removed or interfered with until I take over again.

Why take it?

Do you really need to take valuables with you? Is it necessary to take your best watch, your top-of-the-range digital camera and video camera? You are going on holiday! Will a cheap watch from the market be good enough? If you lose a cheap watch in the Caribbean it won't matter so much.

If you are going on a specialist photography holiday you may need to take the digital camera and a bag full of expensive gadgets and accessories, but the average holiday snapper could do just as well with a disposable camera.

Do you really need to take a video camera with you? It's nice to bring back the moving images to show people the majesty of Niagara Falls and the colour of the ocean in Hawaii, but analyse your use of that video camera.

The newer models are quite small, but carrying them will still cause you problems. You have to carry the extra bulk and weight and protect the expensive equipment. How much filming will you actually do? Think about it. Looking back at previous holidays, is two or ten or even twenty hours of disjointed and shaky video footage that will never be looked at again worth the hassle of carrying the video camera and bag around for two weeks?

Back home people usually find that their video images are a random sequence of mixed-quality shots. Niagara Falls yes, but with that weird guy who walked through the shot, then came back and stood in front of you to take his own picture? You thought the sea at Hawaii was a brilliant sequence but now you view it you can see that dog relieving itself in the foreground! Why bother? Most tourist destinations, especially the photogenic ones, sell a good-quality inexpensive videotape or DVD of just the scene you want to remember.

By buying a pre-recorded video for a few pounds you will benefit from a professionally finished video, with subtitles and commentary. Better still, when the official video was filmed, they closed the area to the public. If there was a problem, they had the time to re-shoot it until it was perfect. They can wait for the absolutely perfect sunset or a beautifully framed view of dolphins leaping over native canoes – you can't.

If you buy a video, it will have all of the images you want, and more. Many outlets have the tape running so that you can see what you are getting. If you absolutely have to have the 'I was there' pictures of you and the family on Mount Everest, or posing in front of the White House, then take a small stills camera. Get those 'evidence' snaps you want, but leave the video camera at home.

Why take it? – countermeasures

✓ By taking expensive equipment with you, you are committing yourself to a holiday spent carrying and protecting that equipment. Carefully consider whether you need to take all of it on holiday.

✓ Consider just buying postcards and locally produced videotapes of the area.

✓ If you have to take a camera, take a cheap one unless you have a real need for an expensive outfit.

✓ Don't assume that holiday insurance will cover you for all actual or claimed losses. Insurance companies might refuse to pay on a claim if for example you claim you lost all three of your Cartier watches off the ferry at the same time. They may refuse to pay if you were stupid too, on the grounds that a reasonable man should not be surprised if he goes swimming and comes back 2 hours later to find that his £3,000 video camera has gone – his negligence makes the insurance void.

Insurance Fraud

Valuable items may be covered by holiday insurance, but insurance companies are beginning to challenge claims. If you want to make a claim and say you dropped your £3,000 video camera and equipment off the ferry, be prepared to prove it.

An insurance assessor told me that the insurance industry has paid out on claims for more 'lost and stolen' Cartier watches than have ever been produced. Making a false claim is a criminal offence, and insurers are not as gullible as some people think.

Insurance companies have sophisticated monitoring systems that will identify multiple claims. If you make a £2,000 claim every time you go on holiday, you had better be really unlucky and making genuine claims. If not, you could end up in court.

The insurance companies also have investigators who will visit the shops where you allegedly purchased that diamond-encrusted cigarette box that you claim got stolen in Greece. They will check with customs and ask at your hotel if anyone ever saw you with such an item. Then they will ask the manager if you asked if you could put it or anything else valuable in the safe. They will ask the local police if the alleged crime has been reported, and find out if the local police believe you, picking up information from them and even viewing local CCTV film to see the alleged incident happening.

In short, insurance companies are investing money in systems and investigations to identify and reject false and inflated claims. They are also quite keen to make some high-profile examples to teach the public that insurance fraud is a crime.

Insurance fraud – countermeasures

✓ Invalid, false and inflated claims cost the insurance industry millions of pounds a year and they know it.

✓ False claims cost all of us in higher fees, because we all share the cost of those fraudulent claims.

✓ Insurance companies are beginning to investigate claims where there is even a hint of dishonesty, or perhaps just where there is a lack of clarity which makes the claim feel suspect.

✓ Don't get a criminal record by making a false claim:

  ➢ Don't take valuables if you don't have to.

  ➢ Make sure that you have the full details of any valuables. Claiming for a Sony Xt-765/03 serial number 333/589387/XT-S3/54 (purchase receipt enclosed) sounds like a real claim. If you can't give any real details your claim looks suspicious.

  ➢ If you lose anything, report it to the hotel, travel rep and the local police. You never know, if you report it lost you might get it back.

  ➢ Never be tempted to inflate your claim. It isn't worth it, and more people each year are finding that out the hard way.

5 At Your Destination

When you arrive at your destination you will probably be tired, a little disoriented and, unless you have been there a few times before, unsure of where to go. Walking around with bags, looking lost, trying to make sense of a foreign bus, train or cab schedule marks you as the classic 'just arrived' vulnerable tourist. Criminals love that, because they know you have pockets full of cash and traveller's cheques, expensive cameras, credit cards and valuable passports and other documents. When you land you must switch to a state of high alert so that you can identify and avoid trouble.

Baggage Collection

This is an area where people sometimes let their guard down. The possibly long-haul flight is over and you are on the last leg to that luxury hotel. The climate change may have hit you, and you think that you can relax while you wait for your bags to come through. Don't!

You don't know who is around you jostling you, pushing to the front. Was that guy who just leaned on you to reach the red suitcase retrieving the suitcase or using it as an excuse to lean on you and dip into your pockets? Stay alert, and don't join the scrum to get to the carousel first. Chances are yours will be the last bag to come off, and there will probably be a long queue for immigration and customs.

Baggage collection – countermeasures

✓ Realise that the scrum of baggage recovery could be an opportunity for thieves to target you and your valuables.

✓ Keep your eyes open. If the criminals see that you are alert and keeping an eye on yourself and your property, they will leave you alone and look for an easier target.

✓ I like to get a baggage trolley then stand back and wait. I keep an eye on the carousel in case somebody tries to walk off with my cases, but initially I stand back. When I see my case, I find a gap and then step forward to scoop it off the carousel and straight onto the baggage trolley. Remember, if you are alone keep one eye and one hand on the baggage trolley and any cases and bags that you have already retrieved.

✓ The last bag makes you vulnerable! Everybody in your party will be impatiently waiting for your bag to come through. Make sure that while you all strain to catch the first sight of it as it drops onto the carousel, somebody isn't taking your camera bag off the unattended baggage trolley.

✓ Keep your baggage claim tags. Some airports ask to see them to check claim tags against the cases you are taking.

Think About Your Location

When somebody was sick, a friend of mine once had to go on a very short notice business trip. He was told at ten past nine that he was on an early afternoon flight to an ex-Soviet satellite state. He was assured that everything had been arranged, and that all he had to do was meet a contact, get some important contract documents signed, then fly back on the return flight the next morning.

He was handed three envelopes. One held the documents to be signed and the name and address of his contact, one contained the tickets and the last one contained his visa documents.

After a flight to Frankfurt he transferred onto a small aircraft operated by an unknown airline. He carried his own baggage to the aircraft and climbed some rusty steps to the cabin. The flight was terrible, nobody spoke English, and no food or drink was available. They landed and rattled down a very long runway and parked near what looked like a camouflaged ex-military hangar to see a horse and cart being loaded with cases. Thinking that nobody would believe him he took some pictures with his pocket camera, only to be confronted by a soldier waving an automatic rifle. The soldier slapped his camera to the ground and then stamped on it before herding him into an office at gunpoint. Then he belatedly spotted military jets on the edges of the airfield.

Nobody had said it was a military base that accepted the occasional commercial flight. Inside, the man waving the gun spoke to an officer sitting at a desk, then the officer asked for his visa. Grateful that nobody had used words like 'spying' or 'jail', he presented the visa envelope. Two minutes later he nearly died when the officer tore it open and took out a few hundred US dollars in ten-dollar bills. Luckily the 'visa' was accepted and he was released.

Think about your location – countermeasures

✓ Know where you are going and know what you are carrying.

✓ Remember the importance of research on your destination. I doubt if many of you will face that sort of situation, but it illustrates the need to be prepared.

✓ Get as full a briefing as you can if you have to substitute for anyone, and be prepared to handle anything if you are going to – what shall we call it? – an 'undeveloped destination'.

Research Local Crime Trends

Your research should have let you know what the crime trends are at your destination. Forewarned is forearmed. When you know what the threats are you will be safer! For example, I did a quick search and found the following:

- Belize City – snatch-and-run thieves.

- Managua – pack slashers (pickpockets) on public buses.

- Thailand – a surge in bogus charity collections, and drugged gifts of food or drink (you eat it then collapse, get robbed and wake up in a back street next day).

- Lahore, Pakistan – backpacks stolen from hotels, public places and transport.

- Guatemala – armed robbery and rape in the hills outside towns.

Debts and Corruption

I have heard several stories about tourists visiting third-world countries where they were waved through immigration controls with no real checks. When they came to leave, their documents were checked thoroughly and, having no entry stamp in their passport, they were held for 'entering the country illegally'. After a lot of shouting and talk of courts and jails, they were only released when a sum of money was paid to the official.

If you have been to the country before, make sure that you didn't leave any unpaid parking fines or bills on previous visits. I was once told by a fellow passenger that on landing he presented his passport, which was checked and stamped, then was asked to go to a side room. He was told that he had been arrested over debts and would be transferred to jail to await a hearing. Apparently on his last trip to that town he had somehow left some car hire charges unpaid. He didn't know he had, and in fact wasn't sure that he had left unpaid debts!

Nobody seemed interested in what he had to say, until he apologised, said it was a mistake and offered to pay what was owed. Money was taken, plus some 'compensation' and 'expenses', and he was released.

In some third-world countries corruption is a way of life. Research can some-times tell you that 'arrangement fees', 'on the spot fines' or 'administrative payments' may be required.

The problem is that generally you don't know where strange official practices stop and where corruption begins. Worse, I have known some travellers who have assumed that their difficulties have been prompted by some minor official's attempt to attract a bribe, so they have offered one and been arrested for trying to corrupt the only honest official in the country.

Corruption – countermeasures

✓ Do your research, and try to find out what is expected.

✓ Never offer a bribe, though if asked to pay an 'on the spot fine' be ready to pay it.

✓ If you are going to be asked to pay an 'on the spot fine' it will help if you have distributed your money in various pockets. I can almost guarantee that the fine will miraculously be set at exactly the sum of money that you pull out of your pocket! Keep some money in other pockets and be prepared to lose all of the money you take out.

Immigration

Immigration in some countries is nothing more than a formality, while in others they almost seem to want to find an excuse to deny entry to everyone. In some countries immigration offences, whether real or imagined, are considered to be very serious, especially now that international terrorism is so prominent in our minds.

Immigration – countermeasures

✓ Do your research, in books, via travel agents, the internet and the embassy of your destination country.

✓ Make sure that you fully understand the current procedures and requirements for entering the country.

✓ Don't assume that the controls will be the same as they were last time you went. As terrorists extend their range of attacks, more countries are looking at tightening their immigration controls.

✓ Make sure that you have all of the documents required by that country, and that they are all in order.

✓ Get entry and exit stamps in your passport if you are supposed to have them.

Customs

Just as immigration controls have been tightened in the past few years, customs controls have been tightened too.

Trying to bring illicit or illegal materials through customs is a fast way to prison in most countries. In some countries there are rules about the import of almost everything, from fruit to seeds and plants, and from natural products to meat. This is of course an attempt to stop the introduction of new pests and diseases. Something as simple as sneaking in a Granny Smiths apple to eat on the coach to the hotel could find you detained and deported on the next flight, so don't risk it.

There are strict rules about exporting a range of items from most countries too, designed to protect their plants, wildlife and historic treasures.

Customs – countermeasures

✓ Travel agents should be able to give you lists of goods that cannot be imported to a given country.

✓ Widen your research if you have any doubts. If you really can't live without Marmite on your breakfast toast, check with your travel agent to see if the destination country has it, and if not check with the embassy or consulate of the destination country to see if you can take a jar with you.

✓ If you are not sure how their rules relate to the antique stuffed penguin that you want to take as a gift to Aunt Maude, ask them, and if possible get everything including their reply, permission, import licence or whatever in writing.

✓ Prohibited articles may be anything from innocent medication to drugs, condoms, currency, religious material, foodstuffs and plants, political material, or even simple Western-style magazines.

✓ If you are bringing any prescribed or over-the-counter medication into the country with you, be ready to show it to the customs staff. Have a letter from your doctor and/or a letter from the country's embassy in the UK stating that you have to carry and use the medication and that importing it will be acceptable.

✓ When you arrive you will usually be presented with a customs list, which describes the items that you cannot bring in. Check it, in case there have been any changes.

✓ Many customs organisations are very wary of the dangers of importing fruit or plants. It is too easy to introduce a disease or parasite into a country where the native plants or animals don't have any natural protection against it. Your casually smuggled apple could wipe out the fruit crop in a whole country under the right circumstances, so treat the rules seriously.

✓ Never carry anything for anyone else. Your best buddy at work might have asked you to take a birthday present to his old grandmother in Florida, but you can't be sure that that stuffed penguin is all you are carrying. Drug smugglers know that there is a high risk of being caught, so if they can trick or fool people into carrying the drugs and taking the risk for them, they will. You should only carry your own personal property that you have selected and packed yourself.

The Hotel

When you reach your hotel or other accommodation, the reception area is usually bustling with activity. Guests checking out, new guests arriving, staff rushing back and forth, visitors milling around and mixing with delivery staff. In that rush, nobody will take much notice of a guy walking out with a suitcase and camera bag, even if that suitcase and camera bag are yours and were taken while you were distracted trying to make sure your room has a sea view.

You probably feel safe in that busy hotel foyer, but it is a security threat to your luggage simply because it is so busy. Nobody is going to notice a guy in shirt and slacks picking up a case and walking off with it, because there are dozens of people doing that every day. As far as anyone watching is concerned, he is just another guy carrying a suitcase and camera bag. People will only pay any attention when you call out in distress asking where your bags have gone, but then they will be looking at you because of the disturbance you are making. Nobody will run out to look for a guy with your bags until you have found a member of staff to listen to you, explained what has happened and described the missing bags.

Some thieves actually specialise in raiding the approaches to hotels, hotel reception areas and hotel rooms, preying on guests and their valuables as they arrive and depart.

Many larger hotel chains have implemented quite extensive security measures, but the thieves are still there. From room burglars to luggage thieves through to plain old muggers who operate on stairs and in lifts and corridors. Beware!

The hotel operators can cause you problems as well. At reception when you are booking in find out exactly what is available in the room, and if you don't want it consider asking for it to be removed or disabled. When checking out I was rather surprised to be told that I had to pay a considerable minibar drinks bill. Being absolutely teetotal I knew I hadn't opened it, let alone used anything, but I couldn't prove that. I argued the point, but didn't really have any evidence to back me up, so I paid and considered it an education fee! It was an expensive lesson, but I now ask for the minibar to be locked, emptied or removed.

Hotel – countermeasures

✓ Check in, but keep your bags close to hand while you do it. If you are alone, stand them against the reception desk and lean over them if you have to, then nobody will be able to touch them without you knowing.

✓ If you find that there are services available in the room that you do not require, ask if they can be disabled, locked or removed to avoid any confusion or inflated bills later.

✓ Always keep your hotel door locked and use the door peephole to check who is outside before opening the door.

✓ Remember to check the rest of the room for security.

> ➢ Check that the locks work.

> ➢ Check connecting doors. Some rooms are designed so that large families or groups of guests can have several interconnecting rooms. Make sure that any connecting doors are solid, secure, lockable and locked from your side.

> ➢ Check to make sure that staff members have taken action over any facilities that you did not want, such as minibars. They seem to be a common cause of disputes over final bills!

> ➢ Check the security and operation of the patio doors or window, especially if you are on a ground floor, lower floor or facing a flat roof. You don't want a room with such a weak patio door or window that thieves or intruders can choose when they enter your room.

> ➢ Check for any possible access from neighbouring balconies. Even if you are on the tenth floor, if anyone with access to the room next door can get into your room from the balcony of the room next door, you have no security.

> ➢ Women alone should pay particular attention to door chains and window security. When abroad on hot nights, windows are often left open to get a little air. Make sure that there is no access from outside the window for an intruder to come into the room while you are asleep.

✓ If travelling alone, you could make sure that somebody knows what your plans are. For example, if you are going to go exploring in the old town or on a day trip into the rainforest, leave a message with the hotel receptionist saying where you are going, how you are going to get there, who you will be with or will be meeting and when you expect to return. In that way the hotel management will report your absence if you fail to return as scheduled.

✓ When you are alone, stay aware of your surroundings. For example, if a group of people in the lift make you nervous, don't take the lift. Make an excuse about leaving something in your room or wanting to get something from the hotel shop if you want to save face, but always trust your instincts.

✓ Don't carry your hotel key in a bag. Leave your key at reception. If the bag is stolen at least you still have your key so you can get into your room and the thief won't know where you are staying or have access to your room with your stolen key.

Use The Hotel Safe

Most hotels have a safe available for the guests to use to secure their valuables while they are on the beach, etc. Depending on what you have and what you want to do I would suggest that you use it, but only when you have inspected it.

I stayed at a hotel in Florida where there was a strong box in each room. Guests were invited to use the safe to store cash, passports and small valuables. One day, three rooms were raided and the valuables were stolen from each 'strong box' using a key. Unfortunately the key was not a security key. At some stage, the thieves had managed to get hold of the keys to those boxes, then get spares cut at the local hardware store so that they could come back and empty the valuables at their leisure.

Hotel safe – countermeasures

✓ Don't take valuables with you if you don't really need them. That gold and diamond necklace might look stunning if you get invited to a formal reception, but do you really need to take it on holiday with you? If you calculate that you might need £500 spending money for your holiday, don't take more than £1,000 with you!

✓ If your room or hotel has secure storage for guests' valuables, check it. Check to see what sort of state it is in, and how complicated the keys and lock are. Ask if it is easy to get a duplicate key cut. Ask if they insure the contents of the safe. If they say they do, ask what their insurance limit is. When I was in Malta they imposed a maximum limit for the loss of items stored in a guest safe equivalent to about £15. That showed me that they had no faith in their guest safes, so I didn't use them. When I got back I reported my findings and the travel agent said that in future he would warn travellers about potential security problems at that hotel.

✓ If the safe looks secure, use it.

Hotel Fire Safety

You have decided that the room is secure, but just as important is your safety in an emergency.

Fire safety – countermeasures

✓ Usually in hotel rooms there are notices explaining emergency procedures.

➤ If there is no fire evacuation notice in your room, go to reception and ask for one. If they say there is no alarm system and no emergency or evacuation procedure I would leave and find a decent hotel. I would also complain to the travel agent and claim compensation. I will not stay at a hotel that does not have fire precautions. (But from my research before I went I would have already requested a safe hotel.)

➤ Read a copy of the emergency evacuation procedures, and make sure that you understand them. Ask a member of staff to explain them if you don't.

➤ Make sure that everybody in your group or party understands the procedures.

✓ When you have read the instructions, you should explore the hotel. When I book into a hotel I tell the receptionist that that is what I am going to do. If they object I say that if they have nothing to hide they shouldn't object. If they object or tell me I cannot look at the emergency exits, I ask **155** to see the manager and ask why not. Then I find a decent hotel to stay in and report the suspicious activity to the local fire authority, the travel agency, the embassy and anyone else who will listen.

✓ When I explore, I find the nearest emergency exit and stairs and go down to make sure that the doors are there, the stairs are not blocked, and the door at the bottom actually opens to safety, not a locked yard containing pool equipment!

✓ When you explore the fire exit, open it and go out to look for the rallying point. In the absence of an official rallying point, pick a family or group rallying point. For example, tell your family that in an evacuation you will all meet next to the big palm tree on the left. (Pick a rallying point at a safe distance from the hotel and away from anywhere that fire engines, etc. will be arriving.)

✓ When I am satisfied, I go back and explore at least one alternative escape route, in case the nearest route is blocked by fire.

✓ Remember that in a fire, you may be in the dark and feeling your way out of your hotel room in thick smoke. Think ahead. When checking the fire exits, try to count how many turns and doors there are between you and the fire exit. For example, out of the door, turn left, move to the right-hand wall and exit through the third door on the right, which leads into the stairwell. With that information I can find the fire exit in thick smoke and darkness.

✓ Remember the standard fire evacuation rules.

  ➢ When you hear the alarm, rouse anyone in your party and make sure that they are awake, aware and leaving. Then you should all get out, rousing other people on the way.

  ➢ Try to make sure that everyone has put on shoes and decent easy pull-on clothes. You don't want to have to walk through debris or hot ashes in bare feet. If any member of your party is infirm or disabled, help them out of the building or assign members of your party to make sure that they are taken out of the building.

  ➢ If there are children in your party, check that they are all present. Then check again. When you have them all, hold their hands and chaperone them out of the building. Children get scared and hide away under beds and in closets.

  ➢ Do not use lifts during an emergency evacuation.

  ➢ Don't stop to take anything with you. DON'T try to take cases and other bulky items. They will only slow you and everybody behind you down. Depending on the weather, take a coat.

  ➢ Consider taking wet towels or woollen blankets with you. They can be used to wrap around your face to make breathing easier in thick smoke, or to wrap around your head and shoulders to protect you from flames and heat if you have to pass near to the fire.

➢ Close doors and windows behind you if it is safe to do so, because closing them will slow or halt the progress of any fire and keep your room safe.

➢ Don't try to fight a fire. You are not trained, you don't know what is burning and you don't know if there are other fires that may block your escape route. Get out!

➢ When you reach any door, test the door and door handle with the back of your hand. If they feel hot there may be fire on the other side of the door. Using a rag if necessary, very carefully crack the door open, standing well back. Check for fire in the escape route. If all is clear, go. If there are signs of fire, use another escape route.

➢ If your escape is blocked and you cannot get out, retreat to your room (better still a room that looks out onto a car park or other clear hard area where fire engines and their evacuation ladders can drive up to the building). Shut the doors, and pack wet towels around the bottom of the door to stop smoke entering the room. Try to use the phone to tell reception that you are trapped and give them the floor number and room number. Wave out of the window and shout for help to attract attention. Do not try to climb out – wait for rescue.

➢ When you get outside, try to reach your meeting point and check to see that all members of your family or group are present.

➢ If you need medical attention, accept it, but if possible ask a member of the group to attend the meeting point to pass on the information that you are out and safe.

Hotel Accidents

Statistics show that more people are injured in hotel falls than in drowning accidents. At first sight that seems strange, but a combination of factors make it a reality.

• Unfamiliar accommodation

• Balconies, which most people are not used to

• Sea views

• Hot nights, which send you to the balcony in search of fresh air

• A party spirit and too much alcohol

It doesn't take too much imagination to see a drunken holidaymaker falling from their balcony or hotel window.

Hotel accidents – countermeasures

✓ Be aware of the problem. Accept that it happens far too often.

✓ Be aware that cheap and free-flowing alcohol, hot thirsty days, hot and humid nights and a stumble or slip on a balcony or beside a hotel window can kill you.

✓ If you don't remember what you did last time you were drunk, you are at risk. Cut back on the alcohol. Take a room without a balcony, or take a room on the ground floor!

Acclimatisation

You may well have to acclimatise to the temperature, humidity, sunshine, different pace of life and sometimes a radically different culture. From your research you should know what to expect at your destination, so take a day or so to adjust.

Acclimatisation – countermeasures

✓ Different time zones on top of jetlag may leave you unexpectedly tired even though local time says it is only half past eight in the morning. Pushing yourself so that you don't 'lose a day' of your holiday could leave you too ill to enjoy the last week of it. If you feel like sleeping, take a sleep.

✓ During the flight it is easy to become dehydrated, and that has an adverse effect on your condition. Try to make sure that you drink plenty of water during your flight. Tea and coffee may be flavoured water, but avoid them and avoid alcohol. Drink pure cool water if possible.

✓ Temperature and humidity can vary wildly around the world. An aircraft can take you from UK summer to a polar ice cap in just a few hours. Be prepared for the condition you will find when you arrive. Take the right clothes for the weather and temperature that you expect to find on arrival.

✓ Familiarise yourself with the strength of the tropical and subtropical sun. It's the same sun that we see, but the strength is radically different. You might be able to go sleeveless all summer at home, but half a day of an African sun can leave you severely burned and hospitalised. Even modest exposure to strong sunshine can result in skin cancer later in life. Cover up by wearing long-sleeved shirts or blouses and cover your legs too. Factor 30 skin protection might not be cool in the clubs in Leeds, but in Barbados it could be a lifesaver.

✓ Exposure to the sun irreversibly ages your skin!

✓ Some companies refuse to allow a holidaymaker to take a camper van out on the road until 24 hours after a long-haul flight. Be sensible – don't expect to get off a long-haul flight, collect the hire car and drive three hundred miles to your holiday destination. If you do have a long drive to make when you arrive, consider booking into a hotel near the airport to give yourself a day to acclimatise and recover from the flight, then you can safely start your journey fresh the next day. Don't risk falling asleep at the wheel of an unfamiliar car on an eight-lane Florida highway!

✓ Be aware of the different cultures. Don't assume that the culture in your destination will be the same as it was when you were there in 1995 or even what it was like three months ago. Governments and laws change. A country may decide that they don't want skimpily dressed bikini-wearing girls walking down their streets any more. Newly enforced religious laws might require women to cover their heads and wear long skirts. In some countries the possession and use of alcohol is strictly prohibited. Make sure you know what you are going into and be prepared to obey the law and culture of the land.

Don't Flash Your Cash

It is never a good idea to let people see how much money you have. In countries where the average annual wage might be a tenth of what you have in your pocket, flashing your money around carelessly is inviting theft. In some countries laws are made by the gang with the most guns, in others the police are people who are a two day journey away and they don't really care if a foreign tourist is shot and relieved of his holiday cash.

Cash – countermeasures

✓ Don't take any more money than you need.

✓ Only change traveller's cheques for cash when you need the cash.

✓ Never carry all of your cash in one pocket. Spread it around in different pockets. In that way you never have to pull out of your pocket what looks like a lot of money. If you are robbed, they hopefully only get the contents of one pocket!

✓ Don't carry expensive cameras, watches or jewellery for the same reason. Remember that your flashy bauble could be worth five years' average wages to a local thief, so he may go to any lengths to get it.

✓ Stay alert, and avoid areas and situations where you may be at risk.

✓ Try to carry smaller valuables in an inside front pocket or in a money belt under your shirt. Never carry anything in a hip pocket, because it is an open invitation to a pickpocket.

✓ Wrapping a couple of rubber bands around a wallet, purse, or even passport or traveller's cheques keeps them tightly together. It prevents them from falling out of your pocket when you bend down, or lay your jacket on a seat. Most importantly, rubber bands mean that a pickpocket cannot easily slide your wallet or purse unnoticed out of your pocket. You will feel the pull of the rubber bands.

Tour Rep/Hotel Staff Advice

I suggest that you always seek advice from tour reps, holiday company representatives, hotel staff and people who have been in the hotel for a week or more. You should already have collected a lot of information from other sources when you were researching and planning your trip. Confirm that information with some current local knowledge. Make sure that you know which areas are safe for tourists and which are not.

Advice – countermeasures

✓ Do as much research as you can when planning the holiday. Contact the embassy or consulate of your destination country. Read tour guides and check the internet. Take a trip to the library – their staff are often quite helpful in finding out about a town or a country.

✓ When you arrive, ask the taxi driver, hotel staff or holiday representative for current and local information. Circumstances may have changed since the books you read were written, and your supposedly middle-class holiday destination may now be riddled with drug dens and violent crime.

✓ Check with hotel staff when you are planning a trip. They can tell you which places are safe and which aren't. They can tell you what the latest tricks and common crimes are, and how to avoid being conned out of your cash. But don't assume that hotel employees are not criminals themselves. They may be working with some of the criminals, so stay aware.

✓ Ask other guests. I always look for guests who have already been there a week or so. They are the ones with a good tan, well-worn ski boots, etc. It usually isn't too hard to identify them and if you get into conversation you get good advice from them. They will tell you where they thought they were unsafe or where they think they didn't get value for money. They will tell you where the best places and excursions are, as well as the ones you should avoid. (Don't forget to pass these tips on to newly arrived guests before you go.)

Common Sense

Use the same common sense when travelling overseas that you would at home. Be especially careful about areas where tourists are likely to gather and stand out, so that it is easier to select and victimise them. Places to be on guard are crowded underground trains, major tourist attractions, railway stations, public lifts and escalators, markets, holiday fiestas and carnivals, etc.

Common sense – countermeasures

✓ Stay on the main roads, where possible using brightly lit roads and paths. Never use short cuts, back alleys and unlit roads.

✓ At night, try not to travel alone.

✓ Avoid any local demonstrations or civil disturbances. Don't even stay around to watch what is happening – some countries use military force to disperse demonstrators and bullets don't avoid innocent bystanders and stupid tourists.

✓ Don't be argumentative. Stay out of political arguments and discussions that may be going on around you.

✓ Never discuss your wealth, possessions, job, family or travel plans with or in front of strangers. In many countries kidnap and ransom is almost considered to be a legitimate family business, so you may end up chained to a beam in some back country cowshed hoping your family can raise £10,000 to get you out – and hoping the kidnappers let you go even if they get that cash.

✓ In many tourist destinations you will be approached by dozens of touts, who offer best prices and cheapest accommodation, car hire, souvenirs, drugs, guides and 'company'. Some are genuine but some will take you down some back alley and rob you – don't risk it. You should have done your research and so should be pretty sure what hotel you want to use and what excursions to take.

✓ Pickpockets have various methods of targeting their victims.

  ➤ They often work in teams.

  ➤ One will bump into you or ask for directions. Their job is to distract you while their colleague steals your valuables.

  ➤ Some wait near a sign saying 'Beware of pickpockets'. People walk past and read the sign, then subconsciously pat their pocket to reassure themselves that their valuables are still in place. Unfortunately that act has just showed the pickpocket which pocket contains the star prize!

  ➤ If there is a distraction or natural crush in a crowd, look out for pickpockets.

  ➤ Even if the victim feels something and catches the dipper, he or she will probably have passed the stolen goods on to another member of their team.

  ➤ In some places if you feel a pickpocket and grab them the criminal gang will attack you, beat you, take everything of value and still escape!

  ➤ Pickpockets may be male, female, small children or women carrying babies, and I have even heard of disabled pickpockets in Italy.

✓ When wearing a shoulder bag, wear it across your chest so that there is less opportunity for a stray hand to slide into it without you seeing or feeling it.

✓ When you have a bag, if walking along the street keep the bag away from the road and walk as far away from the road as you can, in order to prevent the bag being snatched by a cyclist or motorcyclist.

✓ Position a bag so that any flap or zip is nearest to you. If the flap or zip is on the outside, a pickpocket in a crowd could get a chance to open the bag and take whatever is available. If the flap or other opening is towards your chest or stomach they won't even bother trying.

✓ Try not to look lost or confused. This makes you vulnerable and you could attract a range of criminals. Maintain an air of confidence. You may be lost but walk with purpose towards the nearest safe location where you can ask directions or hail a taxi to get you back to where you feel safe.

✓ If you have to ask directions, try to ask somebody with an official role, such as a police officer, traffic warden, transport official, utilities or bank employee, etc. They should give sound advice and directions.

✓ Make sure that you know how to use the pay phones in your destination country. It isn't always as straightforward as you might think. You should also have loose change and the numbers of the hotel where you are staying and the British Consulate handy.

✓ Learn a couple of basic words and phrases in the local language. 'Hello', 'thanks' and 'please' are good but also find out how to ask for the police or a doctor, for example. On the note you have made of the hotel and consulate phone numbers, write the numbers for contacting the local fire police and ambulance services.

✓ Finally, if all of your precautionary measures and preparation fail and you are robbed, be sensible. When confronted by a robber, hand your valuables over. You shouldn't be carrying much and you should be insured anyway. You have your traveller's cheque numbers and details of your passport, etc., so give up your wallet or handbag – not your life.

Vehicle Rental and Driving

Driving abroad can be a risky undertaking because of the differences between driving in the UK and driving in other countries. As an indication of the differences you can experience, I have listed a few that I have encountered below. Read them and accept the fact that driving abroad can make you subject to hundreds of new and unknown threats and risks.

Throughout the world the collection of accident statistics varies from the almost obsessively accurate to the casually indifferent. Some broad accident statistics were collected and the results may surprise you. By mode of transport, from most to least dangerous, the results showed:

- Minibuses (most dangerous – highest fatalities and injuries)

- Motorcycle

- Bicycle

- Walking

- Car

- Aircraft

- Scheduled bus service

- Train (least dangerous – lowest fatalities and injuries)

In developing countries and some popular holiday destinations where the weather is warm and the alcohol is cheap, the risk of dying in a minibus or motorbike accident is said to be up to 15 times higher than in the UK.

A UK report stated that flying is 15 times safer than car travel, 176 times safer than walking and 300 times safer than riding a motorcycle – and that is in the UK!

The only lesson I would draw from these statistics is that drink, drugs, carelessness, vehicle condition, lack of a helmet, not wearing a seatbelt and unfamiliarity with foreign roads and driving laws can kill you. Whichever mode of transport you use, be sensible and take care!

Vehicle rental – countermeasures

✓ If you want to drive, or might want to drive, make sure that you take your driving licence with you. I have always had to present a full UK driving licence to hire a car.

✓ When paying for a hire car, be very wary about allowing the company to take a credit card deposit. Don't sign a blank receipt, no matter how much they claim it is standard practice. I have heard a lot of stories of fraud and abuse of credit card accounts associated with vehicle rentals in tourist areas. Unfortunately the victim doesn't find out until their statement reaches them a month or so after they get back from holiday. Use the larger international vehicle rental companies, or book and pay for your hire car through your travel agent before you leave the UK. It may cost a little more but the peace of mind is worth it.

✓ Make sure that your insurance is adequate. Clarify and confirm what is and is not covered with the travel agent. Arrange it all in advance so that there is no rush with the possibility of things being missed. Carry all of the papers to prove that you are insured, as well as a list of who to contact if there is a problem.

✓ Check the condition of your hire car. Some backstreet companies run cars that would be on the scrap heap in the UK. Use a reputable vehicle hire company which operates relatively new vehicles.

✓ Always inspect the vehicle the company wants to rent to you before signing the papers. I once booked a 'medium family saloon (make and model depending on availability)', but on arrival found I was being given a Ford Anglia. To be fair to the rental company, compared to most other cars on the road there at the time, that was a modern family saloon! I declined the offer, the rust and apparent lack of attention under the bonnet and around the wheels leading me to believe that no mechanic had touched it since it left the factory.

✓ Make sure you know which side of the road to 'officially' drive on. In some places meeting another vehicle is so rare that people tend to drive down the middle of whatever road is available. Suddenly meeting a speeding truck and then collecting your thoughts to decide if you should aim to pass to the left or right can be scary.

✓ Check with the car hire company to confirm local traffic regulations, parking restrictions and speed limits.

✓ Include driving standards and practices in your pre-holiday research.

✓ Weigh up the cost of a taxi, the cost of a hire car and the driving standards and conditions. You may find that taking a taxi anywhere you want to go is an acceptable option. In some countries the cost of hiring a car *with a driver* compares quite well with the cost of a hire car. With a chauffeur-driven car at your disposal you have the added benefits of a local guide and translator, no parking worries and no worries about having that extra drink at the beach party.

✓ If you hire a taxi or private-hire vehicle, always make sure that you agree a fully inclusive price in advance. (The same goes for carriage rides, boat trips and tours.) You should also make sure that the driver is reputable and that the vehicle is properly maintained. Hotels and resorts should be able to advise you about which drivers are safe and honest and which you should avoid.

✓ Your research should have told you of any specific practicalities to driving in your holiday destination. You should know how to treat a cow or an elephant if you encounter one while

165

driving. You should know if women are allowed to drive at all because in some countries they are not.

✓ DON'T DRINK AND DRIVE. In the UK you know the quality and strength of the alcoholic drinks you are swallowing and what the laws and standards are. When abroad you should never drink and drive. I will restrict myself to just three reasons.

1. If it is brewed locally, you have no idea of the strength and effects of the alcohol you are consuming.

2. You are in holiday mood and it is hot so you will drink more than usual.

3. You went on holiday to relax and enjoy yourself. Do you really want to risk killing yourself, a member of your party, another holidaymaker or an innocent local resident for the sake of a few glasses of something or other and a late-night drive back to the hotel in an unfamiliar car along unfamiliar roads?

✓ Fuel can be a problem if you are going to a remote destination. Seek advice about distances, fuel consumption and supply. If necessary get the rental company to mark your map with the locations of reputable garages or sources of fuel and ask them to give you a contact number in case of problems.

✓ If you are going into a wilderness area, ONLY go with a professional guide who knows how to survive if things go wrong. It doesn't take long to die of exposure and thirst if your car breaks down in a desert region.

➢ If you are going to travel to a distant and remote place, get a local guide to take you. They know the route and what preparations to make to keep you safe.

➢ Tell somebody where you are going, what route you will take and when you will arrive at your destination. They should then check up to make sure that you got there. If you didn't, they should get the search and rescue teams looking for you.

➢ Never ever leave the vehicle if you are stuck.

➢ In remote areas a minimum of two vehicles is advised. If one vehicle breaks down, the other can go for help, or if one gets stuck the other can winch it out.

➢ Make sure you carry plenty of food and more water than you think you will ever need.

➢ Aim to take a radio, signal mirrors, smoke flares and shelter. At night in desert climates it gets very, very cold, so you will need warm clothing, a tent, warm food and materials to make a little campfire (which may be used to attract the attention of rescuers as well).

✓ In any vehicle, if there is a seatbelt wear it, and make sure that children are strapped in too.

✓ This is only one tenth of the preparation you need to make before you venture into a wilderness area alone. I *guarantee* that you are not prepared so DON'T DO IT.

✓ Don't hire, accept lifts on or drive a motorbike when abroad. It is one of the most dangerous forms of holiday transport.

✓ If you absolutely must travel on a motorbike, scooter or moped, ONLY do so if you can be supplied with a decent crash helmet, goggles and protective clothes. Whizzing along in shorts and a tee-shirt may be cool, but after skidding down a gravel road, leaving several pounds of flesh embedded in the road surface, you will wish that you had changed your mind.

✓ Avoid bicycles in most places too. They are almost as dangerous, but you probably won't have the option of the crash helmet and protective clothes.

✓ Even when walking, remember to look out for traffic coming from any direction. Think safety, be defensive.

✓ Never under any circumstances, go out on the road after you have been drinking and certainly don't mix alcohol and drugs of any kind.

Vehicle Crime

There are two basic types of vehicle crime: 'theft of' and 'theft from' cars. Though the UK has pretty abysmal car crime statistics, we are not alone. Theft of cars is apparently higher in Sweden and Denmark than in the UK, with Italy not far behind us. In France and Spain theft from cars is on about the same level as the UK, but there is no record of how many of the victims were British tourists who fell victim while in France or Spain.

Target

One problem with car crime abroad is that 'foreign' cars (UK registered) and tourist rental cars are usually easily identifiable. Criminals can spot a tourist's car if it displays a foreign registration number or has some vehicle rental company logo in or on it. They can be pretty sure that it contains money, traveller's cheques, credit cards, passports, cameras and all the other valuables and portables that we take on holiday.

In some countries such as the USA, thieves will go out of their way to target confused and lost, newly arrived tourists. It is not unknown for spotters to wait at an airport to identify wealthy-looking tourists. They tip off their colleagues or follow their targets out of the airport and take what they want, sometimes at gunpoint.

Use common sense and stay alert. When you collect your hire car, make sure you get a good-quality map and clear instructions on how to get to your hotel or holiday complex, avoiding any rough areas. If in doubt, head for somewhere where there are bright lights and a lot of people. A service station, shopping complex or public building offers protection and safety because of the number or people around, officials working in the area and possible CCTV coverage. When you get there, ask for some new and clear directions to reach your destination. If really worried or totally lost, you could consider hiring a taxi to show you the way and follow it to your hotel.

Contents

The other main crime risk is of theft from cars. When you are on holiday you tend to be more relaxed. Forgetting to hide the car park change in the glove compartment, or leaving your camera on the back seat will invite a broken window and loss of property. As in the UK, getting to a car park and then carefully stowing everything in the boot of the car has limited benefits. If the criminals are watching, they know you have put your valuables in the boot. Think ahead. Never carry valuables if you don't need them, and make sure that your insurance covers any threat.

Vehicle crime – countermeasures

✓ Don't be a target. Where at all possible, avoid displaying the evidence that you are a tourist. Don't carry or leave suitcases with flight tags on the handles in clear view. Don't carry or leave holiday brochures, tour schedules and guidebooks on display in your car.

✓ Never leave anything, especially valuables, on display in the car. A sports bag might only contain a pair of smelly sandals and a wet beach towel, but a criminal doesn't know that. He will break into the car to see if it contains a video camera and your passport and wallet.

✓ Don't carry any valuables around that you don't need. Use the hotel safe to keep them secure (if it is safe). If you have to take anything valuable with you, discreetly keep it on your person. Don't display valuables or hold them casually – a thief might snatch them off you.

✓ Stepping off a long-haul flight into a country, city and car with which you are unfamiliar is not the best recipe for safety and security. I often bypass the car-hire desk and head for a hotel. I arrange for a hire car to be delivered to the hotel the next morning when I am fresh and ready. I return the car the day before my flight out as well so I relieve myself of that hassle on the last day, when I probably wouldn't be driving anywhere. And I also save two days' hire charges!

✓ When driving a hire car you sometimes have to carry valuable things with you. If you want to leave anything in your car for any period of time, think ahead. Well before you get to the place you want to park, pull off the road in a busy safe place and store your things in the boot. That way any criminals in the area you eventually park in will not see you storing valuables in the boot. If they see that, they could well target your car.

✓ Always lock your hire car and never ever get out and leave the keys in the ignition. Where some people are dismissive about rental cars, saying things like 'it's only a hire car', I believe that that attitude increases your chances of becoming a victim of car crime. By treating a rental vehicle as though it is on loan from a friend, I am more considerate and careful when I use it. By taking that much more care, I am more aware of what I am doing and what is happening around me, and so I am more security conscious and consequently safer.

✓ Be aware of any local risks. I did hear of one tourist in Africa who took a hire car to a safari camp and the car was charged and rammed by a rhinoceros. Imagine explaining that to the insurance company!

✓ Always double-check your insurance. Due to a shortage of available vehicles I was once offered a free upgrade to a convertible car, so I checked my insurance. I found that I would have needed extra insurance to cover me for driving the convertible sports car they were offering me. I declined the upgrade offer. If I had accepted the convertible upgrade, I would have been driving while uninsured or at least under-insured.

✓ Remember the vehicle you rent will dictate the level of security you have. A saloon car with a large boot has enough seating, air conditioning, and a large boot to hide things in. A convertible car is similar, but a craft knife is the only 'key' needed to get in with a quick slash to the canvas roof. Any jeep-type vehicle offers no protection to any possessions left in the car, little protection to the inhabitants (from assault, accident or sunstroke) and poor protection from the rain.

Use of Credit Cards

Credit card fraud is as common abroad as it is in this country. Credit card companies have systems that watch for unusual patterns of behaviour, and if they spot any unusual patterns they will query the usage, and ask a retail assistant to check. Your card suddenly turning up and being used in Zorkland might be identified as unusual and suspect usage, so you may find that any purchases when on holiday are barred and your card is seized and cut up by the retailer.

If you are going abroad, and want to use your credit and other cards on a once-in-a-lifetime luxury holiday, call the card company and discuss your plans, telling them where and when you are going and how long you will be there.

The new chip and pin cards offer more protection but they don't offer complete protection.

There is some good news though. Credit card fraud abroad for UK citizens over the last year is reported to be the lowest level for five years. However, don't let that lull you into a false sense of security. Stay alert. While there are credit card frauds at home, when you are abroad you are exposed to additional problems:

- A language and possibly different dialects that you do not understand.

- Customs and lifestyles that are alien to you.

- Currency that is alien to you.

- Making credit payments in busy or unusual tourist areas, such as caves or plantations, where the card is swiped in a ticket booth.

- You will only know about any abuse of your card when the statement comes to your front door in a month or two.

Credit card – countermeasures

✓ Take care when using your credit and debit cards at home, take even more care when using them abroad.

✓ Remember that some companies add processing fees and surcharges if you make purchases in a foreign currency in a foreign country.

✓ Try where possible to only use your cards in major international companies such as hotel groups, vehicle rental companies, etc.

✓ At the first sign of trouble contact your credit card company and explain what the problem is. Work with them as far as possible to resolve the problems.

Public Transport

Though there have been some high-profile accidents and terrorist attacks, UK public transport is still infinitely safer and of a better quality than many foreign services.

You must make sure that they fully understand your requirements when you book any tickets using public transport. Misunderstandings may not endanger your life, but they can ruin carefully laid plans, cause you stress and alarm, and generally ruin your day, if not the whole holiday. Remember that statistics show that more tourist deaths and injuries are caused while travelling in, on or being hit by minibuses.

The further you venture off the beaten track and away from traditional holiday destinations, the greater the risk you take by using some services. Some of the more common threats you may face are listed below.

- Some countries do not have the equivalent of our car, heavy goods or public service vehicle (bus) driving test. In countries that do have a driver testing and licensing system, in remote and rural areas the testing and licensing process is largely ignored and rarely enforced. That means that your driver may have first seen the vehicle he is using to transport you the day before.

- In some countries there is no equivalent of the MOT test. Consequently rusty vehicles with bald tyres and little or no brakes will probably be on the road around you.

- In the UK we drive on the left, though most other countries in the world have adopted a policy where they drive on the right-hand side of the road.

- In some countries there is no requirement to have insurance. Make absolutely sure that you have total insurance cover for any eventuality.

- Drink driving laws vary around the world. In some countries the limits imposed in Britain are seen to be far too lenient. In Sweden you will be behind bars before you can say 'but I only had one, officer'. In some countries there are no drink driving laws.

- In some countries overloading of vehicles is an everyday occurrence. When carrying far more passengers than the vehicle was designed for and with

171

additional loads of baggage and cargo strapped to the roof, a vehicle can become unstable on bends and braking systems can fail.

- In some countries vehicles are modified locally to increase capacity with no thought given to upgrading or reinforcing suspension components or upgrading braking systems.

- In some areas what they consider to be a main road would be identified as a country track to most Western travellers. Crash barriers are not fitted, hazard signs are not erected, and frequent random landslides and floods erase some stretches of the roads altogether. Travellers therefore have to take extra care.

- Some countries have few if any traffic laws, so there is no concept of 'right of way' or speed limits. Instead of that, the biggest and bravest simply charge through and take what space they want to take. The small and the weak get out of the way or suffer the consequences.

- Remember that there is also the threat of driving into remote areas and meeting armed bandits! Stay on main roads.

Other driving issues

- In Barbados when I asked which side of the road to drive on, I was half jokingly told 'in the shade'! Lane discipline is quite lax in many countries. UK drivers must look out for vehicles overtaking on either side of them, while approaching vehicles may be in your lane.

- Driving practicalities vary as well. In India, cows have the right of way and cyclists are suicidal. Add to that the odd overloaded donkey, roaming elephant and decidedly mad bus and truck drivers and you have a concoction that will defy all logic, common sense and all attempts to be safe. They say that in India, within five years of production every single car will be involved or present at a fatal traffic accident!

- In some more remote countries and regions, petrol supplies are rare. In former Soviet bloc countries you are likely to find fuel being sold out of milk churns or fizzy drinks bottles at a roadside layby. The supply and quality of fuel is not guaranteed, so before you set off you must make sure that you are carrying enough fuel to reach your destination.

- Be very careful when arranging to drive though remote areas. Seek advice from local experts. Armed bandits are surprisingly common even in some parts of Europe.

- Beware of confidence tricks. The latest assault on UK holiday drivers is fraudulent speeding fines. Criminals spot a UK driver, collect their name and address, take the number and details of the car they are driving, then wait a couple of weeks. When the UK driver gets home he receives a very official-looking speeding ticket, or parking infringement notice. Enclosed with the notice is a demand for the 'fine' to be paid to a given address. More often than not there was no speeding or illegal parking – it is just the latest criminal trick to separate you and your money. If in doubt, check it out with the country's embassy.

- In some countries corruption is so endemic that in some areas the population can do what they want to do, as long as they can afford to pay the appropriate bribes to the right officials.

Public transport – countermeasures

✓ Investigate the quality of the public transport before you go. By looking beyond the brochures at some of the honest guides you will find the truth.

✓ Make sure that whoever books your tickets and transport understands exactly what your requirements and expectations are in relation to safety, quality and the purpose of the journey.

✓ Accept that some drivers are dangerous and in some countries almost all of the drivers are dangerous by UK standards. In knowing this you can take action that will avoid this threat!

✓ Make sure that you book a safe means of transport, even if it means paying a premium. Ensure that the travel agent understands that though it might be 'colourful' and 'adventurous', paying ten pence less for a seat on the roof of the bus isn't how you define safe!

✓ When you arrive, check the vehicle in use and be prepared to find a different route. I once refused to get on a rusty tour coach that had a bald and damaged front tyre. I found a taxi and passed the bus in a shallow ditch a few miles up the road. Nobody was hurt, but on another day on another bend it could have been a very different story.

✓ Accept that minibuses are notoriously dangerous. If confronted by a minibus on holiday and told that it is your transport, satisfy yourself that it is safe.

✓ Be aware of the state of the roads, warning signs, speed limits and presence of crash barriers, etc. If I am going on a journey along winding narrow mountain roads where I know that there are no crash barriers or road signs, I take a lot more care in arranging my transportation than I would if I was at home.

✓ Plan your journeys to avoid risks. On one business trip I made I was told that there was a two-day celebration, after which nobody in the country would be sober for at least a couple of days. I planned my trip to avoid the celebration and 'hangover period'. A local colleague told me that as expected there were hundreds of traffic accidents and dozens of fatalities during that period. Simply changing my travel plans avoided the problem.

Animal Attacks

Though I called this section Animal Attacks, I am also going to include the threat of insect and fish attacks, because they broadly pose the same sort of threat and the countermeasures are similar.

You will find a wide variety of animals wherever you go. Almost all of them could be a threat to you.

Bite

A bite can range from a hypodermic-like single puncture that leaves no mark to something more serious, where teeth penetrate the skin and leave an infected wound. A bite can range from a budgie that nips your finger, to a lion or great white shark that has taken an arm or a leg as a snack.

Scratch

A scratch has a similar range of severity, from a barely discernible mark where a hamster scratched your hand, to the raking and life-threatening gash of a grizzly bear's claws.

Gore

Because by definition 'gore' means to penetrate the body, gore wounds tend to be serious. Apart from the strength and violence necessary to inflict the wound and cause major damage to flesh, muscle and internal organs, the risk of secondary infection is huge. If you say 'gore' to most people they immediately think of bullfighting in Spain, but on a bad day, if you are in the wrong place at the wrong time anything with horns could gore you – a sheep, a goat or even a reindeer.

Kick/Trample

Many animals use kicks as a defence, or some simply kick out while running, like a horse galloping round a meadow. Different species of animal kick, but while most of them have some sort of hoof, not all of them do. An extension or alternative to kicking is to trample. That is to deliberately knock over a victim and then jump and stamp on them. Horses, cows, deer, moose, elephants and goats have been known to kick and trample human victims.

Crush

A few animals use their bulk to crush a human victim. Crush injuries may be accidental or deliberate. Whatever the cause, large animals are a threat, because they can and have crushed humans to death.

Sting

To most people, stings are inconsequential though sometimes painful and annoying. The threat of stings is usually considered to come from bees, scorpions and other insects, but box jellyfish sting too and they have fatal consequences. Any number of small sea creatures can cause you harm, for example blue-ring octopus, coneshell and stonefish. A sting can result in an itching annoyance, a painful swelling or a quick and agonising death.

Poison

Many creatures use poison as a defence mechanism. Some like snakes bite to inject their venom, others spray or squirt it, while some have poisonous skin glands. Some of the most toxic and most potent substances known are found in animal venom. The poisons vary in strength and effect. Some are deterrents that are designed to make a creature taste bad so it won't be eaten by a predator. At the other end of the scale are nerve toxins that can kill an adult man in seconds.

Experts tell me that animals do not attack because they are malicious. They attack because they are:

- Hunting for food

- In pain

- Defending themselves

- Protecting young or a nest

- Seeking a mate

- Startled.

Whatever the reason for an attack, the results can be devastating. If not fatal, a victim could easily be crippled, disabled or blinded. Even a simple bite could infect you with potentially fatal diseases such as rabies.

Animal attack – countermeasures

Though some people are used to being around or working with animals and are able to read their moods, many people never come closer to an animal than walking past a cat or stray dog. To these city dwellers an animal is an alien creature, and they have no idea how to deal with it. I have therefore targeted these countermeasures at people who are devoid of animal experience.

✓ Avoid any animal that you don't know. Given the right circumstances any animal can and will attack. Though the consequences of being nibbled by an irate hamster and being mauled by an angry lion are totally different, both attacks resulted because the animal was provoked in some way.

✓ Be aware that animals have a variety of ways of attacking. For instance, small dogs snap, camels and horses bite, and llamas kick and spit. An elephant could toss you around using its trunk and then trample you, goats often nibble, and even a little old beach donkey can kick or chew your hand if it takes exception to you.

✓ Respect any animals you come across. Don't be fooled by cute and fuzzy cartoon looks or behaviour. An angry kangaroo could disembowel you with one kick. A disgruntled swan could break your leg. Even a cute chimpanzee has phenomenal strength – an adult chimp could easily rip a man's arm off.

✓ Don't be fooled by other people. The man in the bazaar may be handling the snake, but it doesn't mean that it will let you touch it. The trainer might be able to take liberties with the 'tame' wolf, but you shouldn't copy him. Some animals have been conditioned to tolerate humans. They may participate in games and tricks, but inside they are a free spirit with their own drives and nature. In other words, they are still wild animals with the potential to revert to natural behaviour, operating on instinct.

✓ Take notice of signs and warnings when dealing with animals. The sign at the zoo saying don't feed the animals is not just there for the dietary needs of the animals. If there is a fence and strong bars between you and the animal, they are there to protect you from that animal. Don't go too close or reach through the bars to stroke the furry-looking bear or sleepy lion. People have tried and lost arms or died doing it.

✓ Research what animals, insects, snakes, bats, etc. that you are likely to come across. At the same time learn how to cope with them. In the case of the mosquito, a simple spray-on deterrent may work during the day but a mosquito net is usually recommended to protect you while you sleep. For anything bigger, if you aren't sure just stay clear – even that cute puppy could have rabies.

✓ Always seek out and take the advice of tour reps and hotel and resort staff when you are abroad. They can tell you if there is an infestation of fire ants, and tell you what a fire ant looks like so you know what to avoid. Local people can tell you how to avoid the places where snakes like to hide, or where vampire bats look for food each night.

✓ In any country where there are animals that can and have killed people, never go into the wilderness or forest without seeking advice, and being properly equipped. We all know about mountain lions in America, and your average big hairy lion in Africa, but there are other less obvious threats. An unhappy moose can easily kill you if you get close enough to give it a chance.

✓ If you are actually on holiday to see animals, take extra care. Listen to what your guide says, and do everything that they tell you to do.

✓ If you unexpectedly find yourself around animals, they are probably more scared than you are. Animals usually move away when there are humans around. An animal that is busy feeding or was perhaps sleeping might not hear you come along the trail so you could surprise it. When they are surprised by the sudden appearance of a threat (even if that threat is just you and your new digital camera), animals' immediate and instinctive defence can be to attack. When you are walking and approaching any animal, or walking where there may be animals, make a noise.

Whistle, sing, talk, rattle cans, anything that will make a noise! The noise will alert the animals to your presence and approach. When they know that you are coming they have time to prepare for your arrival by watching you or moving off.

✓ Never ever try to stroke, pat, pull, push or otherwise handle an animal that you do not know, especially when it is a species that you are unfamiliar with. The scorpion may look interesting, but pick it up for a closer look at your peril. That bug may look like a fly but it could be a wasp that could incapacitate you for days. Those pretty-looking things in the seawater may be stinging anemones, and that floating string could be jellyfish tentacles. If you don't know what it is, at least ask, but for safety leave it alone.

✓ If you are bitten, stung or scratched, DON'T try to pick up whatever did it. It will bite sting or scratch you again! Take a close look at it, get members of your party to look at it from a safe distance and even use your mobile phone to take a photograph if you can. Then seek medical help and advice as soon as possible. The bite could be harmless – the equivalent of a British wasp sting – or it could be much worse.

➢ DON'T get excited or run around. That will circulate a toxin more quickly.

➢ DON'T cut the bite open, even if they do that in the movies.

➢ DON'T try to suck the poison out either. The person sucking is at risk of exposure to any toxin and the victim is subject to infection from the open wound.

✓ Best of all, avoid animals, insects, snakes, fish or anything that could bite, sting, scratch or otherwise injure you.

Dangerous Plants

In the UK we have some plants that can sting or contain an irritant that can cause blisters, such as stinging nettles. Various berries, fruits and fungus can be poisonous, but we either know them or simply don't go around trying to eat them. In the UK people don't expect to have to be able to forage for food.

We know that around the world there are stinging plants and those with poisonous sap or fruit, but we haven't grown up with them so we don't exactly know what they are. Any American child can identify and avoid poison oak, which produces a very irritating rash, but could you identify and avoid it?

Some plants and fruit are more toxic than you can imagine, but we have no idea what they are. If a plant has huge spikes and thorns we can see them and know that we should avoid them, but there is no general rule we can follow to avoid poisonous plants or fruit. We only know what to avoid if somebody tells us!

If you were taking a walk in the English countryside, and saw a man about to grasp a handful of stinging nettles, would you call out and stop him? Would you 'interfere', or assume he knows what he is doing, or even ignore him?

Now reverse the situation – you are that person. When I was in Barbados, it looked like it was coming on to rain so I sheltered under a big old tree. I stood and watched the black clouds getting closer, when a passing man changed direction to walk up to me. I didn't hear him when he first spoke, so I said, 'Sorry what did you say?' He paused then said, 'That's a manchineel tree.' I couldn't understand why he had gone out of his way to give me a botany lesson, but I guessed what he was saying was significant in some way.

I thanked him for the information and asked him why he'd gone out of his way to tell me what the tree was. I was glad I did. He explained that the manchineel tree was quite poisonous. The leaves, the bark and the sap were so toxic that rain water running down over the leaves picked up so much toxin that if it dripped onto exposed human skin it hurt and quickly caused a large blister to form.

He said he almost didn't repeat what he had said, because he didn't want to interfere or get any abuse or hassle from a stranger. It started to rain, but he was so interesting and the rain was so warm that we just walked along the beach as we talked. I thanked him several more times before we parted.

Dangerous plants – countermeasures

Tourist hotels and resorts are designed to be safe, and the developers and management tend not to plant dangerous trees or plants in areas where tourists could come to harm. Unfortunately, when we travel most people like to explore a little, to drive around, ride horses, walk and otherwise see a little of the countryside. There are a few things that you can do to make sure you stay safe.

✓ On arrival, ask about dangerous plants, poison sap, stinging plants, etc., and ask where you are likely to find them.

✓ If possible, find out what the plants look like, then if you are unsure you can avoid all plants that look anything like them!

179

✓ If you are planning to explore, check to see if there are any dangers in that area. If there are, go with an organised group so that a guide can steer you away from those dangers.

✓ Consider taking a thick plastic bag so that if you are stung you can carefully collect and carry a sample to show the doctor what caused the irritation.

✓ Seek medical help as soon as you can.

✓ If you are stung by a plant or sap, avoid scratching. In most cases scratching only makes things worse and also breaks the skin, allowing secondary infection to take a hold.

Souvenirs
■ ■

When I am on holiday I am on holiday for me. I am not on an expedition to collect gifts for friends and relatives at home, so nobody expects me to bring back gifts and souvenirs.

Souvenirs and gifts are usually a waste of money. You buy something silly, cute or exotic for somebody, carry it halfway around the world, present it to them and they put it in the loft or more often than not in the next charity jumble sale.

Bringing back some gifts and souvenirs could very easily mean you are breaking the law.

CITES is the Convention on International Trade in Endangered Species. Its website, www.cites.org, describes CITES as follows: 'CITES (Convention on International Trade in Endangered Species of Wild Fauna and Flora) is an international agreement between Governments, which attempts to make sure that the collection and sale of wild animals and plants does not threaten their survival.'

In the 1960s, when CITES was first discussed, conservation and international treaty and regulation on wildlife was relatively new. Today the annual global wildlife trade is estimated to be worth billions of pounds and includes hundreds of millions of plant and animal specimens. The trade covers everything from live animals and plants to a range of products derived from them, including foodstuffs, leather goods, wooden musical instruments, timber, tourist curios and medicines. The extent of exploitation of some animals and plants is bringing them close to extinction.

Regulation of trade is difficult because by its nature the trade passes across borders, from one nation and its laws, to the territory of a different nation with different laws and law-enforcement bodies. CITES was conceived in a spirit of co-operation and now offers protection to more than 33,000 species of animals and plants, whether they are traded as live specimens, fur coats or dried herbs.

CITES is an international agreement and members have to implement the convention which provides a framework to be respected by each country. Each country then has to adopt its own domestic legislation to make sure that CITES is implemented at the national level.

No species protected by CITES has become extinct as a result of trade since the convention came into force.

Though the CITES regulations are supported by law in 164 countries, this doesn't stop criminals from trying to trade in endangered species. So tourists must be aware that many souvenirs are actually made from endangered wildlife, and that buying, exporting them from their home country and importing them when you get back to the UK is illegal.

If you do try to import some of these expensive and questionable gifts and souvenirs, you risk the item being confiscated and you being charged with illegal importation. It is difficult to know what is just a tacky souvenir made from the remains of an endangered species, or just a tacky souvenir made from chicken feathers and an old shoe. When you consider that about 5,000 species of animals and 28,000 species of plants are protected by CITES, you cannot be expected to know what is and what is not protected.

The simple general rule is that you should avoid buying, selling, importing or exporting anything made from:

• Sea turtles

• African or Asian ivory

• Fur from spotted cats

- Fur from marine mammals

- Feathers and feather products from wild birds

- Any live or stuffed birds from Australia, Brazil, Colombia, Costa Rica, Ecuador, Guatemala, Mexico, Paraguay, Venezuela and some Caribbean countries

- Most crocodile and caiman leather

- Most coral, whether in chunks or in jewellery.

The list changes, but it would take an expert in some cases to decide if a product was made from leather or the skin of some exotic and rare crocodile. The simple answer is DON'T BUY ANIMAL PRODUCTS. Avoid anything that is, appears to be or could be made from animal horn, skin, bone, feathers, fur or other living material. If we don't buy them, the local people won't be able to sell them, so will leave the animals and plants in the wild where they belong.

Buying Antiques. Though in my experience most 'genuine' antiques on sale to tourists were made in a local workshop less than a week before, there are real antiques available for purchase. However, most countries are very protective of their archaeological and historic treasures, which means tourists have been arrested for purchasing and attempting to export them.

Countries such as Turkey, Egypt and Mexico are particularly keen to prevent the illegal sale and export of what they consider to be national treasures. Chances are that what the shopkeeper is trying to sell you was made by his cousin in the back of the shop, but play safe. Either avoid anything ancient, or seek advice from the local authorities about its age and value and your right to take it home.

6 Travel Back

During your holiday you should have managed to balance your caution with relaxation and liberal doses of enjoyment. In fact you had such a nice holiday that you are in danger of sitting down under a palm tree and forgetting the flight home.

Don't relax too much yet, because you are about to encounter a new range of risks and threats.

Confirm Flight and Travel Plans

Even though you hold a return ticket, some airlines require you to contact them a day or so before your return flight to confirm that you will be travelling. Check with your travel agent and airline to see if you need to do this. You don't want to book out of your hotel room and find yourself at the airport with all of your cases, only to be told that you are not booked on the flight and the next available seat is in three days' time.

Foreign Currency

Some countries prohibit the export of their currency. That means that you could be required to exchange any currency back into pounds at the airport, using government facilities that offer very unfavourable rates. The worst possible scenario is that the authorities could simply seize any local currency in your possession.

At least a few days before you are due to fly back, find out what the rules about local currency are. With any such rules in mind, review your own needs. You may never want to come back to the country again, so you won't need the local money on future trips. On the other hand you may love the country and can't wait to get back, so you could feel that any spare local currency will be used again within a few months. I try to monitor my usage of the local currency and towards the end of the holiday be careful about how many traveller's cheques I exchange. That way I know I won't be left with a lot of local currency.

Local currency at the airport

Your next consideration is how much local currency you will need at the airport, where you may have to pay for a taxi, food and drink, or local taxes, all payable in local currency. If you haven't been very thorough with your research or if your travel agent has left some vital information out, you could be in for a shock.

Trying to book in for my flight home, congratulating myself for having spent my last local currency, I was surprised when the check-in desk clerk asked me for the new departure tax. All foreigners were required to pay about £7 each in taxes to compensate for the environmental impact of their travel (well that was what they said). I had to go and change another traveller's cheque.

Loose change

Travellers often seem to get stuck with a pocket full of change. When I was writing this I had a quick whip around among close family members and collected all the forgotten dusty holiday change. We had coins from 11 different countries, but the most surprising thing was that between us we had almost £53 in change. It quickly adds up and banks and travel agents won't accept or exchange foreign coins, so any change you bring back is lost.

Foreign currency – countermeasures

✓ Some countries impose strict controls on the export of their currency. Find out what the rules are relating to the movement of currency in and out of the country or countries you will be visiting.

✓ Manage your foreign currency so that you don't change too many traveller's cheques and then lose out changing the foreign currency back into pounds when you come back home.

✓ Make sure that you find out if you will have to pay any charges or taxes at the airport on your departure. If so, make sure that you have sufficient foreign currency available to pay them.

✓ Nobody exchanges foreign coins, so make sure you don't collect large quantities of them. It may be easier to use bank notes rather than struggle with strange coins in unusual denominations, but try to use the coins as you get them, so that you don't have too many when you get to the airport on your way home.

Packing

In a security-conscious world, packing and luggage take on a new and crucial importance. All airlines ask if you packed your own bags, and if you are carrying anything for anyone else. This is partly as an ineffective security measure (will a terrorist or criminal really admit to carrying something he shouldn't be carrying?), but mostly to do with deniability. When and if drugs or other illegal imports are found in your case, you have already admitted three things. It is your case, you packed it and everything in the case belongs to you!

Treat travelling seriously, and be aware that the greatest threat is probably drug smugglers looking for 'mules' to carry their substances for them. They use all sorts of tricks, including the old favourite of a free holiday as long as you bring back one small package for them. Drugs detection and intelligence is improving all of the time, and the likelihood of drug smugglers being caught is increasing. Make sure that you strictly follow the guidelines set down by airlines and travel agents. DON'T CARRY ANYTHING FOR ANYONE ELSE.

As with the journey out, pack your things neatly, and make sure that you follow the airline safety rules. Don't pack electrical equipment with batteries installed. Security will make you open the case and remove the batteries. Don't try to carry sharp objects onto the aircraft in carry-on luggage. They are banned because they could be used as weapons by terrorists. You should also remember to make sure that the lids of bottles of shampoo or perfume are securely sealed. There is nothing worse than getting home to find that your new digital camera has had a bath in a mixture of medicated shampoo, nail varnish remover and suntan lotion!

Packing – countermeasures

These are as for packing for the outward journey, plus:

✓ Only use your own cases and bags. Be wary of cases that may have had drugs sewn into them.

✓ Always pack them yourself and never leave them unattended.

✓ Never carry anything for anyone, no matter how nice and trustworthy they seem.

✓ Never try to pack and export from your holiday destination, or import into the UK, anything which is, or you suspect to be, dangerous, illegal or restricted.

✓ Make sure the lids of all containers of shampoo, etc. are screwed on tight.

✓ Keep your passport, flight tickets and a warm coat to wear when you land out of your packed cases.

Clearing Your Room

UK holidaymakers and business travellers leave hundreds of millions of pounds worth of clothes, equipment, money and valuables behind when they travel. In fact one report put the value of items forgotten and lost by holidaymakers as high as two billion pounds a year!

While on holiday, before you leave a restaurant, hire car, beach or anywhere else – especially the hotel room when you pack to come home – check to make sure you are not leaving things behind.

Clearing your room – countermeasures

✓ When you unpack, store things where you can easily find (and remember) them. If you hide your best watch under a loose floorboard you may forget it and leave it there.

✓ When you use the hotel safe, leave a note to remind yourself things are in the safe. The staff may not remind you when you leave.

✓ When you pack, methodically go over the room, villa or house checking every cupboard, drawer, store room, shelf, etc.

Immigration

We all have to pass through immigration to allow the authorities to check that we have a right to enter the country. They do that job, but usually very slowly, so be prepared to wait and make sure that you have your passport ready to present to the staff manning the desk.

Customs and Excise

There are strict rules, regulations and laws governing what can be freely imported, what is barred and what has to be licensed or taxed. Customs and Excise staff members have the widest powers available to any official in the UK. They have more powers than UK police forces!

Don't try to smuggle anything into the country. Some products like cooked and raw meats or plant material can carry diseases that could wipe out whole species of plants and animals. Some products are simply dangerous and do not match UK and EU safety laws and standards.

UK Customs defines lists of goods that are 'prohibited' or 'restricted' in the UK to protect citizens' safety, health and the environment. These rules apply to ALL travellers, whether you are travelling within the EU or from outside the EU.

- **Prohibited.** Prohibited goods are goods that are banned completely in the UK.

- **Restricted.** Restricted goods are goods that cannot be imported into the UK without the appropriate legal documentation, such as a licence.

The rules are quite complex. For more information see www.hmce.gov.uk

The UK Department for Environment, Food and Rural Affairs (DEFRA) has introduced a campaign which aims to reduce the risk of exotic animal disease entering the country and then threatening our public health, livestock, agriculture and horticultural industries. For further information on the regulations of bringing back meat, animal products or plants from outside the EU see www.defra.gov.uk/animalh/illegali/

Penalties for smuggling can be quite severe. Trying to bring things into the country could be a very expensive game to play.

Medication

Remember that some medications may be legal and sold openly in one country, but if you try to take those medications into a neighbouring country it could be treated as a serious criminal act. In some circumstances, travellers have faced the death penalty for possession and transportation of illegal drugs that were purchased innocently in a neighbouring country.

Medication – countermeasures

✓ Check with the appropriate embassy and get them to state in writing that your medication can be legally imported and used.

✓ Review the medication that you may have secreted in your cases. Be absolutely certain that they are legal to export/import between different countries.

✓ On return to the UK, declare any over-the-counter or locally prescribed medication and explain the circumstances in which you got it. Leave it to the Customs staff to decide if you can bring the medication in or not.

✓ If they want to seize the medication, ask if you can keep the packaging/bottle/label so that you can at least show your doctor what you were prescribed and have been taking while abroad.

Acclimatise Again
■■

You might experience another extreme climate change. When you fly into a British winter from Barbados you will undoubtedly need the warm coat you carried just for this moment, or coming from a cold climate you may feel uncomfortably hot. Make sure that you're prepared for the weather, whatever it is or might be when you finally get off the aircraft.

Post-Travel Monitoring

Don't be complacent about foreign diseases when you return to the UK.

Holiday infections and injuries

If you sustained any injuries, suffered any adverse symptoms from altitude sickness, food poisoning, sunburn, cuts or bites while on holiday, make an appointment to see your doctor as soon as possible.

When you see them, explain what happened, what your symptoms were and the treatment you received. If you were given any medication or purchased any medication, show the medication and its packaging to the doctor.

Be safe, not sorry. Your original sickness may merely have been a symptom of a major infection that the doctor can treat easily if he catches it in time. On the other hand, that wound that looked like just a little scratch, may well be 'just a little scratch'!

Infection and food workers

If you are or were recently suffering from a stomach upset and/or diarrhoea and are due to return to work which involves handling food, call in and tell your employer before you report to work. For Health and Safety and food hygiene reasons, they may require you to have a medical checkup to get permission to return to work, rather than risk infecting those who eat the food you handle.

Monitor your health for a few months

Because the incubation period for some diseases is measured in months, you must monitor your health for months after you return. If any symptoms appear, see your doctor as soon as possible.

Explain where you have been and voice your concerns. UK doctors don't often see dengue fever, so if you think you have the symptoms, say so. The doctor may be able to tell you that it is food poisoning or constipation, or you could discover that you do indeed have dengue fever. The speedier the diagnosis, the quicker and more complete the recovery.

If you were prescribed some medication abroad, as with any medication you should always finish it. Don't stop taking it because you begin to feel better. If you stop taking the medication before reaching the end of the prescribed course, any infection can take hold again.

If you are in any doubt about the medication or if you are suffering side effects, you should see your doctor. If you cannot get an appointment to see the doctor within a day or so, consider going to the local hospital.

7   **Terrorism**

What Is Terrorism?

What one group or organisation calls terrorism, another group will claim to be a legitimate strike for independence (or whatever cause they claim). Are they freedom fighters or terrorists? Your view of terrorism will be coloured by a number of factors. For example:

- What the 'terrorist' group claims to represent.

- What damage they cause in pursuing their demands.

- Whether they kill or injure innocent parties or don't care if they do.

- Whether they restrict their activities to their own country.

- Whether the actions they use are warranted and proportional to furthering their cause.

- Whether they have real, or idealistic and unreal demands and aims.

What The People Think

The real question is what do members of the general public *perceive* to be a definition of terrorism? The root of the word terrorism is 'terror' which is a good indication of the apparent aim of these groups. That is, to induce terror in the general population, with an aim of forcing it to submit to their demands.

Terrorist acts can range from making radio broadcasts denouncing the government, through throwing raw eggs at a politician, to planting explosives in a public area. The range of activities is huge, but I suspect that the general public would define 'terrorism' something like this:

Terrorism is any indiscriminate act, whether violent or not, that kills, injures, harms or adversely affects members of the public who have no control over whatever activity a 'terrorist' group may oppose.

Broadly speaking – don't attack the small guys because we don't run the country, control the army or define the laws, and whatever you do keep it inside your own country.

Any group that uses indiscriminate violence against innocent people, or uses indiscriminate violence outside their own geographic or political borders must be branded as terrorists. Any group or individual participating in pure terrorist activities, plus any government, company or organisation found to be promoting, funding or supporting terrorist activities, should be vigorously prosecuted by the international community.

Who Are Terrorists?

An even harder question to answer. For a start the list will change depending on how you define terrorists. As an example of how interpretation can affect your view, allow me to describe one group.

An organised group operating in England. They operate in clandestine ways and are run along military lines. Members often wear a uniform for operations, but wear civilian clothes to merge in with the population when not actively engaged in their group activities. The legitimate wing operates quietly in conjunction with a significant commercial organisation with international links. The 'operational' wing of the group allegedly receives no funding or support from the commercial organisation, though indications are that this is not strictly true. The group actively recruits fit young men, aiming to convert them to their cause. Even children participate in planned operations in mainland UK. Group and regional leaders occasionally send active cells to targets in Europe. These cells travel incognito, and meet up at a predefined location to complete their mission. UK security services are actively investigating this group. UK police forces are investigating the group, and have arrested several of its leaders and many of its members, charging them with a variety of offences including assault, riot, and possession of offensive weapons.

Would you define that group as being a terrorist organisation? Would you say that they have terrorist objectives under my definition or by your own understanding of what makes a terrorist organisation?

Would you think differently if I told you that the group I am describing is the fictional Bradfield County Football Supporters Club? Yes, they are organised and 'uniformed', they travel to away matches, they are not really funded by the football club, they do fight with rival supporters and there have been arrests here and abroad, and the police and security services are investigating them ahead of a European cup final match. A few of them are known criminals.

Now you know that, has it changed your opinion of the group? Did you decide they were terrorists based on my first description of them? The first description was true even if the language used was somewhat misleading on occasion. Remember that I had already primed you to think 'terrorist' by the title of the chapter, earlier discussions and even the question I asked. Now that you know that the organisation is just a football supporters club, which has a few members who pick fights with rival supporters, does it change your mind about their classification as a terrorist organisation?

Terrorist Groups

Are all protest groups terrorists? Greenpeace are an ecological protest group, but could you describe Greenpeace as a terrorist organisation? Not so many years ago a Greenpeace ship was allegedly attacked by agents of the French Security Service. Its agent used explosives to sink a Greenpeace ship and during the operation a Greenpeace crewman was killed. So, by our definition doesn't that define the French Security Service as a terrorist organisation?

Unfortunately terrorism is 'delivered' under the name of a wide range of different groups, promoting political, religious, sociological and geographical ideologies. There also seems to be a sprinkling of mentally disturbed people who just get a sense of power out of random acts of violence. I suspect that the general answer will be that though most of these groups involved in the undue use of fists and aggression are a nuisance, real terrorism is what we see on the front page of the newspapers.

Legitimate Escalation of Force

People have a legitimate right to overthrow oppression by force of arms if necessary. Terrorists declare an aim and therefore all of their actions and activities should support their declared aim. If I were to form the National Front For The Liberation Of Some-where-or-other with the aim of removing President Floribunda and his corrupt administration I would need to undertake a range of activities to achieve that. I could:

- Call for free elections.

- Call for national strikes and demands for the president to resign.

- Call on people to withhold taxes.

- Call on people to write to their political representatives.

- Call on people to stand in elections against the corrupt administration.

- Call on big business to withdraw support and funding from the president.

- Call on surrounding countries to cut off political ties.

- Call on the UN to stop supporting the administration.

- Call on the IMF to withhold financial aid.

- Call on countries to ban imports and exports from and to the country.

If all that fails, and President Floribunda has started sending his secret police to arrest and kill opponents, I could escalate my activities, meeting violence with violence to physically remove the president from power.

- I could kidnap members of his government and demand he step down.

- I could organise a revolution (when many could die on both sides).

- I could assassinate the president.

Because I can prove that President Floribunda is corrupt, is guilty of ethnic cleansing, is siphoning off money to his private accounts, is oppressing the people and sending death squads to deal with anyone who speaks out, I may have legitimate reason to resort to force. Even though I am branded a terrorist, an impartial observer might more accurately decide that it is the president who is a terrorist, or perhaps that the conflict is a civil war.

Pure Terrorism

Where an individual or organisation makes unrealistic demands on a global scale, they are pure terrorists. For example, if I created an organisation demanding that everybody should stop listening to rock and roll or classical music and should immediately start listening to country music every day, most normal people would say that this is an unrealistic and unreasonable demand.

If my group then resorts to using explosions and gunfire to force people to listen to country music, it must be condemned by all nations as totally illegal. Any nation which then harbours or supports that group will itself be committing a crime against humanity and should be punished by the international community.

Where Are They?

As it stands, the fundamental message is that terrorism is all around us. The last time I looked, the Foreign and Commonwealth Office defined the countries and areas most at risk from terrorist threats as:

- Middle East and North Africa

- East Africa and the Horn of Africa

- South Asia.

They might be the areas where terrorism is at an observable peak, but terrorism is a global problem, not a foreign problem. We have to be alert to the dangers and have to do what we can to suppress it, and to cope with it until there is real global agreement and co-operation on how to deal with it.

What Does a Bomb Look Like?

In cartoons a bomb is always a round black ball with a burning fuse sticking out of the top and the word 'BOMB' helpfully printed on the side. But in life it isn't that easy. With home-made or commercial explosives anything could be a bomb – or rather, a bomb can be made to look like anything.

A cigarette packet can hide a small timed incendiary or explosive device. A briefcase can hold enough explosives to demolish an entire building. A bomb loaded into a small van could destroy a tower block.

Bombs can be fired like mortars or rockets from a distance, delivered in the post, attached to the bottom of a car as a booby trap, parked outside in a van, fixed inside the frame of an innocent-looking bicycle, or carried into a building strapped to somebody's waist. The type and quantity of explosives vary along with the style and look of the device.

The intention isn't necessarily to kill or destroy. The intention may be to disrupt, because terrorists can cause immense disruption with minimal effort.

With the right explosives and positioning, something the size of a matchbox could easily kill an adult. Anything bigger than a lunchbox will kill a lot of people and cause a lot of damage. It is therefore impossible to say what to look for when you are looking for a 'bomb'.

So how do you spot a bomb? The usual advice is to tell someone who knows the area, shop or station to look for something that is unusual or out of place. For example a rucksack in the restroom that you never saw before, a cardboard box on the floor beside the reception desk, a briefcase where there shouldn't be one or a strange white van parked close to the back wall of the office.

Be alert. Keep control of your shop, office or work area. Make it tidy, keep it tidy then familiarise yourself with what is there. Be strict about clutter and rubbish. Be strict about access and security too, then when something unusual arrives you will easily spot it.

Make sure that everyone knows that if they want to leave a box of books at reception, or leave their delivery van in your company car park, you have to know before they do it. Then you will know that anything else that does turn up is suspicious. The more of a target you could be, the more suspicious you should be of that box, van or briefcase.

It Really Happens

In recent years there have been an increasing number of fairly indiscriminate attacks on what can only be described as 'Western' targets. These include:

- Bomb attacks in the UK.
- Three bomb attacks on tourist areas in south-west Turkey.
- A suicide bomb attack in Doha, Qatar.
- Bombs detonated in Makati, Manila.
- Separatist group exploded a bomb in a Spanish resort.
- Bomb attacks against tourist sites in Egypt.
- Serious attacks including bombings in Saudi Arabia.
- September 2004 car bomb in Jakarta, Indonesia.
- Bombs downed commercial aircraft in Russia.
- Suicide bomb attacks in Tashkent, Uzbekistan.
- Bomb attacks on commuter trains in Madrid.
- Bomb on a ferry in the Philippines.
- Bomb attacks in Casablanca, Morocco.
- Suicide bomb in Mombasa, Kenya.

All of these and more recent attacks illustrate two things.

Soft targets

The terrorists want to succeed. They are intelligent and experienced in attacking the targets they choose. They are organised, have significant resources and can operate anywhere in the world. They aim to attack a target which will give them a high body count and international press coverage. If they can do that without risk to themselves they will attack those targets, leaving them free to attack different targets another day. If not, they use other means.

Suicide attacks

Most people don't commit crimes because they don't want to be caught and punished. Anyone can commit a crime – the trick is to do it and then get away without being caught.

If the ultimate deterrent to crime is imprisonment or in some countries execution, what happens when there are people who don't care about being caught? What happens when those criminals actually intend to die with their victims, whose only 'crime' may be that they are vulnerable and in the wrong place at the wrong time.

Tourists and travellers who die have no control over American foreign policy or British economic policy or anything else that terrorists may be fighting against. Whether they want to or not, there is nothing they can do about any of those things. Their crime is vulnerability. While the people who actually make those decisions, the presidents and prime ministers, sit back in armour-plated limousines and bullet-proof residences with round-the-clock armed guards, ordinary citizens are vulnerable.

Bad luck, being in the wrong place at the wrong time and not being alert to the risks kill average people. Though the likelihood of any one person becoming involved in a terrorist incident is extremely low, there are some things that everyone can do to protect themselves.

Terrorist Tricks

To stay free, make money, move around the country and travel between countries, terrorists have to have a 'clean' identity. That is, they may so far be unknown to the police so they can use their own identity, or they may be using your stolen identity to move around, plan and make money for their group. Criminals are already trying to steal your identity in order to steal from you or steal using your identity, so you should be protecting your identity. Don't let terrorists steal your identity in order to bring death to more innocent people. Don't make it easy for them. Shred or burn confidential papers, don't give personal details over the phone or internet, and protect your passports and other documents.

Methods

The leaders who are the real targets of terrorists are too well protected. The terrorists' only option is to go for a soft target, which is unguarded and may or may not have a tenuous link to the group they oppose.

That soft target could be a shopping centre underneath offices associated with the government, or a factory that the president is due to visit. The terrorists know that innocent people will be hurt or killed, but they aim to 'make a statement' and declare the innocents who are killed to be martyrs. Alternatively they may just declare the innocent casualties to be opposition soldiers.

To the terrorists 'collateral damage' is an acceptable consequence of their fight. More often than not they will deny responsibility or blame innocent deaths on the people they are targeting. For example, blaming President Floribunda for siting government offices over that shopping centre, or saying that the factory was a legitimate target because it was being used to support a corrupt regime.

With limited resources and probably under some level of surveillance by security services, terrorists have to plan their campaign. They have to raise funds, establish a base of operations, visit the site of their intended attack, buy vehicles and import or buy weapons and explosives to build bombs. These are activities that could and sometimes do attract the attention of security services or members of the public.

If we all accept that terrorists may be operating anywhere, even in our street or building, then by remaining alert to what is going on around us we can all help to defeat them.

General

There is little that the average person can do and probably little that the vast majority of people need to do, to protect themselves from terrorist attacks.

A new good-quality bullet-proof vest will cost you at least £800. But that vest only fully protects your torso from a frontal or rear assault.

A bullet or shrapnel can hit your head or neck, arms or legs and that injury could easily kill or maim you. If hit in the arm or leg by a bullet, without prompt medical attention blood loss and shock will kill you anyway. A shot or injury to the groin, which is not protected by a ballistic vest, is notoriously hard to treat in the field. As vital organs are in the lower abdomen and major arteries run through the thighs and groin, unless you get immediate attention after being hit in the groin area you will probably die.

So a bullet-proof vest isn't as protective as most people think it is, and it won't protect you from a car bomb, a nail bomb, a blast bomb, virus release, poison gas, radioactive contaminants etc.

Don't panic though. As a member of the public you are really *extremely* unlikely to encounter terrorists. Unless you work for a defence contractor or news station in a war zone, you shouldn't lose any sleep about the protective quality or otherwise of ballistic vests. I could just as easily have pointed out that a meteorite falling on you could kill you. It would, but that is just about as unlikely to happen to Joe Public (or Josephine Public) as you are to encounter terrorists.

Nobody can guarantee to protect you from terrorist atrocities. There is only one way in which you can protect yourself and help to protect society, and that is to remain alert.

General – countermeasures

✓ Human beings have nervous systems, which react according to our genetic programming. We are just built that way. That means that we have automatic and natural functions that we cannot control. We breathe, sweat and shiver when the body decides that conditions are right. When we are scared, we are genetically programmed to prepare for 'fight or flight', to fight the threat that has scared us or to run away from it. That means that when we are scared, the body automatically prepares itself for one of those actions. That fight or flight preparation is automatic.

Our heart rate rises and adrenaline is squirted into our systems making us more alert, which also makes us visibly more nervous and apprehensive.

✓ A suicide bomber will probably be nervous. Unless they are tranquillised, and you would probably be able to see that in their behaviour anyway. You will probably be able to see that somebody is on edge, hyped up and ready for action.

✓ If a person was hyped up and nervous while waiting for a job interview, or about to run a race, you would expect that, but you wouldn't expect somebody walking into your government office to be like that. Anyone who is hyped up and nervous just walking into a government office should raise suspicions. If the bomber is that close, it is probably too late to stop an attack, but it shows that there are potential clues that somebody could pick up.

✓ If a suicide bomber is carrying a bag containing a device, they will almost certainly be taking unusual care of that bag. Home-made explosives are often unstable, so they will probably be treating the bag as though it was filled with fresh eggs, not the usual way rucksacks, sports bags and briefcases are casually tossed around. Treating a bag that carefully is cause for suspicion!

✓ If the suicide bomber isn't carrying a bag or case, they have to strap the device to their body. If they do that they would have to hide the bulk of the explosives and the wires and trigger device from general view, so they would probably be wearing a coat, bulky or loose garment. If it is a hot day, they may be sweating. Add that to the unusual clothing and acting nervously and on edge and you have cause for suspicion.

✓ Look at the bag. Does it look unusually heavy or light for its apparent size? Are there any stains on the bag, wires coming out of the bag, any visible switches, etc.?

✓ Is somebody stopping to prime a device, that is to switch it from 'safe' carrying and delivery mode to active mode, so that it can be exploded either by a timer, tilt switch or direct detonation?

✓ Suicide bombers are single-minded. Once they set off on their mission they have increasingly tunnel vision and can only see their goal. This means that they can appear to be rude, pushing and shoving to get to that office door. They might push to get to the front of the queue, then pause a moment before purposefully striding in to kill and be killed.

✓ A person who pauses when he sees uniformed security staff, or turns away when he sees that visitors have to go through a metal detector, has to be suspicious. A visitor who is nervous and appears to be hanging back or waiting for something unknown, may be waiting for a bigger crowd to gather in reception or might be waiting for the chairman of the company to arrive.

✓ Even simple clues are available. A person who does not have a company pass, or doesn't know that staff use the right-hand access gate and only visitors use the left-hand gate. Somebody who just doesn't fit into the normal scene should be watched. Somebody who hesitates at the door not realising that it is an automatic door, or somebody who once through the door has to stop and look around to see which direction to take. All simple clues that a person is either new, preoccupied, lost or doesn't belong in that place! They need further investigation.

✓ When driving a vehicle a suicide bomber has the same tunnel vision. Approaching their target they will only see that office door or the entrance to the underground car park. They may wait, illegally parked and ignoring car horns and insults, so that they can follow somebody through the entrance barrier, or they may be preparing to ram though it. They might cut through traffic and appear to be oblivious to it, or to the rules of driving as they concentrate on getting the vehicle to the target.

✓ Be aware of what is happening around you. Terrorists do not wear a uniform or carry membership cards. You could for example be suspicious of a lot of late-night activity in a lock-up store, or different people constantly coming and going at odd hours from a flat across the road. By being aware of it and reporting it to the authorities you could save the life of a lot of innocent people if the activity you reported is a terrorist cell preparing to make an attack.

✓ Make a note of the UK anti-terrorist hotline: 0800 798 321.

✓ If you have any suspicions, make some notes. These will help you by reinforcing your suspicions and give you something concrete to report. By making some notes you will see if that suspicious late-night activity boils down to a group of students going out and coming in drunk every Friday and Saturday night, or if it really is a random pattern any night of the week. By making notes of numbers, descriptions and vehicles, you could talk to the police and give them those details.

✓ If people regularly come and go and you don't know their names, it makes it difficult for you to refer to them. For the purpose of your notes, identify individuals and make a name up for them. For example, 'Harry is the "30 something man" drives white transit A123BCD, short blond hair, always drives the white van and walks with a limp because of something wrong with his left leg'. You may also for example have identified 'Male "Big Nose" comes on foot and has sometimes left with Harry in his white van. Big Nose has dark hair that is trimmed very short, he smokes small cigars'. In this way you will simplify your notes on the activities, and can say that on Tuesday at 2am Harry arrived took heavy box into flat from van, left at 6am with Big Nose. With that the police could do some discreet checks. They may find that you live opposite a brothel, or that the people who live there run a night express courier service. If that is the case then nobody is hurt, but if there is a more sinister reason for the activity, the sooner the authorities know about it the better. If you do make notes:

➢ Don't let the suspects see you watching and making notes.

➢ Never try to get closer or take photographs or go up and look through the windows of the house or any vehicle. If they are terrorists you could quickly end up dead. Your information will be more valuable to the police if the bad guys don't know that they are being watched.

➢ As soon as it looks to you like something is going on, talk to the police. Don't wait until you see somebody deliver dynamite to the house. Report it and then step back (well back).

➢ If you do report something that turns out to be significant, the police may want to ask if they can use your spare room to keep an eye on what is going on. Be ready to answer them.

✓ If there is a report of a threat to a passenger aircraft, or American business interests, keep that in mind. When you go about your daily life you might not want to avoid buying a burger, but you could postpone your plans to fly to New York for an anniversary weekend with your wife.

✓ If you keep your office and site clean and tidy, it will be easier to spot things that are out of place. A device could be missed among the clutter in an untidy office, so that is a lethal risk. If the office is tidy, a strange bag, case or package that suddenly appears on the otherwise clear area in reception or in the public waiting lounge will be clear for all to see.

✓ Keeping the office and premises tidy will make it easier to perform a search of the premises.

✓ Encourage all staff to read security bulletins so that they know what is happening.

✓ Encourage all staff to report anything that they feel is in any way suspicious. For example, if the dustman seems to be putting a package into one of the bins, or a courier driver stopped in the main car park and 'may' have put something near or under one of the cars.

✓ If you report anything, make a note of and report as much detail as you can. Reporting a driver doing something funny in the car park is of little immediate use. Reporting that the driver seemed to have a shoebox-sized package that he seems to have left near or under the blue Ford or the red Volvo in the second row of the car park near the cycle rack, is a great help. Especially if you can also report the name of the courier company, give a registration number, and provide a description of the driver and his vehicle.

At home

Terrorists may want to target military staff, politicians, business leaders and even celebrities. Generally they want publicity. They want their actions to affect and be seen by as many people as possible. Though they usually attack soft targets, they would have little to gain from attacking the home of the average member of the public. That means that at home – unless you live opposite a government building, main-line railway station or military base – you are probably safe.

That doesn't mean you should lower your level of vigilance, but it does mean you will have greater peace of mind while keeping your eyes open.

For anyone who may be selected as a target due to their status or employment, the following countermeasures should help. Your organisation should also be giving information, support and advice on how to protect yourself and your family. Adopting the countermeasures will help anyone to increase their level of vigilance and protection. Be careful and be vigilant, but don't get paranoid!

At home – countermeasures

✓ Keep up to date with the news, so that you pick up any information available on terrorist threats, plans and trends. If they announce on the news that terrorists are thought to be targeting an airport, and you live next to an airport, you should be more vigilant.

✓ If you work in a government building or work for any 'capitalist' or other official organisation, be aware that you personally are more likely to be selected as a target than Mrs Biggins who works as a cleaner at the local supermarket.

  ➢ Familiarise yourself with the alert states in your organisation, so that you know when the risk level is rising. (Most organisations have a system to show the threat level. For example, Green means there is no real threat, Amber means threat levels have increased, and Red means a significant threat exists.)

  ➢ You will know if you are in a role or position or part of an organisation that is a potential target. If you are, check with your security people and familiarise yourself with and take the security advice they offer. For example, they could teach you how to check your car for any suspicious devices attached to it or placed around the house and garden.

  ➢ Get used to checking around your home for potential or suspicious devices and packages. Terrorists have been known to set explosives under items in the garden of a target individual. For example, they may rig a shed door with explosives or arrange for a device to explode if the garden hose is moved.

  ➢ Prepare an evacuation plan in case you have to leave your home in a hurry. For example, you may make arrangements to stay with a nearby relative until allowed back in your home, or perhaps your employer has accommodation you could use.

  ➢ Familiarise yourself with emergency evacuation or terrorist alert procedures relating to your building – and adopt some of those principles to evacuate you and your family from your house if you need to.

  ➢ Be particularly aware of potential devices such as unattended bags, cases and vehicles.

✓ If you or your employer are potential targets you should take additional precautions.

  ➢ Keep a low profile in everything you do. As far as your job allows, avoid publicity. Don't make it easy for anyone to link you to your rank, regiment, company or job.

  ➢ As far as possible be unpredictable in everything you do. Take a different route to work each day. Do the weekly shop in different places. The less predictable you are, the more difficult it would be to target you.

  ➢ Be ever vigilant about people asking you questions, or asking questions about you. Don't give your plans away when people speak to you. For example, avoid talking about your family, friends and private life. If neighbours say there was somebody asking about you and your family, report it through your organisation. (You should cultivate links with your neighbours to collect this sort of information.)

  ➢ When using the phone be extra careful in what you say. Never answer with name, job title or grade, or rank or for that matter your phone number. They may have dialled a random number so don't confirm the number for them. For example, by answering your home phone with '345 675 Colonel Biggins' or '876 459 Chief Scientist Carol Smith' you are putting your security at risk. (With a name and phone number anyone can look up your address in the phone book, unless you are ex-directory.)

  ➢ Get to know your home and area so you can spot things that are out of place. If you do that you will be more able to spot unusual and suspicious activity. For example, you will be able to spot strange or unusual vehicles, parcels or devices.

  ➢ If you spot unusual vehicles in your home area, without being seen yourself, study them. You will be able to identify the usual council and delivery vehicles. Take a closer look at anything else. For example, a car or van with two men in, sitting at the end of the road watching people come and go may be a council traffic census, but it may be something more sinister. Make notes of vehicle make, number, colour, description of people, etc., and report it through your organisation or to the local police.

  ➢ Without becoming paranoid, or distracting you and causing a car accident, keep one eye open for people who may be following you, especially if they are following you from the office or near it towards your home address. Your house may be a softer target than the government office or military base where you work. If you are being followed, contact your organisation or go to a police station.

  ➢ Make it a rule that your children never accept any deliveries, or try to open letters or parcels that have been delivered. Be aware that chemicals and infectious agents have been used in postal attacks.

  ➢ Check your suspect-mail handling procedures. (See At work below.) Be aware of the threat of letter or package bombs. Check your security procedures to establish how to spot and deal with them.

  ➢ Make sure that your children are well aware of the need to avoid strangers, not give out information, think security, be home when they say they will, never go anywhere without your knowledge and approval, etc.

  ➢ Don't accept unknown deliveries. If you find a parcel left at your door, take a close look without moving it. Look for the signs of letter bombs and any evidence that the parcel may be suspect. If in doubt, contact your organisation or the police.

➢ Be cautious with strangers. Use your door viewer and door chain, and find out who they are and what they want before opening your door. Be ready to retreat to a safe area in the house if they are in any way hostile.

➢ *The Home Security Handbook* discusses keys. You have even more need to strictly control who has keys to your house, car, office, etc. Don't give keys to builders or plumbers etc. Only let them in when you have checked their references and then only let them in when you are there to supervise.

➢ When out and about, blend in with everyone else. Don't wear any uniform, company security passes, name/rank/job title name badges, etc. Don't leave anything in your car or throw anything out in your rubbish that will identify you and your position. Don't have a company car with the company name painted on the side.

➢ Don't cluster – that is, avoid places where a group of you can be targeted. For example, a bar, restaurant or club that has become known as the place where all the scientists or all the army guys go. If there is such a place, stop using it and warn your organisation that it is a potential target. (Maybe the organisation will take steps to secure it so that there is somewhere its people can go to relax).

After an incident

I have heard that people are offering bags of equipment that people should carry to use after any attack. They range from a box with a few plasters and bandages to full chemical, nuclear and biological combat suits. I wouldn't buy one!

You could build a disaster kit to be available and ready to be used at home. You could also make a portable kit for each of you to take with you when you are travelling. I would consider putting a few useful things together and carrying them when possible.

• **Face mask.** Recent explosions have shown us that immediately afterwards the air is full of dust and smoke. Victims and those nearby report having difficulty breathing. A simple DIY face mask held on with a strip or two of elastic would fit in your pocket (in a plastic bag to keep it fresh, un-contaminated and clean) and that would be enough to help you breathe while you got to an exit.

- **Goggles.** As above. Close-fitting DIY goggles held on with an adjustable elastic strap will let you see and keep your eyes safe from circulating dust and debris. With those goggles you might be one of the few people who can see to guide survivors to an exit.

- **Gloves.** There will be debris around, sharp edges, glass and possible contamination. You may have to pull debris out of the way so that you can reach survivors or get to an exit. Gardening gloves would protect your hands. Beware of live electric cables!

- **Torch.** Most survivors and those who go to help after an incident report that a decent torch is worth its weight in gold. Any explosion will have caused the power to go off or destroyed the light bulbs so it will be dark. Add swirling dust and smoke and you will need a good torch.

- **Water.** If you are caught in an explosion or other incident water will be invaluable, for you to drink, or to rinse contaminants out of your eyes or off your hands. If you are stuck in a train caught between stations because of an incident somewhere ahead, you may be there for hours, so a bottle or two of water will certainly help.

At work

The threat against your employer will vary depending on what your organisation is and does. If you work for a government department, the threat and risk levels will be a lot higher than those for a shoe repair shop in a rural village.

Method

- Assess the threat and risk level.

- Physical security – fences, barriers, doors, security staff and passes.

- Structural security – strength of windows and doors.

- Staff security – selection and recruitment, training, vigilance.

- Planning – preparation and readiness.

- Procedures – definition and use of formal procedures.

- Management – to manage and control the whole system.

Assess the threat and risk

The first step is to assess the level of risk and threat that you are facing. By their nature some organisations are potential targets, for example government and military offices and bases, and the offices of large corporations. If you work for such an organisation you are lucky because a lot of the work has already been done for you. It almost certainly has an existing security team, management and procedures already in place, whether you are entirely aware of them or not.

Smaller, independent organisations will have to do this assessment themselves, but even then there is help available. If you are a supplier to a government office or large corporation you may be able to get assistance from them. Even if you are just a small business serving the local community you can get free help and advice from the local police and a variety of websites or business groups.

How do you assess the threat level? In simple terms be realistic. Think about it and decide if terrorists would really be interested in Mrs Biggins' Village Bakery – I think not. In that case, I suggest that no special measures are required – just maintain a healthy level of awareness. On the other hand, a defence contractor or subsidiary of a US-based multinational corporation might be the soft target the terrorists are looking for.

When you have identified your threat and risk level, take steps to address the issues below.

Physical security

The perimeter of the building and site should be secure, which could include boundary fences, barriers, gates, floodlights, CCTV, movement sensors, intercom links to doors and gates, collapsible posts, anti-ramraid posts, movement sensors, anti-vehicle spikes, etc. If you can stop criminals from getting near to your building you have beaten them.

The next level of protection is the access doors and windows. Are fire exits kept secured so that people inside can release them to get out in an emergency, but nobody outside can get in? Is the reception desk manned at all times? Are windows secured or set so that they only open far enough to allow for ventilation?

Structural security

So you have doors and fences, but are they strong enough to do the job? Are they in good repair? Installing a reinforced steel goods inwards door is a waste of time if anyone with a chainsaw can cut a hole in the wooden walls of your barn. Securing all windows on the ground floor with security grilles is a waste of time if one good kick will break open the fire exit which isn't alarmed.

Do you need laminated glass in the windows of your building? Do you need blast-proof curtains in certain areas? Do you need to erect bomb shields over basement stairwells, etc.? The structure has to be as strong and secure as your security procedures.

Staff security

People are a security threat – full stop.

As an organisation you should carefully check the references, background and qualification of all prospective employees. If Mrs Biggins' Village Bakery employs somebody without checking their references, it certainly isn't a major threat. That employee may empty the till and run off with all of the money but that is as bad as it can get. If a government department didn't bother checking references the result could be catastrophic.

As a minimum, references should always be asked for and followed up. Work history should be checked and verified. Skills and qualifications should be reviewed and confirmed. The home address and status of the applicant may also have to be checked as well.

When an employee is taken on, it is in the best interests of the employer that the new employee is properly trained, supervised and managed to ensure that they can and do follow all company processes and procedures.

There should be foolproof access-control systems that only allow authorised people into different areas of the building and premises.

Planning

All organisations should invest time and effort in planning what they will do in any likely situation. The risk assessment will have shown them what threats are likely, so they have to produce plans that they can follow if that threat materialises.

All companies probably have written plans and procedures saying what staff should do in the event of a fire, an evacuation, a power cut, floods, etc. I suggest that you should include terrorist incidents in your plans. I saw one report from 1992 that stated that up to 80% of businesses affected by a terrorist bomb ceased trading within a year.

The plans should be simple, clear, available and most importantly tested and reviewed. A plan won't work unless you test it and iron out the problems. By the same token, if you don't review and update that plan, when you come to use it, it will probably be inappropriate.

Procedures
A 'procedure' is an instruction on how something should be done. It is written, tested and formally agreed and signed off. It fills a number of roles. It is a checklist, a training aid and at the same time a sequence of instructions. The checklist tells the employee what he has to do in what order. As a simple example, a 'procedure' for issuing office stationery may be:

1. Check the stationery requisition.
2. Is the requisition filled in properly and completely? If not, refuse to issue stationery.
3. Is the requisition counter signed by a manager? If not, refuse to issue stationery.
4. If filled in properly and signed and the stationery items are in stock, issue them.
5. If stationery items are not in stock, place an order.
6. Member of staff to sign for stationery issued.
7. Amend stationery stock records.
8. Check to see if order level has been reached on any stock items.
9. If order level reached, place stationery order.
10. If order level not reached, serve remaining employees or lock stationery store if no employees waiting for stationery..

Thus the procedure tells people what to do in what order. It reminds them of things that they may forget, such as checking for a manager's signature and/or forgetting to reorder items when stocks are low.

There should be procedures for all standard functions. For example:

New employee process. There should be a process that describes the induction process for a new employee. Attending the HR office, signing forms, getting issued with a company pass, getting issued with a login ID and password, being given a desk and key, etc.

Fire alarm process. This will describe what bell or alarm will sound, what the different alarms mean, by which doors employees should leave the building, whether employees should lock confidential cupboards, etc. before they leave the building, where employees should meet when they get outside, who should check that each floor or section is empty and that all staff and visitors have gone (fire wardens), etc.

Broken computer process. Depending on what the computer is used for, the process may be different. For example, if a social club computer is broken, you just get it replaced. However, if the computer was used to process and store any restricted information there will be a different procedure. In that case you must personally supervise the engineer as he removes the old hard disk, then without losing sight of that disk you must seize it and hand it to the IT manager, who will take it for disposal at a secure specialist company. In that way classified or confidential data will not be removed from the building on a disk that may or may not be recoverable.

Telephone bomb threat
All procedures should be written, checked, signed off and then as part of the management system reviewed regularly. An example telephone bomb threat form follows on pages 212 and 213. Note that it asks for the important information first and gives the call taker time and space to add extra information at the end.

Management
The security system needs to be managed, which means that there has to be a nominated person in charge. That person will have responsibility for ensuring that the security system is used and monitored. To do that they have to have the right level of authority to accompany the responsibility. Without authority, they cannot enforce compliance with the security system.

All security systems have to:

• Be managed/controlled – to ensure compliance and efficiency.

• Be monitored – to maintain the required level of efficiency.

Sample Bomb Threat Phone Call Form

Date call received:
Time call received:
Time call terminated:
Exact words used by caller:

THE BOMB – IMPORTANT DETAILS – GET AS MUCH AS YOU CAN

Where is it **EXACTLY?**
What does it look like?
When is it set to go off?
What will trigger it (timer, movement, etc.)?
What sort of explosives have been used?

FURTHER DETAIL IF YOU CAN GET IT

Did you put it there?
Why did you do it?
Are you part of a group? If so, which group?
What is your name?
What is your address?
What is your phone number?

FURTHER INFORMATION FROM PERSON TAKING THE CALL

WHEN THE CALL IS ENDED DIAL 1471 TO SEE IF YOU CAN
GET THE CALLER NUMBER. IF SO, FILL IT IN HERE

....

IMMEDIATELY

that has been done, call taker to fill in the rest of the form, while somebody else reports this to your management and dials 999 to report the call and the details above to the police.

Call taker should then have completed the form and be ready to give the details below to the police and to answer further questions about the call.

Name of person filling in this form:

Company name:

Telephone number on which call received:

What did caller sound like (circle appropriate or fill in different description)?

**Male   Female   Old   Young   Child
Other:**

Any accent detected:

Caller nationality (stated or assumed – please say)

Other comments on how the caller sounded (drunk, excited, scared, stammer, etc.):

Do you think you know the caller (e.g. Bill from accounts who was fired last week)?

Any other people with the caller, and background conversations heard or names used:

Any background noises – indicating where the caller may be (clocks chiming, railway station announcements, supermarket PA announcement, etc.):

- Be reviewed – to ensure they are still relevant and appropriate.

- Cover the period after an incident, with appropriate plans, processes and procedures to allow the organisation to recover.

In terms of terrorism, a few issues are important. There should be procedures telling staff how to handle a range of incidents – advice is widely available. For example:

- Phone calls giving a warning of a bomb or an attack.

- Reports of a suspect package near, outside or in the building.

- Reports of suspected letter bombs or mail contaminated in some way.

- How to perform a methodical and thorough search of your building and premises.

- Full or partial evacuation in case of terrorist incident that affects your building or a building nearby.

Travelling

Transport systems are a favourite terrorist target. Because people have easy access to public transport, so terrorists can easily get in to plant their devices. Stations, ports and airports are a hub of activity, which means that any explosive will almost certainly kill and injure a lot of people, no matter when it goes off, as well as disrupting life for an entire city. Stay alert.

Travelling – countermeasures

✓ Be aware of any unattended bag, case or package wherever you see it. They have been left on seats, in luggage stores, under seats, in luggage racks, on platforms or on concourses. If you do see something unattended, report it to a uniformed member of staff. Make sure that they know exactly what it is and where it is, then move away. It is probably just an innocent bag that someone has forgotten, but it might be something more sinister.

✓ During a high alert, if you see an unattended bag on a train or bus and you are between stops, I would loudly ask who owns the bag. If the owner stands up to claim it – no problem. If everyone denies all knowledge I would ask again. If it's still not claimed I would consider voicing my suspicions and suggest that everybody move away as far as possible from the bag. I would then report it to a member of the crew immediately, again making sure to say exactly what it is and where it is. Describing a 'red rucksack with the word *HIKER* sewn in large blue letters on the top, left on the rack above the third row of seats on the platform side of the train' is a lot better than reporting 'a suspicious bag'.

✓ When flying, where possible book yourself onto direct flights.

➤ Because airports are a potential terrorist target.

➤ Direct flights will reduce your exposure to risks at and around airports.

➤ Direct flights mean that you take maximum advantage of British airport security. If you have to wait for hours in a remote third-world airport and then fly on one of their aircraft, there may be no security protecting you.

➤ Flying direct takes you to where you want to be, so your security enquiries are not complicated by potential trouble at stopover locations.

✓ Avoid going to, stopping at or transferring to different aircraft and carriers at high-risk destinations as defined by the Foreign and Commonwealth Office.

✓ When at any airport get away from the potentially risky public area of an airport as soon as you can. Check in, book your luggage in and then go through to the departures lounge. Strict controls and security procedures in force there mean that the departure lounge should be one of the safest places for an ordinary citizen in any country in the world.

✓ When you arrive at your destination, try to leave the airport as soon as you can. The airport is a potential terrorist target and therefore a high-risk area, so you should leave it without delay.

Abroad

I have already stated that the only way of spotting a bomb or bomber is to look for something or someone that is out of place and unfamiliar. That won't usually work when you are abroad, because it is you who is out of place and unfamiliar. You are in a place where you are not used to customs, language or sometimes behaviour. That puts you at a disadvantage. You must therefore take advantage of the other indicators that are available to you.

Travelling abroad – countermeasures

✓ Seek advice from your travel agent and/or airline. They should be aware of problems in your destination town or country.

✓ Seek advice from the Foreign and Commonwealth Office to find out if there are any travel advisory notices or warnings. See the website at www.fco.gov.uk and click on Travel Advice and Travellers' Tips.

✓ Watch the news reports for developments in your destination country or city.

✓ On arrival, seek advice from local holiday representatives.

✓ Try not to stand out.

> ➢ Don't dress in skimpy or revealing clothes.
>
> ➢ Beware of nude sunbathing – it often offends older locals.
>
> ➢ Avoid engaging in 'amorous' activity in public.
>
> ➢ Show respect to local people and traditions.
>
> ➢ Don't flaunt wealth.
>
> ➢ Keep your opinions to yourself.
>
> ➢ Keep your plans to yourself.
>
> ➢ Don't get drunk.
>
> ➢ If you see a disturbance, make it your business to be somewhere else as soon as you can.
>
> ➢ If there is any sort of civil disturbance, make your way to your hotel or the British embassy or consulate.

✓ Seek advice from people who have been in the location for a while.

✓ Ask for a daily update if you have any doubts about the situation.

✓ Avoid places that could be considered targets, for example the American embassy or the local offices of American or British international business interests.

✓ Avoid travelling to remote areas. Stay in the tourist areas where local governments usually provide a level of protection.

✓ When at your destination, keep a low profile, remain aware of your surroundings and avoid any trouble.

✓ If in doubt, quietly move away from people, places or situations that concern you.

✓ If advised by the consulate or in news broadcasts, leave the country.

Travelling to high-risk areas

You already know that there are considerable risks associated with travel to listed high-risk areas. The sensible countermeasure is to stay at home. However, in some cases, such as with some urgent business deals, travel is almost unavoidable. If you do have to go, take precautions.

High-risk areas – countermeasures

✓ Talk it over with family and friends, and make sure that they know what you would do in an emergency. If there is a problem and everyone says you will curl up in a ball and wait for rescue or you will head north to the border, rescue services know what you are likely to do! That will make it easier to help you.

✓ When you arrive, contact the British embassy or consulate so that they know you are there and know what your plans are. More importantly, they know how to contact you if they need to update you about changes to the threat level or send you home if the situation has become critical.

✓ Adopt a friendly but cautious attitude with everyone you meet. Stay non-controversial at all times, and don't get drawn into arguments or discussions about politics, religion, America, world-trade, etc.

✓ Never talk about the reason for your visit or discuss your schedule and plans.

✓ Never leave personal or business papers in your hotel room. There is no point in not talking about things if you leave it all on your bed for anyone to read.

✓ Be aware of your surroundings, and look out for people who seem to be following you or hanging around watching what you do, people who are out of place.

✓ Find out where official buildings are in your area. In a crisis you should be able to go to one of them for safety. Places such as an embassy, consulate, police station, government office, major hotel or hospital are the best (though in a riot you may want to avoid government buildings and police stations).

✓ Make sure that you have left a copy of your travel and meeting plans with somebody at home, and if you change those plans let that person know. If you go missing, the authorities can at least follow your schedule to see how far you got before you vanished, and that will give them a starting point as to where to look for you.

✓ The higher the risk factor in an area, the more you should avoid adopting habits. For example, if a terrorist knows that you go to the café opposite your hotel for a coffee at 08:30 every morning, they could plan to attack or kidnap you there. With no observable pattern to your activities it will be that much harder to reach you.

✓ If you use a taxi, make it a habit to use different pick-up points, or a terrorist could warn off genuine drivers and be the only 'taxi' on the rank when you come out of your hotel in the morning.

✓ When you use a taxi, most countries have a licensing system. Before you get in, check the driver against his licence – especially if it is a photo-licence. If the face and photo match, you can at least be sure that the driver in the taxi is a licensed taxi driver. If the face isn't the same he may have killed the real taxi driver, just to get hold of the taxi to attack you. If the driver and licence don't match, don't get in the car. You just have to hope that your legitimate taxi driver isn't also a terrorist!

✓ Where possible, travel in a group. A single person is an easier target than a group.

✓ Never invite people back to your hotel room, and don't let people into your hotel room if they come to the door. All contact with people should be in a public area.

✓ If anyone delivers or tries to hand you a package, do not accept it unless you are expecting it. A bomb that looks like anything larger than a well-filled standard envelope can easily kill!

✓ Plan your days so that you are in control of your schedule. Get local business contacts to come to you if possible. If you are winning a contract, you can claim that you are hosting the meeting as a courtesy. If they want something from you, you can just insist that they play by your rules.

✓ Set a plan of action, saying what you will do in the event of an escalation in the threat in the country/town/area, as well as what you will do if there is any attack against you. A copy of that plan should also be left with the person at home who is holding a copy of your proposed schedule. For example, if there is a bomb explosion or an assassination, you could say you will go to the British embassy, or maybe phone the consulate to seek advice as to where to go.

✓ When using any vehicle have a walk around before you touch it, open doors or get in. You don't have to make it obvious, but an overall visual inspection could disclose threats or cause for alarm. Start your inspection from a long way off because that allows you to see underneath the car. When you are closer you can stoop down to tie your shoelace then take a look to see if there is anything suspicious. Your visual inspection could disclose cut break pipes, a device attached to the underside or packages pushed up to the back wheel or balanced on the front suspension arm, etc. You might see a trailing wire that seems to run around the corner. In the past terrorist bombs have been set off by a command wire. The terrorist sets the bomb then stands around the corner with a switch on a long wire and detonates the bomb when he sees you get in the car.

✓ Make sure that you have a quality vehicle. If you need to escape you might have to drive at high speed, or even push past (not crash into) a car blocking the road. A rusty old car with a suspect engine might not get you to your meeting, and it certainly won't get you away from a terrorist attack. (If you are a very high-risk individual, consider taking defensive driving training from the organisations that exist.)

✓ Get a car with air conditioning if at all possible. That will make it more comfortable when you are driving safely with the windows all shut. An open car window is a temptation for somebody on foot or on a motorcycle to drop a bomb or hand grenade in through the window. Car windows are surprisingly tough. If somebody throws a grenade at a car window sometimes it will break the window and come in, but it could bounce off a side window and fall into the street. Devices will certainly bounce off the front and rear screens.

✓ If you are at the scene of or involved in a shooting, if you can do it safely, get away round the corner and run.

✓ If you are too near the action or are not sure you could reach that corner safely, or if there is another gunman around the corner, get down on the ground if at all possible behind something really solid.

✓ Stay down until you are sure it has all finished.

✓ Don't pick up a fallen gun thinking you will protect yourself, because with a gun in your hand you become a target for the local police or army when they turn up.

✓ When you hit the ground, stay there. As you lay there with bullets whizzing around it may start to look safer over the road under that concrete wall, but getting there could get you killed! If you absolutely have to move – for example if the car you are hiding behind has caught fire – crawl along the ground and use any cover you can. Even a kerbstone offers some protection so crawl along the gutter. Take a quick look to see which way to go – away from the shooters is a good idea, but make sure that you take the safest and shortest path to the next available solid and safe shelter.

✓ Avoid laying on the floor or near walls if you can, because ricochet gunfire tends to hug walls and floors.

✓ Despite the fact that on the television and in the movies everyone hides behind a car when the shooting starts, try not to. Bullets will pass straight through car doors, seats, glass and into you. A car offers little protection from bullets. If you have to, the engine offers best protection.

✓ Under certain conditions, bullets and shotgun blasts will bounce off the bonnet or roof of a car and hit a target above and beyond the car.

✓ Finally, remember cars are full of petrol, and you don't want to be there if the petrol tank catches fire.

✓ If you are shot, clamp a hand over the wound to stop any blood flow. If necessary stick your finger in the hole to stop the blood flow. When it all goes quiet and you know you are safe, call for help.

✓ In grenade attacks, if you have the chance and a choice, dive for the nearest cover, putting it between you and the grenade.

✓ If no shelter is available, dive flat on the ground with your feet nearest the grenade and head furthest away. In that way your head, chest and vital organs are protected by the meat and bone in your feet, legs, ankles and bum.

✓ If possible consider holding your arms crossed over your chest to protect vital organs from stray shrapnel.

Hijack or hostage

There is no standard hijack or hostage situation. They are all different, but there are some things to bear in mind.

Hijack or hostage – countermeasures

✓ We have already covered passport details. You should review what details you have in your passport. You should be aware that in a hijacking or hostage situation terrorists have been known to check passports and use passport details to select people to threaten or kill. Lord Biggins Cabinet Minister is more likely to be selected than Fred Biggins who is a librarian! You have to choose what details you put in your passport.

✓ Remember that the terrorists are probably looking for somebody to use as an example. You may have already changed your passport to protect yourself, but make sure that you do nothing that will make you stand out. In the absence of anything else, they may select the noisy hostage, or the one who continually complains.

✓ Governments do not like making concessions to terrorists. If they do, there will be more hijackings and hostages taken in future because the terrorists know that that government will meet their demands Some governments are willing to negotiate, but the government in whose territory the incident has occurred will make decisions on how the incident is ended.

✓ The highest risk in a hostage situation or hijacking is at the start when the terrorists are excited, everything is confused and nobody is really in control. There is another peak in risk at the end, however it ends, whether by negotiation, special forces rescue attempt or terrorist bombs going off.

✓ Do not resist or make any sudden movements that could be seen as a threat.

✓ Generally speaking you should not try to escape, unless you are absolutely sure that you can do it. At the same time you have to consider that if you escape the terrorists might take retribution against remaining hostages.

✓ Try to sit back and relax. You may be in for a long wait. Some hostages are held for months, and hijacks have been known to last several days.

✓ Don't drink alcohol because it could lead you to do something foolish. Eat a little food, and drink enough water to keep you fit. Apparently that leaves you ready for anything, not too fat to move, and not always wanting to go to the toilet (which would make you stand out from the crowd).

✓ Aim to be passive and co-operative. Don't complain, or demand anything. Never use the 'Do you know who I am?' line – that will get their attention immediately. Don't resist anything, but don't appear to be humouring them either. Do everything that they ask you to do but stay alert.

✓ If they start talking to you, answer their questions but don't volunteer information. For example, if asked if anyone has a mobile phone, say yes or no. Never volunteer anything extra, for example 'His Lordship High Court Judge Biggins in seat 5A will probably have one.' Aim to be invisible.

✓ Even if you are a 3rd dan black belt in karate or some other martial art, NEVER try to be a hero. You might think you can disarm both of the terrorists, but do you know if there is a number three with his finger on the bomb switch? Be invisible, and leave the rescue to the professionals.

The following points are valid if you are a single hostage. However, if you are in a group I suspect that these activities could make you stand out from the crowd and that is something you want to avoid!

✓ The experts say you should maintain a level of dignity, and as time goes on you should gently begin to ask your kidnappers for more personal comforts.

✓ If the hostage or hijack situation goes on for more than a week, you should try to build a relationship with the kidnappers. Avoid political and religious discussions, and talk about any non-controversial matters. The longer you are with them you have become a bit of a friend so they are less likely to harm you.

✓ While you are a hostage you need to keep fit and be alert, if nothing else so that you are ready to react when the rescue squad comes through the door. Try to establish a daily routine, which will help you to maintain a level of dignity and control. It will also allow you to work with the terrorists and build that relationship.

✓ By establishing a routine, any rescuers observing you will know for example that at ten o'clock each day you will be taking a shower. That helps the rescuers, because they can raid the premises and know that you are in the shower so the guys in the basement bedroom or living room are terrorists. If you want medicine or a book to read or a pen and paper, ask for it. They may refuse, they may not – you really have nothing to lose.

✓ You should at least try to eat whatever they give you. Later you can ask for more fruit or tell them that you don't like pork, but at first you have to be invisible and go with it. You will lose your appetite, and you will therefore lose weight but that is normal.

✓ *Always look on the bright side*. It will be hard not to despair. Whatever you can use to get through, use it. If it is religion, the thought of hugging your partner, or a desire to get home and have a whole tub of chocolate mint ice cream, keep that in mind and use that as a psychological prop when you get low.

✓ The last thing is to remember that they took you as a hostage and you will be of no use at all if you are dead. That means they want you to be alive and healthy – so you have something in common at least.

After an Attack

If there is an attack, be it by bomb, rifle or anything else, everyone who was at the centre will probably be dead or severely injured.

Everyone who was in the immediate area will be injured to some extent. If it was a bomb they will be deaf, suffering from shock and concussion, confused and disoriented with their eyes full of dust and grit.

Everyone who was in the area may have been injured by debris. Office and shop windows for streets around may have been shattered by a bomb and falling glass will have caused a lot of injuries.

Anyone further out will be scared. Though they heard the incident, due to the way noise moves in built-up areas, they will not know what has happened and probably won't know where it has happened. You may find people running towards an incident thinking they are running away.

There will be people running in every direction, some wanting to get away, some moving towards the incident to locate loved ones or to offer assistance, and some just running in a panic.

The immediate threat is that when bombs are used, terrorists often place secondary devices at the scene. Secondary devices are placed to cause maximum death and injury to the emergency services, police and officials who attend to deal with the initial incident.

Your main responsibility is not to become a casualty because you will only be adding to the problem. If you stay in the area you are at risk, so in this book the advice has to be to go to a place of safety and get home as quickly as you can.

After an attack – countermeasures

If you insist on offering assistance, some actions are priorities.

✓ Somebody has to make sure that a report has been submitted. If you are not sure that the incident has been reported, contact the emergency services and calmly explain what has happened, for example if there has been an explosion (it may be a gas leak – don't assume it was a bomb unless you know it was).

➤ Call 999 (or the local equivalent) and explain what has happened. For example, 'There has been an explosion in The Whisky Bar, in Bogtown High Street, on the junction with Lower Road.'

➤ Now give details. For example 'The Whisky Bar has been destroyed, the building has collapsed and is on fire.'

➢ Tell the operator how many casualties you can see so that they know if they have to call one ambulance or invoke the emergency medical response in the surrounding towns. You should also try to indicate the type and number of injuries. For example, 'I can see five people who I think are dead. There are another fifteen with serious injuries, one man has lost both legs, there are a lot of burns and facial cuts, several broken arms and legs. Looking around there are at least another twenty people who are bleeding from smaller injuries.'

➢ If you know the area, you may be able to help the emergency services by telling them if there is an obstruction that will prevent them using an approach. For example, 'Lower Road is blocked because the end wall of the bar fell on a lorry which is completely blocking that road.'

➢ You may be the only coherent point of contact at the incident. The emergency service operators may want to keep you on the line to ask further questions. Ask if they want you to stay on the line. If they do not, they may want to call back to check to see if you have any more information.

➢ Protect the scene. Send somebody to the end of the street to direct traffic away from the incident and try to keep it clear for ambulance, police and fire engines. Where possible send two people, the first to do the job and the second to come back and tell you it is being done. When you get the report that traffic is being stopped you can cross one problem off your list, and send the second person back to help the first unless you have another job for them. Use common sense in where you stop traffic. If you stop it halfway down the road, it will have nowhere to go. If you stop traffic at the junction at the end, any vehicles can turn around or turn left and right so traffic will continue to move away from the area.

➢ With a major incident there may be a gas leak or petrol spillage. Smoking can cause further injuries so insist that people do not smoke – shout at them if you have to. When you give any instructions or advice to people for the rest of the incident tell them nobody is allowed to smoke, no matter how much they claim it will calm their nerves. Tell them they will blow everything up because of gas or petrol leaks and do anything you can to make them understand.

➢ When in shock, casualties may wander off. They should be collected together so that they can be watched as they wait to be treated. Usually by this stage people are beginning to want to help, but often they are not sure what to do. Remember that you are also in a potential crime scene. If it was a bomb, you are at the scene of at least five murders because you can see five dead people. Anyone around may be a witness. If they are not injured, get them to stay and help or at least wait to be questioned, then they will be available to talk to the police when they arrive.

➢ Keep your ears open and listen to what is being said. If anyone seems to know what happened, insist that they stay with you to talk to the police when they arrive. Try not to let anyone who knows anything go. Keep them around you or at least insist that they give you their contact details.

➢ A major incident is entirely outside the experience of most people. They are lost and do not know what to do. Many want to help but are in shock. Most people will take sensible orders from somebody who seems to be calm and seems to know what to do. To start with you may be the only person at the scene who can organise assistance for the casualties.

➢ With a major incident, normal first-aid skills and abilities are usually overwhelmed. The average first-aid-trained person will not know what to do with an amputation, serious burns or crush victims. Don't try to be clever. The one part of basic first-aid training that works in a major incident is that the noisy ones can usually look after themselves. Stop to look at them, staunch bleeding, reassure them and offer them support, tell them that they will be OK but move on to the more serious injuries. Stop bleeding as best you can. If somebody is not breathing, clear the airway and if necessary give mouth-to-mouth resuscitation. If at all possible, instruct somebody to carry on with it while you do something else. People in shock can follow orders but may be in no fit state to decide what to do on their own.

➢ Look for anyone who is trapped, or at risk from fire or further collapse. Make best efforts to rescue them without putting anyone else at risk and without causing additional injuries to the casualty.

➢ After the first shock, more people should be arriving to help. I would direct them to moving the walking wounded to a safe area, where paramedics and ambulance staff will have the space to set up and treat them. A supermarket car park would be ideal for this. You will be updating the emergency services all the time, so you should have told them that 25 walking wounded are now sitting on the wall outside Biggins supermarket waiting for treatment. Get the new helpers to stay with the walking wounded to reassure and support them.

➢ If you have any time left, you should go back to check on the seriously injured, make sure that their helpers are still with them, and make sure that the two key actions are being done – keep them breathing and stop them bleeding.

➢ When the emergency services turn up, go and talk to them. You possibly know more about what has happened than everyone else at the scene. Update them, then hand over to them so that they can do their job. Each emergency service will have its own incident control for a major incident, so there will be a senior police officer, senior fire officer and senior ambulance officer.

➢ Though any explosion and fire should be self evident, point them out to the police and fire brigade. Explain what you know about fires, gas and petrol escapes, dangerous walls and other dangers and leave them to it. If you are still in telephone contact, tell the emergency operator that the fire brigade (or whoever) has arrived and pass on other similar details as long as they want you on the line.

➢ Tell the paramedics where what you consider to be the serious casualties are, and if you have any idea explain which you think should be the priority cases. Point out where you have sent the walking wounded. Explain that you picked that area because it has vehicular access, plenty of space for turning and parking, with direct access back out onto the main road (if you are lucky enough to have that nearby). Tell the emergency operator that the ambulances have arrived, including how many ambulances if you are still on the phone.

➢ When the police arrive, if you are still in touch with the emergency operator update them and hand the phone over to the police officer. He or she can tell them what their name and call sign is, because they will now take over from you as command and contact point for the incident.

➢ If you have any witnesses make sure that you point them out to the police officer. The emergency services are under stress too, so make sure that they realise that this person or these people are potential witnesses and have vital information. If any witnesses did leave the scene, pass on their details to the police so that they can be tracked down and questioned before evidence is lost or forgotten.

➢ If you did all of that, congratulate yourself. Whether you get one or not, you earned a knighthood today for your bravery and clear thinking. You undoubtedly saved lives, prevented further injury, protected the scene and maybe collected vital witnesses.

➢ When the emergency services are at the incident, stand back and let them do what they are trained to do. By all means offer assistance, but don't get in the way.

➢ When you are no longer required, or are ordered to go, seek medical care for any injuries you may have then leave the area.

8 Next Steps

Some people read a book thoroughly from cover to cover, while others skip through scanning sections that take their interest. Are you sure that while reading each section, you reviewed your life and travel plans to identify potential vulnerabilities, threats and risks appropriate to you?

It may be worth your while to read through again, to make sure that you have identified and recorded all of the problems appropriate to you.

When you have recorded all of the relevant problems, you must review them, then define, prioritise, adopt and implement the countermeasures as discussed in Chapter 1.

You have probably already started resolving some of the problems that you have identified.

Identifying security issues

Knowing what journey you are planning, and having thoroughly researched the destination, you will have identified those threats, vulnerabilities and risks that apply to you and your journey.

You should have listed them as you identified them, then directed your research and planning to resolving them. Perhaps after researching the altitude sickness problems that you could have in your chosen destination, you asked your doctor for advice. On his advice, you may have selected a new lower-altitude destination, but now you have to research that destination too.

It is still supposed to be a holiday, so don't turn it into a tedious high-security military operation. At the same time don't get killed on a jungle track because you didn't check the Home Office website to see the warnings about armed criminals operating around your holiday destination.

You should review your list of vulnerabilities, threats and risks and identify possible countermeasures that will avoid, reduce or overcome them. Then you must consider each outstanding countermeasure, decide what actions are necessary to implement them and compile an action list.

What is an action list?

You will have to draw up an action list for each countermeasure you have identified and listed. The action list is simply a list of the tasks you have to complete to introduce or implement the stated countermeasure.

For example, taking as an example the countermeasure of 'making up an emergency medical kit', we have to look at the jobs, tasks and actions that we will need to introduce that.

The action list shows each of the steps needed to do that, in the order in which they have to be completed. When finished, the action list becomes a plan, a checklist and a work schedule that will help you to introduce that counter-measure. For example, you may have to collect the following items for your emergency first-aid kit:

- A packet of sterile alcohol swabs to clean the skin.
- A variety of good-quality sticking plaster dressings.
- A large roll of surgical sticking tape.
- Aspirin/Ibuprofen (painkillers)
- Anti-inflammatory cream/spray (soothing bites and burns)
- Anti-acid medicine (settle upset stomachs)
- Antiseptic ointment
- Scissors
- Cotton-wool wipes

A possible action list of the steps and tasks needed to make an emergency medical kit may be:

- Go to the doctor and ask if you can buy some syringes and needles.

- Also ask for needles and sutures, as well as skin-closure strips.

- Get advice about the rest of the items and if possible buy them from the doctor.

- Go to the hardware store and buy a strong plastic waterproof box that is big enough to contain all of the items, and two pairs of small scissors (they are cheap and you may lose or contaminate one pair).

- Buy and collect all of the items.

- Set out a time and place to check and pack all of the items in the box to create your emergency first-aid kit.

When all of those steps have been successfully completed, you will have created the first-aid kit and the countermeasure will be in place.

You will see that in some cases the necessary steps and actions required to deliver a countermeasure could take some weeks to complete, or it could be completed in an afternoon if, for example, your doctor now sells ready-made holiday emergency kits.

Action list considerations

The action list will also help you to understand the effort, cost and time required for you to introduce the more complex countermeasures. Because the action list breaks down the tasks required to deliver each countermeasure, you have a manageable list of understandable tasks. For each task you can look at the time, cost, skills required and impact of the task. Noting them against the actions, you can soon define total cost, time required for delivery, specialist skills required and any impacts and knock-on effects.

Using the above example, the table below indicates the results you may get from this exercise.

No.	Action	Cost	Time	Skills	Impact
1.	Go to the doctor and ask if you can buy some syringes and needles.	£10	4 days	Nil	Nil
2.	While there, find out just what a cannula is and ask if you can have one.	£3	1 hour	Nil	Nil
3.	Also ask for needles and sutures, as well as skin-closure strips.	£15	1 hour	Nil	Nil
4.	Get advice about the rest of the items and if possible buy them from the doctor.	£45	1 hour	Nil	Nil
5.	Go to the hardware store and buy a strong plastic waterproof box that is big enough to contain all the items, and two pairs of small scissors.	£5	2 hours	Nil	Nil
6.	Buy and collect all of the items and make up the kit.	Nil	4 hours	Nil	Nil

In this case it is a simple countermeasure so it is a simple list of actions. The table shows us the work required, the cost involved, the time taken, skills required and any possible impact, which may be significant with a different and more complicated countermeasure.

Though the time required seems rather long at 4 days and 9 hours, that is only our estimate. We may be able to do some of the tasks in parallel. For example, if your doctor has decided to make up and sell holiday emergency medical kits, you could complete this countermeasure in one quick trip to the doctor.

Whatever your action plan looks like, in some cases even if the countermeasure takes a month or more to implement, it may not matter. For example:

- If it is a longer-term goal, for example to learn CPR, you may need to find, book and attend a ten-week first-aid course. In that case a duration of three months to find, book, take and pass a first-aid course may be acceptable.

- Most of the time allocated in this case is allocated to making and attending an appointment with the doctor. This could of course be a background task while you concentrate on researching local transport arrangements at your holiday destination.

- Lastly, you have to look at the sequence!

  ➤ Action 1 is to make and attend the appointment.

  ➤ Action 2 is to ask the doctor what a cannula is and to get one. Actions 3 and 4 are also enquiries, which means that actions 1, 2, 3 and 4 could all be run in parallel.

  ➤ Action 5 is to get a waterproof box to contain your emergency first-aid kit. When you phone up to make the appointment the doctor may be able to tell you what size to buy, so you may actually finish action 5 before you see the doctor and complete actions 1, 2, 3 and 4.

  ➤ Action 6 requires you to go out and buy all other items and then to put the emergency kit together.

No special skills are required, and there is no impact.

When considering actions, you should remember that the details for each action could include:

- **Time.** How long (measured in hours) will it take to introduce the counter-measure?

- **Cost.** How much will it cost to introduce the countermeasure – including all costs, such as buying materials, or paying the doctor for his time taken up telling you what you should have in your emergency kit?

- **Skills.** Are any special skills required so that you can introduce a counter-measure? For example, you may need to consult with a doctor or a pharmacist.

- **Impacts.** You must decide what impacts, if any, the new countermeasure will have on you. For example, if the doctor gave you a vaccination while you were there, the impact might be that you felt ill and had to stay off work for two days afterwards.

Prioritising

When you have completed the listing process, you have to review and prioritise the countermeasures (and the actions needed to implement those counter-measures), and sort them into priority order.

You may realise that some things have priority because they take a long time to arrange. For example, if you have to take first-aid training the course may be three months long so you will need to start at least three months before your travel date. If you need to arrange for vaccinations, some of them have to be given in a series of injections over several weeks, and even then you may have to have tests to see if the vaccinations worked. That means you may have to organise first-aid training and vaccinations well ahead of a travel date, so they are your priority tasks.

Last Word

Has all of this put you off your holiday? If you were planning to tour the latest war zone or cycle up Everest, I hope it has. If you were going to try an exotic holiday and assumed that there would be nice hotels, friendly people and a familiar 'Boots the Chemist' on every corner if you needed anything, I hope you now realise the error of your ways.

If you were just going to try something different, I hope the above information has helped you to organise the trip of a lifetime, and left you confident that you have done all you can to make it a safe and pleasant trip.

If you were going to the usual Costa to flop on a beach for 14 days, maybe the information above has entertained you, educated you and made you appreciate the worry-free, nice warm feeling that a package deal to a safe resort can give you (even if you have bought 20 gallons of factor 30 sun block since you read about sunburn and heat stroke).

If you are going to visit Aunty Biggins in Bognor, this book contains more than you will ever need to know. But you are now a lot better informed than you were before you read this book. And maybe, just maybe, next year it will inspire you to look at the fjords in Norway or visit the Rocky Mountains.

To finally put this into perspective, remember that you insure your house against fire, flood, theft, damage, subsidence and a list of other threats. You don't expect any of those things to happen. They are probably guaranteed never to happen to you, but being insured gives you peace of mind, knowing that you are prepared for anything.

This book is like that insurance. It will give you the peace of mind in knowing that you have done all you can do and that you are ready for anything – well, almost anything. Maybe I should have included a chapter on alien invasion from the planet Zog?

It's Your Decision!

Remember that this book only contains general advice. Laws and circumstances change, and people differ. Experts learn new techniques so advice will evolve and change over time. You may have a totally different lifestyle to everyone else in the country. You may have strange allergies and a love for dangerous sports. Because there is only one 'you', this has to be **just advice** and you must treat it as such. You must decide if you want to act on any of this advice. You must make sure that any actions are appropriate to you, and check with relevant experts to make sure that you do the right thing for you.

Websites

The internet makes a world of information available to everyone. Some people may think that they are excluded because they do not have a home computer or advanced computer skills, but they are wrong.

There are a wide range of places and organisations which make internet connection services available to the general public, from coffee shops with computers to libraries, colleges and schools. Most make the facilities available and offer support and training to those who need it. If you want to learn how to use the internet, ask in your local library first. Even if they don't do it, they should be able to give you a list of places that do.

If you worry about trying to use the internet, don't, because most people are surprised at how easy it is. By the time the average person has had a little practice, they usually say that they don't know why they were so nervous in the first place!

I have only mentioned a few internet sites in this book, because a world of information that is specific to your own personal needs and circumstances is freely available to you on the internet.

The sites I have mentioned are:

ATOL

www.atol.org.uk – Air Travel Organisers' Licensing scheme protects flights and air holidays. It is managed by the Civil Aviation Authority (CAA) and protects flights and air holidays that are sold in the UK through members.

ABTA

www.abtanet.com – ABTA is the Association of British Travel Agents. It is a scheme that protects holidays. Travel agents can join the scheme, but they must provide financial protection for their customers. Booking through an ABTA member means that if they cease trading while you are away on holiday, ABTA will guarantee payments so you can carry on with your holiday and return to the UK as though nothing has happened.

Foreign and Commonwealth Office

www.fco.gov.uk – The Foreign and Commonwealth Office website contains information on the political and civil situation in countries around the world, and advises UK citizens on travel threats in those countries. The threats in these countries are varied but real, so you should always check the lists and seek advice before planning any travel.

World Health Organisation

www.who.int/health_topics – The World Health Organisation website with pages describing specific diseases.

CITES

www.cites.org – The Convention on International Trade in Endangered Species of Wild Fauna and Flora is an international agreement between governments which attempts to make sure that the collection and sale of wild animals and plants does not threaten their survival.

DEFRA

www.defra.gov.uk/animalh/illegali – The UK Department for Environment, Food and Rural Affairs (DEFRA) has introduced a campaign which aims to reduce the risk of exotic animal disease entering the country and threatening our public health, livestock, agriculture and horticulture industries. This web page gives information on the regulations regarding bringing back meat, animal products or plants from outside the EU.

HMCE

www.hmce.gov.uk – HM Customs and Excise website describes the rules on the import and export of materials in and out of the UK. Materials coming from and going to countries outside the EU are described as imports and exports, while materials transferring between countries within the EU are classified as arrivals and departures.

Stopping unwanted mail, fax and phone advertising

If you want to try to stop or at least reduce the amount of unsolicited advertising you receive by mail, fax and telephone, visit the following specific sites to register your details. It will take a few months to work and isn't guaranteed to stop all junk mail, but it helps.

www.fpsonline.org.uk – Register your number and state that you do not want unsolicited fax advertising material.

www.mpsonline.org.uk – Register your number and state that you do not want unsolicited mail advertising material.

www.tpsonline.org.uk – Register your number and state that you do not want unsolicited telephone advertising material.

Index

If you want to know how . . . to beat the pension crisis

'The aim of this book is simple: to help ensure that when you retire you have sufficient resources to afford a reasonable retirement.

'Perhaps the most striking feature of the not-so-brave new world of pensions is that we all need to build up our financial judgements. You can buy advice, which some people prefer; but even then you may fare better if you have some knowledge, both to ask the right questions and understand the answers. Talk to your friends, read newspapers – buy books like this!'

Anthony Vice

7 Ways to Beat the Pension Crisis
Anthony Vice

Since the year 2000, falling stock markets, failing final salary schemes, later retirement dates and lower annuity rates have all affected pensions, and by 2006 the Government will have substantially changed the rules under which pensions operate. Also people are living longer, and therefore costing the state and private pension schemes more at the very time when they are underfunded and underperforming. In this book Anthony Vice explains clearly the new 2005 rules and outlines *seven effective ways* in which you can secure a more prosperous retirement.

ISBN 1 85703 942 4

If you want to know how . . . to keep your home and your
family safe from crime

"There is a lot that the average person can do to protect themselves, their
family and their property. This book will teach you how to perform a security
review on your home and show you what countermeasures you can take to
ensure that you are *highly unlikely* to be a victim of crime."

Des Conway

The Home Security Handbook
How to keep your home and family safe from crime
D. G. Conway

Surveys have revealed that when asked what people worry most about for
themselves and their family 45% of them said 'CRIME'. Crime statistics
certainly indicate that people have good reason to worry: A burglary takes
place on average every 30 seconds in the UK.

Alarming though this and other statistics may be, this book will show you
how you can use them to reduce the risk of becoming a crime statistic
yourself. It will teach you how to audit and review your home and lifestyle, to
identify a range of vulnerabilities, threats and risks and then show you how
to provide effective countermeasures to avoid the threat and reduce the risk.

The countermeasures suggested are designed to be realistic, achievable at
minimal cost and effort and simple enough to be introduced or implemented
by the average person.

Des Conway has over 20 years security experience, which combines police
service with commercial security consultancy. He has experienced countless
security reviews of domestic and commercial properties, delivering reports
highlighting vulnerabilities, and recommending simple, affordable and
achievable countermeasures.

ISBN 1 84528 024 5

If you want to know how . . . to keep yourself and your family safe from crime

Based on his experience as a security consultant and over 20 years police service, Des Conway describes a range of crimes against the person, offering advice together with over 600 countermeasures that the average person can take to avoid that crime.

The Personal Security Handbook
How to keep yourself and your family safe from crime
D. G. Conway

Des Conway will teach you how to perform a security review on various different aspects of your life to identify and resolve any threats, vulnerabilities and risks. It includes:

Protecting yourself against credit card theft and fraud
Protecting yourself and your children from physical harm
Keeping your car secure
Dealing with bogus callers and nuisance telephone calls
Reducing the risks from terrorism

Quite simply, Des Conway's goal in this book is to help you identify the circumstances in which you are vulnerable and in everything you do, to take simple and reasonable steps to make sure that you don't become the victim of a crime.

ISBN 1 84528 056 3

How To Books are available through all good bookshops, or you can order direct from us through Grantham Book Services.

Tel: +44 (0)1476 541080
Fax: +44 (0)1476 541061
Email: orders@gbs.tbs-ltd.co.uk

Or via our website

www.howtobooks.co.uk

To order via any of these methods please quote the title(s) of the book(s) and your credit card number together with its expiry date.

For further information about our books and catalogue, please contact:

How To Books
3 Newtec Place
Magdalen Road
Oxford OX4 1RE

Visit our web site at

www.howtobooks.co.uk

Or you can contact us by email at info@howtobooks.co.uk